THE
COMPLETE BOOK
OF
HERBS AND SPICES

ALSO BY THE AUTHORS

Claire Loewenfeld

FUNGI

NUTS

EATING YOUR WAY TO HEALTH by Ruth Bircher
  Translated and edited by Claire Loewenfeld
HERB GARDENING

with Philippa Back

HERBS FOR HEALTH AND COOKERY

THE
COMPLETE BOOK
OF
HERBS AND SPICES

CLAIRE LOEWENFELD AND PHILIPPA BACK

Illustrations
by
Sarah Kensington
and
Christine Robins

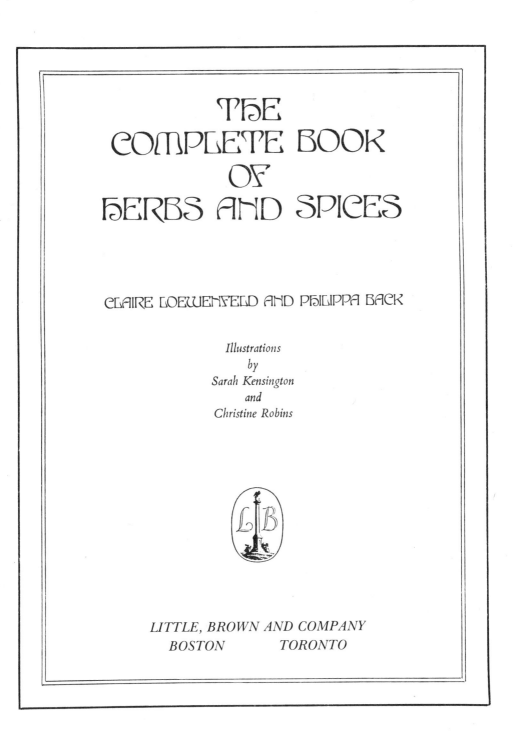

LITTLE, BROWN AND COMPANY
BOSTON   TORONTO

A

LIBRARY OF CONGRESS CATALOGING IN PUBLICATION DATA

Loewenfeld, Claire.
  The complete book of herbs and spices.

  Bibliography: p.
  Includes index.

    1. Herbs, gradening. 2. Herbs. 3. Spices
I. Back, Philippa, joint author. II. Title.
[SB351.H5L67 1974C]   581.6/3   76-7030
ISBN 0-316-53070-0

PRINTED IN THE UNITED STATES OF AMERICA

CONTENTS

CONTENTS

PART THREE
CHARTS

PART FOUR
APPENDICES

LIST OF ILLUSTRATIONS

9

ACKNOWLEDGEMENTS

This book is based not only on the research, practical experience and previous writings of the authors, but also on the knowledge and assistance of other people.

We thank Paula Schüler, a practical expert on the uses of culinary herbs: Jill Menghetti, our research worker and Janet Bryce, our literary assistant, for their excellent work. We are grateful for the help given by Dr Edmond Bonner, the Senior Curator of the *Conservatoire Botanique* in Geneva; for the assistance of Mr Joe Hill, BSc, the Senior Horticultural Officer for Buckinghamshire, who presented the weekly Southern Television programme 'Come Gardening' for several years; to Dr Peter Newmark, Lecturer in Biochemistry at London University, for scientific advice; to Mr and Mrs Evetts of the Ashfields Herb Nursery, Hinstock, Market Drayton, Shropshire, who kindly helped us with detailed knowledge of some herbs; to Patience Bosanquet who assisted with collecting material and editing the book; and last but not least, to our 'team manager', the husband of Claire Loewenfeld, Dr G. E. Loewenfeld, a horticulturist and joint founder with her of Chiltern Herb Farms and Garden Services, who gave his time unsparingly to this book.

INTRODUCTION

Claire Loewenfeld started research work on herbs in 1939. With the outbreak of war, she foresaw the coming shortage of imported oranges, a rich source of vitamin C, so vitally important for growing children. She remembered the many shrub roses planted along the German autobahns seen when motoring through Europe, which were grown to provide rose hips, a home-grown source of vitamin C. Claire Loewenfeld then realised the importance of rose hips in wartime, and arranged for laboratory tests to be made, with the help of a biochemist at Reading University, to determine their vitamin content. With this scientific proof, she wrote a leaflet on 'Rose Hips in Wartime' and sent it to *The Times*. A few days later nearly 400 letters arrived with requests for the leaflet, from hospitals, schools, women's institutes, educational committees, doctors and private people.

During the war she sent out more than 18,000 copies of this leaflet. So many people enquired about the properties of other wild plants and fruits in the hedgerows, that she wrote six further leaflets on these subjects, which were distributed by the thousands with the help of W. H. Smith.

As a result, the Government organised a nation-wide campaign for picking the rose hips with the help of the country's Women's Institutes, and rose hip syrup was then manufactured for babies and children.

Claire Loewenfeld carried on her research work on herbs when she was asked by the Great Ormond Street Hospital to treat at their country base, two wards of children with serious cases of coeliac disease. She used the special vegetable and fruit diet introduced by the Swiss Dr Max Bircher Benner, from whose Zürich clinic she held a special diploma. At that time the cause of coeliac disease was not known and children suffering from it could not absorb food and usually died from starvation. The children in her wards were so ill that they generally refused all food, but she flavoured the juices with the most aromatic herbs and, bit by bit, the children started to like the drinks which saved their lives.

During winter, she could not get fresh herbs and had to use dried ones. As the dried herbs available on the market looked dusty and had no aroma, she grew the herbs herself and dried them in her kitchen and airing cupboard. Her herbs were so much better that she and her husband later started Chiltern Herb Farms, succeeding in bringing to the market the first English aromatic green-dried herbs, recognised today as the best English dried herbs.

Together with her co-author, Philippa Back, who joined the publicity department of

Chiltern Herbs and holds a Cordon Bleu cooking certificate, she gave innumerable lectures, many exhibitions and wrote and published various articles and books on the subject.

Based on their special experience with herbs in theory and practice, the authors have tried in this book to include all herbs and spices of general interest to make it as complete as possible.

PART ONE

GENERAL INFORMATION

What Are Herbs, What Are Spices?

HERBS are fragrant plants of which the leaves, stems, flowers, seeds and roots are used for flavouring dishes, or for medicinal purposes. Botanically, a herb is a plant more or less soft or succulent, mostly grown from seeds and not developing woody, persistant tissue. Some flavouring herbs, such as mugwort and woodruff, can be found wild, but most herbs are home-grown and usually used fresh. They can be green-dried and are then available throughout the year for seasoning dishes. For medicinal purposes herbs, both wild and cultivated, are used fresh, dried or processed.

In daily life, the terms herbs and spices are often mixed up; some parts of herbs are called spices, such as the seeds and roots. In some countries herbs for seasoning are called spices.

SPICES are dried parts of aromatic plants, usually tropical, including the seeds, flowers, leaves, bark or roots. Often pieces of bark, berries, roots or even flower buds are called spices if they are used for flavouring.

A general distinction between herbs and spices is that herbs are usually used fresh and are considered to be a better flavouring in their fresh state, whilst spices, grown and processed mostly in the Orient, are more pungent and used for different purposes such as preserving food, helping digestion and providing ingredients for medicines. Herbs are milder and used for delicate flavouring, whilst spices are strong and give an additional piquant taste of their own to the food.

To put it in a nutshell, herbs are flavouring agents whilst spices are seasoning or spicing agents, but we have to keep in mind that the terms 'herbs' and 'spices' are not scientific, but only culinary terms. They have been used by tradition and this tradition has changed slightly down through the centuries. A century ago, the famous Mrs Beeton, who often referred to herbs and spices as 'condiments', dealt with onions, carrots and turnips under the heading Herbs, and up to fifty years ago these were sold in the grocers as pot herbs.

History and Traditions of Herbs and Spices

From the dawn of civilisation thousands of years before Christ, from Egypt, China, India, Arabia, Persia and Greece, documented records exist to witness the sophisticated knowledge and traditions connected with the cultivation and use of many herbs and spices.

The Bible records that Joseph was sold for twenty pieces of silver to a spice trader from Gilead, and that the Queen of Sheba brought King Solomon gold, precious stones and spices. Mention is made, too, of the opium poppy, hyssop and bay, prized for their many medicinal properties. Herbs and spices played an important part in the religious life of those times—the holy anointing oil they used was made with myrrh, cinnamon, cassia and calamus, and the spices frankincense, myrrh and aloes were burned for incense.

Spices were valued as highly as gold and acquiring them has influenced history dramatically. Possession of the spice islands and territories meant world trade and power; nations fought wars over the occupation of these spice territories, slavery followed and political power shifted from the East to the West when spices started to be carried mainly by sea rather than transported by caravans overland, so that the seafaring nations became rich and powerful and built up empires.

How did the Phoenicians suddenly become so powerful, and how could even a small city like Venice employ an army with such a strategist as Othello? What made it possible for the Dutch people, being a small nation, to develop at one time a great empire? Why were Vasco da Gama and Christopher Colombus so interested to find a new sea route to India? How could it happen that the British East India Company became a political power? The answer is spices, spices and again spices.

From 1000 BC, trading in spices between East and West was dominated by Arabia and carried along the famous 'Incense Route' to the Orient. The Romans broke the Arabian spice trade monopoly by discovering their long-held secret of the monsoon winds, and increased the demand for the various herbs and spices.

After Rome fell to the Goths, trading in aromatic plants declined and finally came to an end with the Arab occupation of Alexandria in AD 641. Trading was revived by the Crusades after the fall of Jerusalem in 1099, and from then on, European eating habits changed with the new Mediterranean fruits, vegetables and oriental herbs and spices. The most famous spice trader of all was Mohammed (570–632 AD) the founder of Islam, and by the middle of the eighth century his empire extended from Spain to China. For 400 years Islam flourished, and many scientific techniques were perfected there—among them the extraction and distillation of scents and oils from aromatic plants. A famous medical school was founded by Avicenna (980–1037) who wrote an authoritative book mentioning many herbal extracts for medicinal purposes. In the thirteenth century the stories and writings of the Venetian traveller Marco Polo (1253–1324), who often mentioned spices, were said to have inspired the Spanish and Portuguese explorations which discovered the New World and the long sought sea passage round Africa to India. Trading began, the power shifted from Venice, and the reason? Again spices. Pepper, cinnamon, cloves, ginger, nutmeg, mace and many herbs were used in large amounts for flavouring and preserving food and helping in its digestion. Hundreds of herbs and spices were used for making drugs, medicines and cosmetics; for adding to the water used for washing and bathing; for fumigating the often evil-smelling houses, and also for religious purposes. In ancient Greece, around 460 BC the writings of Hippocrates, the Father of Medicine, of Theophrastus, known as the Father of Botany, and later of Dioscorides and Galen, showed that their extensive botanical knowledge was mostly used for medicinal purposes, though there is evidence that many herbs and spices were used in the kitchens of that time. The Romans, too, made extensive use of spices and herbs, particularly in their cooking. They traded the herbs and spices all over the western world as the Arabians and Greeks had done before. Pliny (23–79 AD) had written his thirty-two books on natural history, eight of which are on medical plants, by the time the Romans occupied Britain in AD 43. They brought with them many spices and 400 different herbs which they grew from seeds and used them in the diet of their soldiers for the treatment of illnesses. In this way they managed with fewer doctors, essential for an occupation army.

The knowledge and use of these many herbs and spices are the essential part of the Roman tradition which Britain inherited. The Romans required so many culinary and medicinal herbs and spices that they imported them from their colonies along the shores of the Mediterranean, and even from Macedonia. Later, they also imported British grown herbs which proved to have a finer flavour. Herbs made palatable foods stored or pickled over long periods, and we possess some description of these herbs and spices in the book of Apicius on Roman cookery (first century) and learn that they preserved peaches in salt, vinegar and the herb savory.

There is a long tradition of using herbs and spices in India, and we know that the Chinese used them for thousands of years. A work of fifty-two volumes on the subject was published in 1550 by the Chinese scientist, Li Shi Zhen, who spent thirty years studying it. In China today their old traditional herbal treatment is used side by side with orthodox medicine.

In Britain the knowledge and use of herbs and spices almost died out during the Dark Ages, the Saxons and Danes using very few herbs or spices. When the monasteries were founded in the sixth century, the use of herbs was revived. They filled the gardens near the hostels taking in pilgrims, and near the hospitals where people received treatment. Charlemagne (742–814 AD) who learned in Europe how to procure seeds and plants, ordered the growing of herbs on the Imperial farms of Germany. His experience, mainly from St Gall in Switzerland where he produced a wonderful plan for a large monastery garden, was used in Britain by the religious orders.

Herbs and spices found their way into old manor houses and many old herbals witness the interest in and importance of herbs and spices in those days. We know from existing records that in 1289 a rich English merchant, Richard de Swinfield, used regularly in his household cloves, cubebs, mace, saffron, sugar, garingale, cinnamon, ginger, pepper, cumin, liquorice, buckwheat, aniseed, gromil and coriander.

Out of the monasteries many centres of medicine were developed, as for instance, St Bartholomew's Hospital in London. The Kitchen Garden of the fourteenth and fifteenth centuries supplied herbs, onion and leeks. The Herb Garden not only included the ordinary savoury herbs which we use today such as sage, marjoram, rosemary, but also cultivated varieties of many other herbs which we now know as common roadside plants, such as bugloss, borage, fennel and even chickweed. Herbs were used in the same way as spices for making preserved meat palatable and digestible, and for making the herbal beers, wines and meads. Both herbs and spices also provided the stillroom, the place for the care of the sick and wounded people, with the necessary household remedies as well as cosmetics, candied flowers, perfumed candles and insect repellants.

At this time herbs were added to the rushes laid on the floors to make them antispetic and sweet smelling. Judges and city solicitors carried herb posies. One of the most important herbs in these posies was rue, valued for its disinfecting quality and as a guard against gaol fever. The Queen is today given a herb posy for the Maundy Thursday Ceremony and until recently there has been a Royal Herbalist, belonging to the Queen's household.

Before foreign spices were imported English cooking was flavoured with aromatic English plants and these were listed by Tusser, an East Anglian farmer of 1537. Amongst the many herbs mentioned are burnet, burrage (our borage), clarye, fennel, saffron, marygold, mintes of, all sorts, penerial (pennyroyal), rosemary, sage, summer savory, sorrel, tansy and timme which is thyme. Tusser's medical herbs include aniseed, archangel (our angelica), horehound, lovage, mogwort (mugwort), rue, stitchwort, valerian. He also mentions dill, fumetory, eyebright and about twenty other herbs for distilling. Woodruff he notes especially for its sweet flavour and mentions basil as a pot plant. He then finishes a list of 300 herbs with the rhyme:

> Thus ends in brief of herbs the chief,
> Who more would have, of field go crave.

William Turner, one of the first English herbalists, published a herbal in 1559, and the most famous medieval herbal is written by John Gerard of London. He spent more than thirty-six years in growing, classifying and writing about the virtues of plants from all parts of the world. During his life (1545–1612) he supervised the gardens of Lord Burghley's house in the Strand, London. His famous herbal *A General History of Plants*, published in 1597, mentions 'Bugloss in Piccadilla, Clary in Fields of Holborn, Mullein about Highgate, Lilies of the Vale on Hampstead Heath, Sagittario in the Tower ditch, Mallow near the place of execution in Tyburn and the Pimpernel Rose in the pasture of a village called Knightsbridge'.

Popular books such as Culpeper's *Herbal* (1616–1634) introduced questions of astrology into the study of herbs, while the old herbalists like Gerard had described in detail the plants and their properties.

One of the most up-to-date and interesting books on herbs and salad plants has been provided by John Evelyn who lived from 1620 to 1706. He wrote the *Acetaria—a Discourse of Sallets* in 1699 and did much to awaken an interest in herbs and encouraged people to grow thyme, mint and savory in their gardens.

During Charles II's day the knowledge of plants was more scientific and great herbalists of this period dedicated their herbals to learned Fellows or Presidents of the Royal Society. From the physician's garden developed the physic gardens, which in turn became the apothecary gardens for the purpose of making medicines. The most famous of these in London is the Chelsea Physic Gardens.

Herbs and spices were important also to the pioneers who settled in the early American colonies. An example of a colonial herb garden layout can be seen today in the American Museum at Claverton Manor, Bath, England. With the help of herbs the pioneers enriched their diet, made medicines, sweetened the interiors of their houses, and dyed their clothes. One group of these immigrants, the so-called Shakers, made a special business out of preparing herbs, drying them, mixing and selling.

By the middle of the nineteenth century, people were no longer interested in herbs and few herb farms existed. Herbs were, however, cultivated in manor house and cottage gardens and this continued until the industrial revolution. The importing of oriental spices continued unbroken as they were ready-made condiments improving the flavour of most dishes. The mass production of chemical substitutes for herbs played a large part in their declining use, and the idea grew that man could improve on nature. This development was slower in Europe, particularly in the Balkan countries, but in Britain it became cheaper to import the herbs than to cultivate or collect them here.

The new interest in vitamins and minerals revived the growing of herbs in England, also in the United States and Canada. It became possible, with the help of electric drying, to achieve green-dried herbs. In former times imported herbs were sun-dried over long periods, badly packed in sacks or bags, were brown, dusty and of little use. It was discovered that drying herbs in the sun burnt and damaged many herbs.

Gradually the public became more interested in the use of herbs and many gastronomic recipes with herbs appeared, although it was not always stated how important it was, if fresh herbs were not available, to use only green-dried herbs which retained aroma and colour. These green-dried herbs are now available everywhere marketed first in the United States, and in the fifties in Britain, by Chiltern Herb Farms.

There is now also a slight change in the scientific attitude to the nutritional value of herbs and spices. Modern research carried out by the German Research Institute of Plant Products at Gesenheim, on the volatile or essential oils contained in herbs and spices, has shown the nutritional importance of adding herbs to the present day diet.

Herbs and Spices for Health, Cooking and Cosmetics

It is important that the food we eat should contain the necessary nutritive and bactericidal properties. It was Hippocrates, the Father of Greek medicine, who said 'Let food be your medicine and medicine be your food', for in his life time herbs and spices played a major role. They helped to preserve food, to make it digestible, and at the same time provided the basis of their medicines. Even today herbs and spices not only flavour and improve the taste of our food, but supply us with many nutritional prophylactic substances.

In his book *Nutritional Values of Crops and Plants*, Professor Werner Schuphan, a leading authority on this subject, stresses the importance of the essential oils and other principles contained in herbs and spices for the nutritional value of today's food.

We need vitamins as everyone knows, but we also need a combination of the active substances of alkaloids, essential oils, minerals, trace elements, sugar, fatty oils, protein and starch, all to be found in varying degrees in most herbs and spices. Some *alkaloids* produce a stimulating effect on the nervous system, while others stimulate the appetite, and it is thought they enable the body to build up protein. Spices activate the lower digestive glands without which food is not digested properly. Small amounts of alkaloids only are needed to stimulate these glands; large amounts may do harm. Our glands are the control centres of our bodies. Their condition determines a man's energy, nerves, elasticity, beauty and youth.

The *essential* or *volatile oils* are the odoriferous substances of herbs and spices. These ethereal oils have beneficial effects on the metabolism. They increase the production of white blood corpuscles and improve the circulation of the blood to the skin; they also increase production of mucus and bile. They promote perspiration, sooth inflammations and possess bactericidal and disinfectant qualities.

Of the minerals present as inorganic salts in herbs, potassium which is diuretic, and calcium which builds up bones, are important examples. Other minerals in the form of salts of organic acids such as citric and oxalic acids, can increase resistance to infection, influence the blood count, strengthen tissue, particularly of lungs, and act as effective laxatives.

Mucilage, found in many plants, dissolves in water to produce a viscous mass, and is a natural lubricant for the intestines and mucous membranes. There are substances in the herbs known as *glycosides* and their effects are mainly anti-inflammatory and febrifuge. *Saponines* contained in these plants are also glycosides, and these lather slightly in water and can have a cleansing, diuretic and expectorant influence on the system.

Another substance, *tannin*, has an astringent effect on mucous membranes and is antibiotic by nature. Finally, there are the so-called *bitter principles* which improve secretions in the mouth and stomach and generally help organs such as the liver and spleen. They also increase the red and white blood corpuscles, helping circulation and easing painful cramp.

Culinary herbs are important for our health and for helping those on restricted diets, and can be used instead of certain condiments and strong spices. Basil, summer savory, thyme and marjoram can replace pepper for those with ulcers and digestive troubles. A mixture of herbs such as dill, lovage, nasturtium, celery leaves, summer savory, thyme and marjoram can take the place of salt, but remember that thyme, marjoram and celery are relatively strong herbs and should be used sparingly in the mixture. Nasturtium has the additional value of containing much vitamin C and the effect of the blood and digestive organs is both antiseptic and tonic. Sweet cicely and angelica are sweeteners and can be used to reduce the amount of sugar needed with tart fruit.

The subtle flavour of herbs can be overpowered by stronger ones such as vinegar, which can blunt the palate and in time make it insensitive to more delicate flavours. Lemon juice is a good substitute for vinegar, both for salad dressings, as a condiment or as a preservative addition to food. Lemon juice, too, enhances the flavour of herbs and fruits as for instance in herb butters and with strawberries. Many herbs, when infused, provide a comforting or refreshing tisane or tea and their effects, whether relaxing or stimulating, are superior to tea or coffee. In France and Switzerland peppermint, chamomile and melissa teas are often served after meals.

Most dishes, including processed and frozen foods, are improved by the addition of the appropriate herb or spice, singly or in mixtures. Green herbs add either their own special flavour, as with mint, chervil or basil, or they can work as a catalyst, when the natural taste of a vegetable is brought out. An example of this is the use of summer savory with beans of every kind. The amount of the herb or spice used varies according to its strength and one's individual taste.

When mixing different herbs for bouquets, the amount of each herb depends on its flavouring strength and the right proportion of each herb is essential; only through experimenting will this be achieved. Single herbs are best for single vegetables, whilst the herb mixtures add aroma and flavour to composite dishes without leaving any special taste of their own. In the charts on pages 275-88 suggestions for using single herbs, herb mixtures, herb teas and tisanes are given.

Herbs and spices were once the main source and foundation of all cosmetics, before methods were discovered of synthesising their properties. Recipes for making and using these natural aids were handed down from generation to generation. Most of the recipes give instructions for infusing the herbs in water or mixing them with oil.When this is done the active principles within the herbs are released and act directly on the skin, clearing spots, pimples or refining it, according to the herb used.

Whilst a course of treatment with herbal cosmetics is being followed for the first time, it is important that herbs are also included in the daily diet. This will ensure that improvements to skin, hair, nails etc., will come about more quickly.

There is also no doubt that herbs and spices with their lovely natural perfumes and volatile oils, produce a sense of relaxation which is so important if the full benefit of the cosmetics is to be felt.

Cultivation of Herbs and Spices

The cultivation of herbs and spices hardly differs from the cultivation of other plants. Herbs are even easier to grow as most of them do not demand any special soil or protection. Organically grown herbs keep their freshness longer and even when dried they will retain their aroma,

Key to the diagram of the herb garden

1	Russian tarragon	21	Eau de cologne mint
2	Rosemary	22	Fennel
3	Mugwort	23	Angelica
4	Bay leaves	24	Sweet cicely
5	Verbascum	25	Acanthus
6	Hyssop	26	Fine chives
7	Red sage	27	Onion tree
8	French tarragon	28	Coarse chives
9	Onion green	29	Chervil
10	Fat hen	30	Chamomile
11	Garden thyme	31	Tansy
12	Sage	32	Summer savory
13	Borage	33	Lavender
14	Peppermint	34	Wild marjoram
15	Nasturtium	35	Marigold
16	Lovage	36	Pot marjoram
17	Lemon balm	37	Lemon thyme
18	Lady's mantle	38	Apple mint/Bowles mint
19	Parsley	39	French sorrel
20	Caraway	40	Horseradish

scent and colour well. It is preferable to grow all plants in well-drained, not too heavy soil. It it not often recognised that the physical condition of the soil is nearly as important as its fertility. In heavy or cakey soil the plants can hardly breathe or feed and the ground should be forked over regularly to loosen the soil and keep it weed-free. A slightly sloping bed helps with the drainage, and plants on top of the slope protect those at the lower end from too much sunshine and wind. A sunny side is generally accepted as the best position, but too much sun can dry out the soil and make it more difficult for the plant roots to function. A degree of warmth and a light position without too much direct sun is the best to mature both herbs and vegetables. Herbs prefer the lighter, warmer soils and a warm, humid atmosphere. They do not need direct sunshine unless fruit or seed has to ripen, as with spices. Even plant ecology plays a part in their cultivation. For instance, every garden should have nasturtiums growing amongst the herbs, for nasturtiums not only contain a large amount of vitamin C, but it is said that they will keep the surrounding plants healthy.

An experienced old gardener used to say 'Never grow small, delicate plants in heavy soil without peat'. Peat helps to keep the soil in physically good condition, like the soil in woods. It prevents the soil being subjected to sudden changes of temperature and from becoming waterlogged, both of which may damage the plant. The soil under peat remains in a crumbly condition which encourages root growth, and weeding is also easier. The authors regularly use plenty of peat in their domestic herb garden which is on heavy soil. Both moss and sedge peat are advantageous, but peat should always be moistened before application.

Another important part of cultivation is protection from wind which can be very cold in spring, disturbing young plants with their small roots, and also causes a constant change of temperature. Old-fashioned kitchen gardens were generally kept sheltered and warm by high surrounding walls which also prevented the encroachment of weeds from outside.

The composition of soil differs from place to place in one garden. We found in a garden of one acre, all kinds of different soils—light and acid soil only a few yards away from heavy, alkaline soil. Natural garden fertilisers such as farmyard manure, can never harm any kind of soil life; not so chemical fertilisers, different types being required for the different soil compositions. Chemical fertilisers can cause a lavish growth of plants, making them grow to an unnatural height. For this reason market gardeners and herb growers generally prefer organic fertilisers, or those with an organic base. Cow manure makes soil heavier and horse manure makes it lighter. Preferably, well rotted or at least partially rotted manure should be used. Fresh dung incorporated in the soil needs at least a year to break down before it helps to feed the plant.

Wood ashes from bonfires are good for the soil but the best organic fertiliser is obtained from well broken down compost, and no other type of fertiliser can be compared with a good compost. Compost needs the right temperature, the right mixture and the right position. It is useful to have an overhanging branch, such as a quick growing elder, shading the compost heap as it requires warmth but not sunshine.

There are two well known methods for making compost. The method of Rudolf Steiner, the founder of the Anthroposophical philosophy, and that of Sir Albert Howard which he developed in India, known as the Indore method. Both methods suggest starting with a layer of well dug soil with leaves, leaf mould or small twigs on the bottom; then a layer 4-6 in (10-15cm) of garden refuse with some lime spread on it; next a layer of soil approximately 1 in (2½cm) thick. Howard suggests to put a layer 3-4 in (8-10cm) of manure on this, but this manure should never touch the lime. The layers should be repeated to the desired height of 4-5 ft (100-120cm). A good way to keep it compact is to construct a bin of approximately 4 ft × 6 ft (120cm × 180cm). At the corners, ram in wooden posts 3 in (8cm) in diameter, and to these nail wooden boards on three of the sides. The fourth side should have removable boards which can be achieved by ramming in two more posts to hold the loose boards.

To allow the compost heap to breathe, 6 or 8 holes should be made with a crowbar through the heap. Some activator, a juice or powder which helps the decomposition, if possible an organic one, should be poured into these holes. Rudolf Steiner suggests an organic activator made by a mixture of flavouring herbs which are mixed with water and stirred for at least an hour. The results with Steiner's compost described in his books, are excellent, but not many people are prepared to stir the mixture for the prescribed time.

The compost in the bin has to be turned over once decomposition has started. A second, adjoining compost bin makes this easier, as the compost can be shovelled from one bin to the other through the open sides. When the compost has rotted down into good dark soil, having reached an internal temperature of 60°F (16°C) then it is ready to use.

Many people cannot afford the time and labour to compost, and in this case the application of market organic fertilisers such as seaweed preparations, Biohumus or 6X Organic fertiliser is a good substitute. With these fertilisers, it is sufficient to mix them with the soil while planting, and then sprinkle it from time to time around the plants. In particular, herbs such as chives which are cut frequently during the season, need fertilising as they have to repeat their growth.

In periods of drought, freshly planted herbs may need watering. The roots of plants grow vertically in dry soil searching for moisture which they find at lower levels. This growth does not take place when the plants are watered, but once started, watering should be continued regularly, otherwise newly planted herbs will dry out and die. Watering should also be done either early in the morning or late in the evening to prevent the sun burning the leaves. If large amounts of herbs are needed for use or storage, they should be cut in the morning after the dew has evaporated when they are fresh and at their best.

GROWING HERBS OUTDOORS

The herb garden, or the herb bed, should be near the kitchen with an easy, dry approach either by well-cut lawn with stepping stones, or gravel or clinker path which need be no wider than 18 in (45cm). If herbs are too far away from the kitchen, or the cook cannot collect them without getting her feet wet, she may prefer to go without!

A small bed approximately 10–12 ft (3¼–4m) long by 5–6 ft (1½–2m) wide can supply a family with sufficient herbs. Plant at the back, one lovage, two sweet cicely, two lemon balm, one mugwort. In front of these taller herbs, plant the medium sized ones such as mint, sage, thyme, salad burnet. In front of these plant groups of chives and Welsh onions and in the gaps sow the annual herbs. If there is some more space left between the rows, use it for second crops of parsley or chives of which you will make the most regular use, but leave sufficient space to allow access to the plants. If there is only room for a small bed, the most important herbs for the family are: thyme, sage, mint, marjoram, lovage, parsley, chives and Welsh onion. As a general rule all garden sowing and planting should be done at the appropriate time as it is difficult for the plants to catch up if you once get behind in the season.

The distances between herb plants for either planting out or thinning seedlings, varies according to their size, and they should not be allowed to touch each other. 18–24 in (45–60 cm) is the right space between large herbs; 12 in (30cm) for the medium ones and for the small herbs, 6–9 in (15–20cm).

To help with the weeding, a layer of garden peat is desirable. Peat has the advantage of keeping heavier soils more friable.

The sowing of herb seeds does not generally entail any difficulties, the important thing is to use only fresh seeds from a reliable firm. Most herb seeds are very small and require no over-night soaking before sowing. The only exception is parsley, so slow to germinate that soaking the seeds the night before may help to soften the hard seed coat. If the seeds are to be sown outside, the area can be pre-watered with hot water to help accelerate germination, but do not use boiling water which is inclined to kill the living organisms in the soil.

Generally it is best to sow herb seeds mixed with a little sharp sand which keeps in moisture wanted for germination, and at the same time, deters slugs. Sowing should be done in March or April in shallow drills made with the edge of a hoe, and when the ground is not too dry. As soon as the seeds have germinated, watering is essential in dry weather as the young plants, with their small roots, would dry out. They should be thinned out when the plants are about 2 in (5cm) high. The use of cloches is sometimes useful for the growing of plants with a short season, such as basil. A cloche gives more warmth for the plant and protects it from early frosts.

There are only a few herb plants which remain above ground in the herb bed or herb garden during winter; most of them die down. Still available during winter is salad burnet, a perennial whose luscious green leaves remain all winter, disappearing only when the new growth has started. Bay leaves do not mind the frost, though sometimes the leaves become brown without doing further harm, and will sprout again during the following season. Thyme and sage can be picked throughout the year, and also rosemary does not disappear, though it is better to protect it from severe frost.

Annual herbs such as dill, summer savory and marigold stay only for the summer months. Biennials such as fennel can stay two years, but it is advisable to sow it every spring as aroma and taste are reduced in the second year. Borage, an annual, disappears entirely but re-seeds itself so generously that it does not have to be resown. Woodruff can be found wild in shady woods and growing under trees, and to cultivate it, it has to have similar conditions. Pieces of the creeping rootstock can be planted in suitable shady places in the garden, where they will spread to form a ground cover.

The few evergreen herbs stay, as we have already said, throughout the winter, but they provide only a few herbs with a relatively strong aroma and flavour, and we would miss many of our herb friends in the kitchen for nearly six months, from November to May. For this period, herbs dried or kept in the deep-freeze are recommended. Some of the most important herbs can also be grown indoors.

GROWING HERBS INDOORS
The indoor growing of herbs makes it possible for people without gardens to have fresh herbs nearly all the year round. One should keep in mind however, that there is less fresh air and sometimes too high a temperature in rooms, and this makes regular watering and ventilation essential. This is important where there is central heating. Plants can be grown in pots and bowls, or in larger portable containers which are best placed along or near the windows.

It is relatively easy to grow the small herb plants of chives, parsley, mint, dill and Welsh onion, but avoid very small pots and use a well balanced compost like John Innes No 2, or a soil-less proprietary compost. Always water into the saucer in which the pot stands, removing surplus water after two hours, but do not over water. Only rarely, when the top soil appears to be dry, should you water from the top. Feeding can be done easily with liquid bio-humus— about four to six drops for one to two pints (20–40 fl oz) of water in the watering can should be sufficient. Keep the room well aired, but remember drafts should be avoided, and a thermometer will help to check the temperature which should be under 65°F (18°C) but not fall below 50°F (10°C).

You can start in September with two herbs to be sown in pots like chervil and dill, and if you have a garden, two transplanted herbs such as chives and parsley. Chives can be cut twice during the winter if the soil is treated with fertiliser but parsley rarely more than once. Keep twice the number of pots filled with parsley and chives, but only cut off a little at a time to make further growth possible.

Growing herbs in window boxes is another possibility, especially for flat dwellers and you can grow all the smaller herbs under 12 in (30cm) in height, in much the same way as the indoor plants. The window boxes should have drainage holes in the bottom, and be filled with a good soil or compost on a layer of pebbles, keeping it well watered and fertilised.

IN THE GREENHOUSE
We should give greenhouse herb plants similar conditions to those they have out of doors during the summer season. The small herbs can be easily grown in pots. A minimum night

temperature of 50°F (10°C) has to be maintained for herbs to grow satisfactorily but even a temperature of 45°F (7°C) will not kill plants. A suitable method of heating is provided by electric fan heaters which air the greenhouse whilst warming it, and a regular stream of air in the greenhouse is important for the respiration of plants. If electric tubes or oil heating is used, some fresh air should be circulated with a fan. To prevent the air from drying out, keep water in open containers.

Herbs are modest in their demands as to soil unless cut very often, and generally obtain sufficient plant food where ample soil is available. The soil in the greenhouse should be well fertilised, but avoid over-fertilising which causes lush growth, thus reducing the aroma and nutritive quality of the herb. Most herbs will grow satisfactorily in John Innes Potting Compost No 2 and in the modern proprietary soil-less potting composts. It is better to use the lower recommended quantities of fertiliser when making up the compost, and to top-dress as necessary as growth proceeds. Preferable to the chemical fertilisers are the organic ones, such as seaweed and bio-humus—better also for the aroma and taste. The development of the plants has to be observed all the time and the grower will soon discover how much organic fertiliser he has to add to the soil.

The soil, whether on the floor of the greenhouse or in pots, should be just moist. For pot-grown plants, drainage should be provided by placing stones or pieces of broken pot over the hole in the bottom, without blocking it. Pots can stand on saucers in which case watering can be done into the saucers as necessary. The surplus, unabsorbed water remaining after 2 hours however, should be removed. The pots can also stand direct on staging on a layer of pebbles or gravel. These materials are kept damp from the excess of top watering and by spraying over from time to time to create a humid atmosphere. If the pot is large enough, or the plants are in relatively large quantities of soil, it is preferable to water only every second or even third day, but small pots have to be attended daily. The larger the pot the easier it is to grow the plants. Larger amounts of soil keep the necessary moisture longer and also contain more bacteria and the plants therefore have more natural conditions. A more modern method of watering is to lay a ½ in (1½cm) plastic hose pipe, pierced with small holes every 6 in (15cm) along the bench in grid fashion spaced at about 18 in (45cm). Cover the hose with 2 in (5cm) of medium sharp sand and tightly twist the pots into it. Plastic pots must be used with no crocks. Turn on the tap for 5 minutes or so 2 to 3 times daily. This is called 'trickle irrigation' and is now used extensively in place of more traditional methods.

All herb plants can be grown in the greenhouse in winter but chives, Welsh onions, parsley, chervil, tarragon and mint are easier to grow than other plants which feel happier in the lighter and sunnier summer months. The taller herbs such as lovage, sweet cicely and angelica, make more demands on the soil and conditions in the greenhouse. To provide a regular supply of fresh herbs, established plants can be transplanted from the herb bed to the greenhouse in September, potted into suitable compost and protected from direct sunlight.

It is quite possible to sow herbs in the greenhouse, such as chervil, dill and parsley, but it has to be kept in mind that parsley has a very long germination period, and is restricted to a relatively short time during winter. However, provided a minimum night temperature of 50°F (10°C) is maintained in the greenhouse, and artificial light installed to augment winter daylight, annual herbs can be grown satisfactorily. Cold greenhouses, unsuitable for winter growing, are useful for transplanting the herbs from the greenhouse to harden them off before planting out in the open ground in spring. Cold frames, widely used in former times for growing cucumbers, lettuces and a few herbs on a hot-bed during the winter, have the advantage of providing early plants several weeks ahead of the outdoor grown ones.

The Herb Garden

The well kept herb garden is not only useful but picturesque. It can be made in many various ways, small or large, artistic or formal. The authors have a domestic herb garden which measures 10 yds (9m) square and contains seven different-sized beds with 40 varieties of herbs, as you can see in the keyed line illustration on p. 24. This variety of herbs gives a wide choice, both for cooking and natural remedies, and provides sufficient for home drying for use all the year round.

Of the many possible designs for a herb garden, a practical layout is a rectangle with stone paths on all four sides approximately 18 in (45cm) wide, allowing you to walk all round it. Herbs can be planted outside and inside these paths. Inside, it is suggested beds of different sizes surrounded by stone paths of a smaller size, say 12 in (30cm) wide. These stone paths should be ½ to 1 in (1½ to 2cm) higher than the soil level, thus giving the plants a little protection from the wind. On the outer side of the herb garden tall herbs should be planted, and at the two corners have perhaps rosemary in one and a bay tree in the other. At the other corners have two lavender plants of the smaller growing *Lavendula nana* variety. Between these, on one side of the herb garden, tall herbs such as sweet cicely, lovage and mugwort can be planted along the outer side of the stone paths. Between the rosemary and bay tree, plant verbascum which grows up to 7 ft (210cm) and on the third side, between the bay tree and lavender, have angelica. The open side, between the two lavender shrubs, should be the entrance to the herb garden.

Inside the irregular beds, one bed can be planted with thyme, annual marjoram and a few herbs which have to be sown in spring, such as summer savory, chervil, parsley and marigold; and in the second inside bed, smaller groups of chives, approximately 6 to 8 plants, and about 3 Welsh onion plants; also salad burnet which remains fresh and green throughout the year. On one of the inside beds you can sow dill and basil. A little further away from this bed, sow fennel which should never be near dill, as the aroma and taste of dill and fennel will mix if they are close together. In this bed, peppermint, fennel, caraway and borage can be planted or sown in the centre, and on the outside, thyme, which gives a nice appearance. In another bed keep common mint, lemon balm, tansy—which has a sharp aroma but looks beautiful with its lace-like leaves. Somewhere at the corner of a bed, have some horseradish which is disinfectant and useful for sauces. Nasturtium should also be sown in every herb garden as it not only looks nice but is reputed to keep away pests and infection. Last, but not least, leave a space near the entrance for the beautiful, unique herb thistle, *Acanthus mollis*.

All these herbs will not cause any difficulties, although the mints have to be watched as they are strong growers and will intrude on to territories of the other plants. Slates or tiles can be pushed deeply into the ground around the mint corner to avoid this kind of overgrowing. Mugwort, verbascum and angelica seed themselves to a great extent and it is advisable to cut off some of the seed pods before they spread all over the herb garden, unless some reseeding is wanted, important for angelica, which should be renewed every second year.

A soil cover of garden peat 1 in (2½cm) thick saves work, as this will not only keep the soil friable and allow the weeds to be pulled out easily, but it reduces the growth of weeds by keeping the soil underneath dark. Peat is best applied in spring, after a shower but not when the soil is too wet. It should be watered a little to make it just damp before application. It is hardly ever necessary to water the herb garden when it has a good peat cover.

In late autumn, the herbs except the evergreens such as thyme, sage, bay leaves and rosemary, have to be cut off at ground level. In springtime only some forking-over is required and perhaps another cover of peat. Rosemary should be protected from the frost by bracken, leaves or straw, kept together with wire netting, and if there is danger of a severe frost, tarragon roots should also be given some protection with a mulch of straw or other material. If only a small herb garden is wanted, take any shape and replace, if desirable, the stone paths with cinder or brick paths, but keep different sized beds as smaller beds make picking and cutting the herbs easier.

Harvesting, Drying and Storing

DOMESTIC DRYING

A natural and simple method of preserving herbs is drying. In this way they can be used in the kitchen all the year round. In order to retain the green colour and all their qualities, the herbs have to be picked at the right moment, mostly before blossoming, and dried immediately afterwards. This can be done at home in a heated airing cupboard, in an oven with low temperature, or with a home-made drying cabinet.

The principle of drying, once the herb is harvested, is to dry without any delay in the dark and not allow sun or wind to reduce its valuable properties such as the volatile oils. *Airing cupboard:* Spread the herbs thinly on trays covered with nylon net or stainless steel wire mesh, then stack them, leaving some space between for the warm air to circulate, at the same time allowing for ventilation. You must decide when the herbs are dry by your own judgment for they are all different in thickness of leaves and stalks. Generally speaking, when the herbs are really brittle in leaf and stalk but still green in colour, they can be considered dry. If the herbs turn brown, they are burnt.

Oven drying: A less satisfactory method as the temperature of the oven should not exceed 90°F (32°C). Herbs are inclined to lose their colour when dried in higher temperatures but if you can achieve this low temperature, spread the herbs on trays in the same way as for the airing cupboard and leave the oven door ajar for ventilation.

A simple domestic herb drying cabinet can be made at home, consisting of a wood-framed cupboard lined with hardboard approximately 3 ft 6 in (115cm) high and with an inside measurement of 12 in (30cm) square, or to suit the size of a small heater. Trays should be made to fit the inside diameter and wooden batten supports fixed to the sides to carry them. The height of the lowest tray should be 12 in (30cm) from the floor. A small greenhouse-type heater can be used or any suitable electric convector or blown air heater which fits the area. It may be advisable to reverse the top and bottom trays after some time of drying, which should be done without interruption. The herbs when dry, are rubbed by hand, discarding the hard stalks, then sieved and stored.

STORING HERBS—Where to keep them

Herbs, once dried, are best kept in airtight glass containers in a dark cupboard. This is advice against the herb racks which are so often displayed by shops selling herbs. Nothing is more detrimental for dried herbs than to keep them in a place where light has access to them, fading their colour and spoiling their special qualities. Glass is the best material, being clean and lasting, and if the container is well closed by a plastic screwtop lid or even a glass stopper, the scent cannot escape. If it is not possible to find space in a dark cupboard, a large label round the container will help to keep out the light. If harvesting very large quantities of herbs for drying, these can be kept satisfactorily in any kind of bin or container, provided the herbs are first put into linen or cotton bags, and the container well closed.

Fresh herbs can be stored for some time in the refrigerator in large glass jars with airtight closures and parsley and chives packed tightly in such a jar—a preserving jar or empty honey jar will do—will keep for several weeks without losing much colour or crispness.

DEEP FREEZING

A good method for keeping herbs in their original condition is to deep freeze them. Although they will not be crisp enough when thawed to sprinkle over a dish, they are perfect for adding to a variety of recipes, either singly or as mixed bouquets of herbs such as bouquet garni.

How to do it: Cut the herbs when the dew has evaporated, wash and shake free of excess water and harden for a few minutes by putting them on a plate in the deep-freeze. Make individual bunches of the herb, tie with thread, put into small cellophane bags and close with deep-freeze wire closures. Six or more of these bunches can then be put into a large bag, closed and labelled. It is important to get the air out of the bags before closing.

Frozen herb bouquets can be stored in the same way except that the individual bunches will consist of a mixture of herbs. Various home-made mixtures and many ideas for their use are given in the chart on pp. 282–85.

Frozen herb cubes—a good way to freeze small quantities of single herbs. Chop up the herbs after washing them, ladle into ice cube trays with small divisions. Then fill each division with concentrated stock made from a cube and ¼ pt (5 fl oz) water. When frozen remove cubes carefully, wrap in foil and deep-freeze in the usual way in cellophane bags. This method is especially good for making chervil soup when fresh chervil is not available. Make a roux of 2 tablespoons butter and 2 tbs flour. Gradually smooth in 1½ pt (30 fl oz) cold stock. Then add 3 frozen cubes and cook for 20 min, adding salt if necessary and a little cream at the end.

The Significance of Wild Herbs and Spices for Survival

We are becoming increasingly aware of the dangers of pollution of every kind and a world-wide food shortage, but not much is done to preserve the wild flora, so important for animals, birds, insects, and subsequently, mankind.

Nature's wild larder and its possibilities for feeding and healing seems to be neglected. Many wild herb plants, rich in essential proteins, vitamins, minerals, alkaloids, etc can help to supply valuable food as well as a variety of natural remedies for healing. It is interesting to note that animals still have what mankind has lost, the instinct for the nutritional value and healing qualities of the different plants available to them.

Ancient documents from the time of the Egyptian pyramids, reveal again and again man's knowledge and experience connected with the virtues these plants possess. The botany taught in today's schools could be extended to include this ancient knowledge of herbs, wild plants and weeds for general feeding and healing. In the countryside, local authorities should not be allowed to use poisonous weed killers for wild plants along the roadsides, and we should be encouraged to ramble and search for ourselves to find and recognise wild plants.

NATURE'S LARDER
One can find in hedges, meadows, woods, on banks, moors, waste lands and building sites, large numbers of different edible plants allowing a rich menu of vegetables, flavourings, seasoning and sweetening herbs, fruits and nuts, plants for both hot and cold drinks, and grasses to provide meal and flour for baking. The worst weeds in the garden such as ground elder, couchgrass, chickweed, nettles and dandelions, to name but a few, form an important part of nature's wild larder, and even cooking oil can be provided by the humble beech nut.

Many wild edible herbs and plants provide either a kind of spinach, such as Good King Henry, shepherd's purse, goosefoot, alexanders and chickweed; or an asparagus-like vegetable such as burdock, willowherb, salsify and hops whose shoots should all be cooked. (But peel and eat raw the succulent shoots of horsetail.) Even peas can be included on the menu if you gather the seeds of the wild lupin. For extra variety, make use too of the edible mosses and seaweeds such as dulse and sloke.

For raw salads and a plentiful supply of vitamins, minerals and trace elements, choose plants like chicory, vitamin-rich nasturtium, purslane, wild cucumber, the young leaves of stinging nettles, dandelions and ground elder, and the roots and stems of the yellow goats-beard. In winter you can find corn salad and salad burnet which survive under snow.

Root vegetables and substitutes for potatoes can be found in the water plantain, pignut, wild carrot, Jerusalem artichoke, arrowhead and the roots of the evening primrose and comfrey. The tubers of solomon's seal and silverweed taste like parsnips. In times of famine, the roots of the troublesome couchgrass and the soaked bistort root will nourish you.

Wild vegetables are not pleasant to eat without the addition of flavouring and seasoning herbs. Natural condiments are wild garlic, horseradish, rock samphire, stonecrop, wild fennel, thyme and mint, hyssop and yarrow in place of parsley. For seasoning use the salty dried leaves of nettles and the peppery stonecrop or shepherd's purse. Don't forget too, arrowroot, for flavouring biscuits, puddings and to thicken soups, stews and sauces.

Soups can be made from the young fronds of the common bracken and the narrow buckler fern, as well as from herbs like sorrel, lady's smock and watercress or bittercress. (Not to be confused with the poisonous marshwort or fool's cress.) As a substitute for animal protein which may become scarce, make good use of nuts and all edible fungi, but learn first which fungi are poisonous. Mushrooms are found all the year round and provide stimulating flavours to a vegetarian diet. Recognise immediately the poisonous Amanita group of fungi, the death cap, fool's mushroom, destroying angel and fool's deathcap with their distinctive white gills and bulbous volva at the base of the stem, usually underground. Then try the large variety of culinary fungi as a tasty addition to any dish, from the common field mushroom to the unlikely-looking puff balls. But remember all fungi should be eaten fresh and not kept, and they are more easily digested when cooked.

Cereals and home-made flour and meal can be obtained from wild oats, buckwheat, the red and green amarynths, from the dried seed of the sunflower and the bulrush (reedmace) pollen. Oil for cooking can be extracted from ripe sunflower seeds and the beechnut. Natural sweeteners come from herbs such as sweet cicely, stems of yellow goatsbeard and salsify, and the delicate orange-flavoured root of the common sweet flag. Use them to sweeten the plentiful wild fruits to be found in their seasons, wild strawberries, raspberries, bilberries, rowans, sloes, crabapples, elderberries, haws and the highly nutritious rosehips.

There is a wide variety of drinks to be made from wild plants. Coffee substitutes are dande-lion root, acorns and the ripe seeds of goosegrass—all should be dried, ground and roasted. The many herb teas to be made are both refreshing and possess medicinal qualities of great importance to any survivor. These teas or tisanes can be brewed or infused from leaves such as mint, sage, thyme and tansy; from flowers of chamomile, lime, mullein and yarrow; elderberry and juniper amongst many; from seeds for the comforting seed teas such as fennel, caraway, dill, linseed; and finally from the roots and stems of plants like valerian and marshmallow.

You will find at the end of this chapter an alphabetical list of many wild plants with suggested uses.

NATURE'S MEDICINE CHEST

From time immemorial, certain wild herbs were known for their healing powers, and this knowledge, still used and acknowledged by Chinese doctors today, has survived the ages. Healing with natural remedies is relatively cheap, and the need for people to administer to their own minor ailments with herbal treatments may spread all over the world with the increase of populations, allowing effective orthodox medicine to be mainly used for acute illnesses.

From early times it was common knowledge that men's wounds could be healed effectively with agrimony, comfrey, St John's wort and woundwort as their names suggest. There is an impressive list of plants to help the digestive system and intestinal complaints, such as oakbark, bilberries and herb bennet for dysentery or diarrhoea; feverfew as an aperient and centaury to tone up the whole system. Disorders of the urinary tract, bladder and kidneys are relieved with infusions or tisanes made of a large variety of wild berries, leaves and flowers. It could be of great help to know that betony and goutweed are beneficial for rheumatic pains, lesser celandine (pilewort) and hops for varicose veins or piles, burdock root, ground ivy, silverweed for skin complaints, and feverfew or yarrow for reducing a fever. Coughs and colds, sore mouth, eyes or ears, can be relieved by the use of such herbs as chamomile, coltsfoot, comfrey, horsetail, which is said to be a cure even for tuberculosis, elderflowers for toothache, eyebright for an eye bath and self-heal (*Prunella*) to soothe a sore throat. Deficiency diseases such as scurvy can be corrected with preparations of rosehips, bilberries, scurvy grass and chickweed, and even the diabetic finds help from the stinging nettle, dandelion and teas made of bilberry leaves and elderberries. For the sleepless, try infusions of cowslip or valerian; for the heart, extracts of hawthorn or yarrow juice, and for general tonics, centaury, juniper berries, calamus rhizome, yarrow and plenty of nettle tea.

Nature can also provide antiseptics in the form of violet leaves and agrimony; antibiotics from juniper berries and nasturtium leaves; a pleasant alternative to aspirin is the lime flower, and a valuable detergent in the leaves of soapwort.

A knowledge of poisonous plants and fungi is important, but it is also useful to know some of nature's antidotes for plant poisoning, for insect bites and stings, metal poisoning and against pests and germs. It is said that fennel is an effective antidote against poisonous herbs and mushrooms, and for insect bites or stings soothe them by applying directly leaves of plantain, dock or melissa. Powdered oakapple in large quantities will counteract lead, copper and tin poisoning; the meadow saffron, rue and blessed thistle can be used as emetics in cases of food poisoning; aconite, though poisonous to humans, may help as a poison against rats, and smoked juniper berries produce germ-killing fumes.

To make effective use of the many herbs and plants to be found growing wild, a basic knowledge how to make the various applications for the remedies is important. In general, a decoction is a solution made from various parts of herbs by boiling them in water; an infusion is made by steeping the part of the plant in water without boiling, and a poultice or plaster is applied externally and made by spreading the medicinal preparations on a cloth.

There are so many wild plants which are recommended for a large variety of ailments that even if you are not sure which plant to use for which symptom, each contains so many different properties that without a detailed knowledge, it would still help to select a few plants and give them either singly or together. To help the inexperienced user, we summarise symptoms and the plants recommended for them.

Chickweed, eyebright and plantain leaves can be applied directly to fresh wounds; comfrey, figwort, ground ivy, marshmallow and solomon's seal for poulticing inflamed or ulcerous wounds. Dandelion juice, extract of burdock root for eczema; silverweed, lemon balm, bistort for toothache and sore gums; betony, bilberry leaves, common mullein for varicose veins; coltsfoot, elecampane, horsetail, lungwort, Iceland moss, red clover, violet flowers for coughs and colds; agrimony, chamomile goutweed for rheumatic pains, and if there are no rosehips to be found, try instead bilberry, buckbean or shepherd's purse for vitamin deficiency.

There are many herb teas and preparations which will help the digestion and generally strengthen the organs. Centaury is especially good, but so are costmary, fumitory, herb bennet, hop flowers and shoots, juniper berries, melilot, St John's wort. For urinary obstructions, infusions of goosegrass or ground ivy; for gravel stones, lady's bedstraw or solidago. Extract of hawthorn, oil of valerian or the fresh juice of yarrow act as heart stimulants; for liver disorders an excellent infusion is made with leaves of fumitory. Try woodruff or tansy tea if convalescing from jaundice. To calm nerves, drink tisanes made of vervain, chamomile, cowslip flowers and hops; the astringent witch hazel is made from the bark and leaves of the spotted alder (*Hamamelis virginiana*). These natural remedies will take effect more slowly than we are used to, but they are reputed to improve the general health and cannot do any harm.

TERRITORIES OUTSIDE EUROPE

Nature has not neglected any part of the earth for the survivor. Many plants in these territories, including desert and arctic regions, provide both food and medicine.

Vegetable-like plants found in the Americas are brooklime—as good as watercress—mountain sorrel, a potherb—the spinach-like common milkweed, the loofah plant—a gourd, tasting like cucumber; wild hyacinth bulbs or camass, wild caper whose leaves and stems are edible, and the oil-rich sesame. In the tropics you can find water lettuce, the lotus lily and water chestnut. In northern parts of America and Canada can be found wild rice, or try the boiled seeds of the common bamboo.

Root vegetables abound. There are wild yams, taro root, bitter root, salsify, prairie apple which is like turnip, squawroot like parsnips and some consider the American groundnut or wild bean better than cultivated potatoes. Many seeds such as wild oats, squawgrass and large cane amongst others, provide flour and meal. Nuts and a large variety of nutritious wild berries are plentiful in many regions, and sweetening plants and trees can also be found, such as liquorice and balsam plants, and several different sugar maple trees which can be tapped. Wintergreen, a valuable plant for both feeding and healing, provides a delicious tea.

At certain times of the year, edible flora can be found in the desert and the arctic. You can find the nutritious seeds of the South African butternut and many thirst-quenching cacti in desert regions. In the arctic there is more variety. Vegetables such as the edible sedges, stone-crops and lichens, woolly lousewort, leaves of mountain sorrel and young shoots of the arctic willow, rich in vitamin C, can be found. Wild rhubarb grows there and many berries such as cornel berry, crowberry, wild red currants and raspberries, cloudberry, whortleberry and the mountain cranberry. Liquorice root also grows there, and for a refreshing drink try the well known Labrador tea which is made from the leaves of the *Ledum decumbens*.

Of the healing plants to be found on the American continent we mention only bitter root, gentian (the yellow *Gentiana lutea* variety) and quassia, as effective tonics for the whole system. From Ceylon, calumba root and cardamom seeds will do the same. Slippery elm for all catarrhal conditions, and its bark powdered makes one of the best poultices for boils and skin eruptions. Coughs and colds are relieved with bistort root, grindelia (gum plant), mountain balm and orris, said to be good for whooping cough and asthma. Skin affections are helped with powdered root of the American blue flag which also has a stimulating effect on the liver. The rootbark of the American sloe or black haw, and squaw vine are a help for uterine disorders, especially in pregnancy. In South Africa, the leaves of the buchu plant are good for ailments of the urinary tract. Gravel root is said to relieve painful kidney or bladder stones, and mandrake, or the rootbark of old man's beard for congestion of the liver. Wild ginger can be found too, and will relieve stomach pains. For aperients learn to recognise the plants of senna, *Cascara segrada* and mountain flax. Pains of rheumatism are soothed by black cohosh (snakeroot), poke root and the well known wintergreen. Finally, for an effective sedative, try scullcap or buglewood.

The following chart gives at-a-glance general information about many healing plants.

Plants with an asterisk are described in detail under individual herb plants.

HERB	PARTS USED	FEEDING	HEALING
AGRIMONY* *Agrimonia eupatoria*	Leaves		Infusion for coughs, colds, arthritis, rheumatism; for washing wounds. Antiseptic, tonic, blood purifier Gargle, diuretic, liver complaints

BILBERRY* *Vaccinium myrtillus*	Berries Leaves	Bilberry tea Wild fruit	Infusion of leaves for diabetes; berries for dysentery, urinary complaints Poultice of leaves for ulcers
BRACKEN *Pteris aquilina*	Roots Young shoots, Young fronds	Roots ground for bread Young shoots as vegetable like spinach Young fronds seasoning in soups	
BUCKWHEAT *Fagopyrum cymosum*	Seeds	Ground for bread and cakes	
BURDOCK *Arctium lappa*	Leaves Root Seeds Stalks	Young stalks boiled like asparagus	Infusion of leaves for digestion, skin diseases, blood purifier Wound herb for bites and burns Decoction of root or seeds for boils, rheumatism, kidney troubles Externally for ulcers Poultice of leaves for bruises, swellings
CHAMOMILE *Matricaria chamomilla*	Flowers	Chamomile tea	Infusion for toothache, digestion, sedative, tonic, constipation Steam bath for skin troubles Inhalation for catarrhs, colds
CHICKWEED* *Stellaria media*	Whole herb	Young leaves as vegetable like spinach. Chopped in salads	Ointment for chilblains, skin diseases Poultice for rheumatism, stiff joints Decoction of fresh plant for constipation, diuretic
COLTSFOOT* *Tussilago farfara*	Leaves	Coltsfoot wine	Infusion for coughs, colds, asthma, bronchitis Herbal tobacco for chest complaints
COMFREY* *Symphytum officinale*	Roots Stalks Leaves Flowers	Roots cooked as asparagus Potato vegetable Stalks for chutney, wine Young leaves in salads cooked as spinach Dried leaves and flowers added to cooked vegetables before serving	Infusion made from leaves and root Use fresh for bronchitic colds, pneumonia, dysentery. Arrests internal bleeding Poultice, liquid decoction or ointment for: sprains, bruises, swellings, arthritis, rheumatism. Helps to mend broken bones. Thought to be helpful for malignant tumours and progressive ulceration
COUCHGRASS* *Agropyrum repens*	Roots	Ground for bread	Decoction for kidney, bladder, colic, gout, cleansing the blood
DANDELION* *Taraxacum officinale*	Leaves Root	Leaves boiled as vegetable, raw for salads, wine Roots roasted and ground make coffee substitute	Infusion of leaves for liver complaints, laxative, tonic, diabetes, rheumatism, arthritis Juice from leaves for skin diseases, loss of appetite

DULSE *Rhodymenia palmata*	Seaweed	Raw or cooked, vegetable or soup	
ELDER* *Sambucus nigra*	Berries Flowers Roots	Elderberry tea, wine Wild fruit substitute for currants Elderflower tea	Berries for neuralgia Infusion of flowers for colds, influenza, tonic, toothache, bronchial ailments, sedative, diuretic Roots as a laxative
ELECAMPANE* *Inula helenium*	Roots	Candied as sweets Herbal tobacco	Decoction for colds, coughs, bronchial ailments, kidneys
EVENING PRIMROSE *Oenothera biennis*	Leaves Roots Young shoots	Roots boiled and eaten like parsnips Young shoots raw in salads	Infusion of leaves as sedative
EYEBRIGHT* *Euphrasia officinalis*	Whole herb	Eyebright tea	Infusion for eye lotion, astringent, digestive tonic, head colds, hay fever
GOATSBEARD *Tragopogon pratensis*	Leaves Stems Roots	Leaves as raw salads and greens Stems as natural sweetener Roots as boiled vegetable like parsnips	Decoction of roots for heartburn, loss of appetite
GOOD KING HENRY* *Chenopodium bonus henricus*	Leaves Roots	Leaves raw in salads, vegetable like spinach. Young shoots cooked like asparagus	Poultice of leaves for sores Decoction of roots for indigestion, anti-scorbutic, laxative
GOOSEGRASS *Galium aperine*	Leaves Seeds	Vegetable like spinach. Seeds as substitute for coffee	Infusion of leaves for colds, swellings Ointment for scalds and burns
HAWTHORN* *Crataegus oxyacantha*	Leaf buds Berries Flowers	Leaf buds in spring salads, sandwiches Wild fruit	Infusion of leaves for acne, dizziness, heart palpitations, tonic Decoction of flowers and berries for sore throats, diuretic
HEDGE GARLIC *Alliaria petiolata*	Leaves	Boiled vegetable like spinach Flavouring stews and meat dishes Fried with bacon or herrings	Leaves rubbed on bites and strings
HORSETAIL* *Equisetum arvense*	Young shoots	Cook like asparagus or toss in flour and fry	Infusion for anaemia, sore throats, haemorrhoids, diuretic, chest complaints
LIME* *Tilia europoea*	Young flowers and bracts Leaves	Limeflower tea	Infusion of flowers for mouth ulcers, bronchial complaints, catarrhs, colds, influenza, migraine Sedative, blood purifier, refreshing Poultice of leaves for swellings and sprains

MARSH MALLOW* *Althea officinalis*	Stalks Leaves Roots	Young leaves and tops as salads or cooked vegetables Marsh mallow tea	Decoction of root for urinary complaints Syrup for bronchitis, sore throats, digestive organs, soothing Ointment for chapped hands, chilblains, burns, boils
MULLEIN* *Verbascum thapsus*	Flowers Leaves		Infusion of flowers for coughs, cramp, gout, bronchitis Poultice of leaves for neuralgia, toothache Ointment: soothing
NETTLE* *Urtica dioica*	Young leaves	Boiled vegetable, raw salads, flavouring Nettle tea	Blood purifier, rich in minerals Infusion for liver, gall bladder; arrests bleeding
PLANTAIN* *Plantago major* *Plantago lanceolate*	Leaves		Insect bites and stings, haemorrhoids Infusion of leaves for diarrhoea, fever
PURSLANE* *Portulaca oleracea*	Leaves Shoots	Leaves in raw salads Shoots as cooked vegetable, seasoning in soups	Infusion of leaves is tonic, sedative, soothing
RAMSONS *Allium ursinum*	Bulbs	Garlic flavouring	
ROSEHIPS* *Rosa canina*	Fruits	Rosehip tea, syrup Wild fruit	Source of vitamin C Infusion for tonic, soothing, dysentery female disorders, diuretic, kidney
SWEET CICELY* *Myrrhis odorata*	Leaves Roots	Natural sweetener Leaves raw in salads or as cooked vegetable, in soups	Infusion of leaves in tonic, antiseptic
ST JOHN'S WORT* *Hypericum perforatum*	Leafy tops Flowers		Infusion for nervous disorders, toothache, menstrual pains Oil made of flowers soaked in olive oil for rheumatism, lumbago, gout Internally for colic, wounds, ulcers, skin rashes Ointment for bruises, sprains
SHEPHERDS PURSE *Capsella bursa pastoris*	Leaves	Peppery seasoning Young leaves eaten like spinach	Infusion of dried leaves for diarrhoea, internal haemorrhages Ointment for cuts and abrasions
SILVERWEED* *Potentilla anserina*	Tubers Leaves	Tubers boiled vegetable like parsnip	Infusion of leaves for jaundice, gall stones, skin troubles Astringent, tonic
SLOE *Prunus spinosa*	Leaves Berries Roots	Leaves as tea Berries for wine Wild fruit	Infusion of leaves for laxative, styptic, astringent, asthma, nosebleed

WILD FENNEL	Leaves	Seed tea	Infusion of leaves and/or seeds as
Nigella arvensis	Seeds	Seasoning	antidote to poison
WILD MINT	Leaves	Flavouring sweet	Infusion for indigestion, stimulant
Mentha arvensis		and savoury foods	
		Mint tea	
WILD THYME	Leaves	Flavouring sweet	Infusion for digestion, bronchial ailments
Thymus serpyllum		and savoury foods	
WILLOW HERB	Tops	Flavouring drinks	Infusion of leaves for asthma, whooping
Epilobium	Leaves	Young shoots eaten	cough
angustifolium	Roots	like asparagus	Soothing, tonic
			Ointment for skin infections
YARROW*	Leaves	Yarrow tea	Infusion of leaves and flowers for skin
Achillea millefolium	Flowers	Young leaves in	complaints, flatulence, constipation,
		salads	kidneys
			Stimulant, tonic, circulation
			Wound herb. it stops bleeding
			Fresh leaves chewed for toothache

PART TWO

THE
INDIVIDUAL
HERBS AND SPICES

The botanical names of the plants given in this book are all taken from the Dictionary of the British Royal Horticultural Society, and the classifications of Linné.

ACANTHUS—Bear's Breech
Botanical name: *Acanthus mollis*
Family: Acanthaceae

GENERAL

Acanthus mollis is a herbal thistle of rare beauty and should have a place in every herb garden. Though it has medicinal properties, it is not used as a healing herb today, nor is it used in the kitchen. It was introduced to Britain from Italy and south Europe during the Middle Ages, and the Greek physician Dioscorides in his De Materia Medica, wrote a description of it. The unusual shape of the large handsome leaves is reputed to have inspired the Greek architect Callimachus when designing the capitals of the columns for his temple at Corinth. These columns are still known today as 'Corinthian columns'. The Greek word *akanthos* means spine.

DESCRIPTION AND HABITAT

The acanthus is a stately ornamental perennial with beautiful foliage. The tall flower spikes of the *candelabrum* variety of *A.mollis* bear striking purple and white densely clustered flowers which are tubular and have a single three-lobed lip, appearing in August and September. The broad shiny green leaves are deeply pinnatifid. Native to Mediterranean regions, they are cultivated in gardens everywhere, being a hardy species.

CULTIVATION

Acanthus can be grown in bold groups in a herb garden or herbaceous border. Propagation is by division of the plant in autumn, and for best results, full sun and well-drained deep loam soil is best. In very cold weather it may be wise to protect the plants by mulching or covering with litter. They make good indoor decoration grown in pots.

USES

The herbalist John Evelyn grew this plant in his Physick Garden. It had the reputation as a mollifying herb and was once used for gout, burns and scalds though it is not used any more for this purpose, and it does not appear to have any culinary uses.

ACONITE—Monkshead, Wolfsbane (POISONOUS)
Botanical name: *Aconitum napellus*
Family: Ranunculaciae

GENERAL
Aconite is a powerful poisonous plant which nevertheless has a beneficial effect on some symptoms. The toxic substance it contains is aconitine and is present in the whole plant, particularly the root. The name aconite is derived from the Greek *akontion* a dart, because it was used by barbarous tribes to poison their arrows. It was introduced to England centuries ago and has been mentioned in herbals since the tenth century. It was known to the Ancients as a deadly poison. Also in the East Indies natives used aconite to poison wells to halt the progress of a conquering army.

DESCRIPTION AND HABITAT
Aconite is a hardy perennial plant with a fleshy, spindle-shaped root and a tall stem. The leaves are a dark glossy green on the upper side and light green underneath The flowers which are dark blue and grow in erect clusters are irregularly formed and look like a monk's hood. In Great Britain another variety *A.Anglicum* may be found wild in the west counties and South Wales. Now it is chiefly grown in the Swiss Alps, North Tyrol and Vorarlberg and Spain and Italy, preferring north-facing slopes. It is also cultivated in America and Britain for medicine.

CULTIVATION
Aconite prefers a moist, loamy soil and flourishes in the shade. It can be raised from seed but it will be two or three years before it flowers. Propagation is usually by division of roots in autumn after the stem has died down. The plants are perennial, but every year the 'parent' root dies and the growth is continued by new 'daughter' roots. These roots are selected for replanting in December or January, and planted about 1 ft apart (30cm).

HOW TO STORE
The leaves and flowers should be cut just when the flowers begin to bloom in June. The roots should be collected in autumn, after the stem dies down. They should be washed and trimmed and then dried. Drying can be done in the usual way with electric heat, and stored in dark securely closed containers, keeping in mind the poisonous properties of the plant.

USES
Aconite is strictly medicinal and should be used only in accordance with a doctor's prescription.

Preparations of aconite are applied externally to diminish the pain of neuralgia, lumbago, rheumatism, arthritis and gout. Tincture can be provided for various illnesses. Aconite has also been used for treatment of typhus, measles, diptheria, inflammation of any of the organs, croup, disturbed menstrual cycle due to emotional causes, and also milk-fever.

AGRIMONY—Cocklebur, Stickwort
Botanical name: *Agrimonia eupatoria*
HEMP AGRIMONY—Boneset, Gravel Root
Botanical name: *Eupatorium cannabinum*
Family: Compositae

GENERAL
There are two species of agrimony which differ mostly in the conditions needed for their growth. Both plants have diuretic properties. *Agrimonia eupatoria* has been known from time immemorial as an outstanding healing plant for wounds. The origin of *Eupatorium cannabinum* is difficult to trace as it played a lesser part in folk medicine.

DESCRIPTION AND HABITAT
Both plants are perennial and grow wild in Britain and Europe. *Agrimonia eupatoria* can also be found in Asia and Africa as it enjoys a sunny climate while *Eupatorium cannabinum* is more to be found in damp places such as ditches and river banks. It is the taller of these two plants and has dull lilac or purple flowers. *Agrimonia eupatoria* grows to a medium height and bears clusters of yellow flowers.

CULTIVATION
Neither is cultivated, but found growing wild.

FLAVOUR AND HOW TO STORE
A medicinal herb, agrimony has a pleasant aromatic taste, but very little scent. It can be dried and stored in the usual way.

USES
Agrimony leaves are used to make a herbal tea which has tonic properties and it is said to be good for problem skins, also for rheumatism, arthritis and colds and coughs. It was widely used in the Middle Ages in a solution for washing wounds.

Agrimony

RECIPE SUGGESTION
For the tea: to one teaspoon of agrimony leaves or root, add 8 fl oz (225ml) of boiling water. Allow to draw for about 5 min. It is best infused with a little liquorice root or lemon and sweetened with honey.

ALEXANDERS—Horse Parsley, Black Lovage, the Black Potherb
Botanical name: *Smyrnium olusatrum*
Family: Umbelliferae

GENERAL
Before the days of onions, carrots and turnips, alexanders was widely cultivated as a potherb. Its Latin name *Smyrnium*, comes from the Greek word for myrrh which describes the scent, and *olusatrum* means 'black potherb'. It was mentioned by the ancient Greek botanist Theophrastus (322 BC) as an officinal plant, and later Dioscorides recorded the edible properties of its roots. It became popular during the time of Alexander the Great. It was introduced to Britain by the Romans.

DESCRIPTION AND HABITAT
A biennial, alexanders grows to medium height. The flowerheads are umbels of greenish-yellow flowers; the dark green leaves are unequally divided into three, and serrated on the upper part. The fruits are small and black. Originally native to Macedonia, alexanders has been naturalised in Britain for two thousand years and grows abundantly on meadows and waste land near the sea.

CULTIVATION
Sow in an ordinary soil in autumn as for other biennials. When seedlings are large enough, transplant in spring. Later, earth up for blanching as is done with celery.

FLAVOUR AND HOW TO STORE
The young shoots and leafstalks which are the edible parts, have an agreeable, celery-like flavour, though more pungent. It is best used as a fresh vegetable.

USES
Alexanders may be boiled as a vegetable or used as a potherb to flavour soups and stews. Medicinally, it is diuretic and carminative.

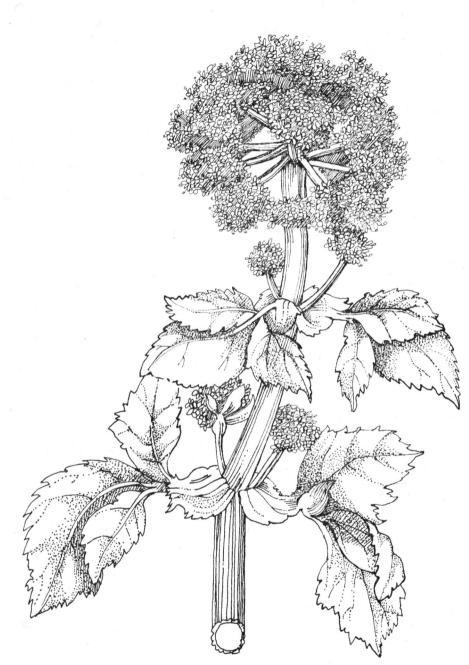

Alexanders

RECIPE SUGGESTION
To cook alexanders shoots, take young shoots and leafstalks. Wash and cut them into small lengths. Cook in boiling salted water until tender. Strain and serve in a white sauce.

ALLSPICE—Pimento, Jamaica Pepper
Botanical name: *Pimenta officinalis*
Family: Myrtaceae

GENERAL
Allspice is the dried, unripe berry of the West Indian pimento, or allspice tree. Its name comes from its combination of flavours and its variety of uses, and it is not a mixture of spices as is sometimes thought. Amongst the most aromatic of spices, it has a world wide reputation yet is grown exclusively in the Western hemisphere.

It was first brought to Europe by Christopher Columbus who found it in Jamaica, its true country of origin. In Mexico the Aztecs used it to flavour their national drink, Chocolada. It was first known as piment, probably from the word pimento which was used in the Middle Ages for every spice.

DESCRIPTION AND HABITAT
The allspice tree is native to Central and South America and the West Indies, particularly Jamaica where the berries are smaller and more aromatic, and considered to be of the highest quality. Allspice forms one of Jamaica's main exports. The evergreen allspice tree belongs to the myrtle family and can grow to a great height depending on the climate. It has small white flowers and the fruits are round with a rough surface, a little larger than peppercorns, each containing two kidney-shaped seeds. The fruits are gathered unripe and dried in the hot tropical sun till they turn a dark reddish-brown.

CULTIVATION
Allspice trees can only be grown in tropical climates or in a heated greenhouse. Propagation is by seed taken from the fresh, ripe fruit and immediately planted. The seedlings are ready for transplanting after about a year and start to bear fruit after six or seven years. The trees continue to produce for up to a hundred years.

FLAVOUR AND HOW TO STORE
Allspice has a mild yet biting, spicy taste reminiscent of a combination of cloves, cinnamon and nutmeg. It can be bought whole or ground and should be stored in glass, screw top jars.

USES

Ground allspice is found in many of the blended spice mixtures and whole in pickling spice. It is used in marinades for, and in the boiling of, fish and shellfish; also in beef, lamb, ham, game and curry dishes. Two or three berries in green pea soup add a spicy flavour, as does a pinch of ground allspice to carrots and other sweet vegetables. It is used to flavour cakes and biscuits, milk and chocolate puddings, fruit pies and a popular West Indian drink called Pimento Dram. Its leaves are used in the production of bay rum, and at one time the white bark was sold as clove cinnamon.

Medicinally, the volatile oil is aromatic, stomachic and carminative and is added to other medicines for flatulence and diarrhoea. It is also used for head and toothaches.

RECIPE SUGGESTION

Stuffed Spiced Lamb: For a 2 lb (900g) boned best end neck of lamb, make the following stuffing. Sauté lightly 1 tbs chopped onion in 1 oz (30g) butter. Remove from heat, mix in 3 oz (90g) breadcrumbs, 2 tsp raisins, grated rind of 1 orange, 1 tsp mixed herbs. Add 1 beaten egg and seasoning. Place stuffing on lamb, roll and tie securely. Rub joint with 1 oz (30g) soft butter and sprinkle over 2 tsp ground allspice. Place in baking tin, pour over juice of 1 orange, bake in moderate oven 350°F (gas mark 4) for 45-50 min.

ANGELICA
Botanical name: *Angelica archangelica*
Family: Umbelliferae

GENERAL

Legend reports that angelica was revealed by an angel to cure the plague and though it has medicinal qualities, it is best known nowadays for its bright green candied or crystallised stems. It came to England in the sixteenth century from countries in the northern hemisphere.

DESCRIPTION AND HABITAT

Angelica, a biennial, is a tall plant, with deeply indented, very large leaves and strong stems. It provides an attractive border to any herb garden, at the same time protecting the other herbs from wind. The colour of the stems, leaf segments and the flowers is greenish-white, or light green. Angelica is rarely found growing wild, its natural habitat is in shady places in Iceland, Lapland and other northern regions.

CULTIVATION

As angelica grows tall, the plants should be at least 18 in (45cm) apart. Propagation by roto

Angelica

division is the usual method since the seeds lose their germinating power very quickly. In the temperate climate of England, it reseeds itself so profusely that to avoid this the flowerheads are often cut off. The self-sown young plants can be easily transplanted, when they will normally flower in the second year. Angelica likes a shady position in relatively good soil. The flowering stalks and leaf stalks should be harvested in April or May, but the leaves in May or June before flowering. The plant will continue growing until the flowerheads are allowed to go to seed, and the plant may die after the second year.

FLAVOUR AND HOW TO STORE
The flavour of angelica resembles juniper berries and it has been used with them for gin. The sweet flavour of the crystallised stems is more well known. After careful drying, angelica leaves can be used for tisanes or pot-pourri.

USES
The leaves can be used dried or fresh as a tisane, resembling China tea, which helps to produce perspiration in feverish colds. Its lovely colour and scent can also be used in pot-pourri. The candied leaf stalks are often used to decorate cakes and pastry, and for flavouring jams. The roots and stems of the plant can be cooked with rhubarb to remove the tartness. Angelica has also been used in flavouring drinks and the muscatel flavour of Rhine wine is supposed to be due to its use.

RECIPE SUGGESTION
Angelica Jelly, served as a dessert with cream, or on top of a sponge cake, is made from 20 fl oz (575ml) of liquid made up of half apple juice and juice of half a lemon and water; 3 tbs sugar and 1 envelope gelatine. Line bottom of jelly mould with very thin rings of angelica, using about 3 in (8cm) of fresh stalk. Sprinkle evenly with 1 level dessertspoon sweet cicely. Make up jelly as usual, bringing liquid to the boil once—pour carefully into mould and leave to set in refrigerator.

ANISE—Aniseed
Botanical name: *Pimpinella anisum*
Family: Umbelliferae

GENERAL
An oil-bearing seed plant, anise is widely used today. Apart from its excellent flavour in cooking, it is valuable in medicine as a digestive, curing flatulence and helping in the assimilation of food. These properties were recognised in classical times by the Romans who, after

their rich meals, would eat a spiced cake containing aniseed, which may well be the origin of our spicy wedding cake of today. On the Continent, and renowned in Austria, anise is used in cakes, bread, rolls and in Christmas cooking. Anise is native to the Middle East and has been grown in Egypt, Asia Minor and on the Greek islands for thousands of years. With the absorption of the Greek way of life by the Romans, anise came to be grown throughout the Roman Empire, along the shores of the Mediterranean, in France and in England. Nowadays aniseed comes from India, North Africa, Spain and Italy.

DESCRIPTION AND HABITAT
An annual, anise grows to medium height. The light green leaves are serrated and the flower heads are umbels of creamy-white flowers. The aromatic fruits, with the seeds inside, are known as 'aniseed' and generally no distinction is made between the minute fruit and its seed. They have a distinctive sweet-scented fragrance which comes from the colourless anise oil contained in them.

CULTIVATION
Anise grows well when sown in April on a light soil with plenty of lime, in a sheltered south facing position. Only in a really hot summer will the fruits ripen in August. When this happens and the tips of the fruits have turned greyish-green, they are ready to be harvested. Cut the flower stems at ground level, tie in bundles, then pile, heads down, in a large crock and leave for a week, when the ripening should be complete. Carefully shake out the tiny aniseeds and they are ready to store. In the summer months, before the plant comes into flower, some of the leaves can be dried for use during the winter.

FLAVOUR AND HOW TO STORE
The flavour of anise is sweet and spicy and is popular with children. Aniseed is best stored in glass screw-top jars away from the light in a dry place. They should always be bought in small quantities and whole, for they soon lose flavour; when needed ground, they are easy to crush at home.

USES
Anise is probably best known for its use in flavouring various liqueurs and cordials with its attractive, sweet aroma; such drinks are Pernod, Anisette and the Greek Ouzo. Chopped leaves of anise can be added sparingly to cooked vegetables, soups, stews and salads; also to sweet dishes such as fruit salad and apple pie.

Medicinally, aniseed aids the digestion and is good for small children suffering from diarrhoea. With honey, the tea disperses flatulence and for asthma, the tea should be drunk warm; if fennel is added, it helps to ease bronchial catarrh. Chewing aniseed induces sleep and a few seeds taken in water will cure hiccups. The distilled and dried seeds contain up to 20

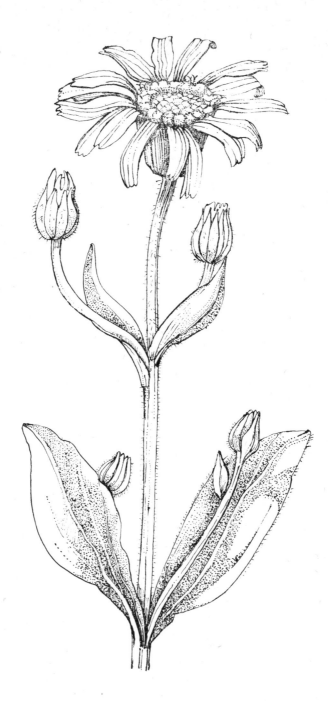

Arnica

per cent protein and therefore are a valuable addition to animal feeding stuffs. Because of this concentrated protein, it is believed that aniseed is good for nursing mothers, stimulating the milk production.

RECIPE SUGGESTION
Anise Biscuits: Ingredients 9 oz (250g) butter, 8 oz (225g) sugar, 3 drops vanilla essence, 1 tbs milk, 1 tbs rum, ⅓ oz (8g) crushed aniseed, 12 oz (340g) flour, whole aniseeds, little caster sugar, egg yolk for glaze. Brown butter in pan, then cool. Beat in one third of the sugar then remainder with vanilla, rum, milk and crushed aniseed. Mix in flour thoroughly. Turn out on board and knead well. Shape into long thin rolls and cool in refrigerator for an hour. Cut rounds 1½ in (4cm) thick—put on greased tin, well spaced, and brush with egg yolk mixed with milk. Sprinkle over whole aniseeds and caster sugar. Bake in 350°F (mark 4) oven until golden brown (8–10 min). Allow 2–3 min before removing from rack. (Makes about 60 biscuits.)

ARNICA—Mountain Tobacco—Leopards Bane (POISONOUS)
Botanical name: *Arnica montana*
Family: Compositae

GENERAL
Arnica is a medicinal plant containing a volatile oil, the bitter principle arnicin as well as tannin and phulin. A tincture, made by preserving the plant in alcohol, is an effective external application. Arnica was known by the ancients as a healing plant whose virtues are recognised and used today.

DESCRIPTION AND HABITAT
Arnica is a perennial herb. The leaves form a flat rosette near ground level from which rises the flower stalk, about 1 ft (30cm) high. The flowers are yellow florets and have brownish fruits. The plant is indigenous to central European woods and mountain pastures, and has been found in England and southern Scotland.

CULTIVATION
Arnica is propagated by root division in the spring, or from seed. The seeds should be sown in early spring in a cold frame and planted out in May. The flowers are harvested whole and dried. The root is collected for use in the autumn, after the leaves have died down.

USES
The tincture, available at chemists, is only applied externally to sprains, bruises and other wounds. Repeated application may produce inflammation of the skin. It has been employed

in the treatment of epilepsy, seasickness, and applied to the scalp it is said to make the hair grow.

ARROWROOT

Botanical name: *Maranta arundinacea*
Family: Marantaceae

GENERAL
Arrowroot, a tropical plant, the root of which is the source of the powdered arrowroot we all know, is a valuable food and natural remedy for convalescents, young and old. It is also a culinary starch valuable for thickening clear fruit sauces and meat glazes. Besides starch, it contains fat, albumen, sugar, gum and ash. The botanical name Maranta was given to the genus in honour of a famous Venetian physician in about 1559. In its native South America, the Indians once used it as an antidote to arrow-poisoning. It was introduced to England early in the eighteenth century though it can only be grown under hothouse conditions.

DESCRIPTION AND HABITAT
Arrowroot, a tall perennial, has a creeping fleshy root. It has oval leaves and creamy flowers grow at the end of long branches. Its natural habitat is South and central America, India, West Africa and West Indies; the finest arrowroot comes from Bermuda.

CULTIVATION
This plant can only be cultivated in warm, moist climates. During its growing period it requires copious watering, but when fully grown it is left dry until harvested.

FLAVOUR AND HOW TO STORE
The flavour is mild. The juice, pressed from year-old roots is washed with clean water, strained and the residue allowed to dry to a powder. This is available at chemists.

USES
Arrowroot is easily digestible and suitable for infants and invalids. Many people can hardly be without this well known natural remedy for bowel disorders. It can be added to warm milk, or made into milk puddings and jellies, and is often an ingredient in plain biscuits.

RECIPE SUGGESTION
To make a sauce, use a dessertspoon arrowroot mixed to a thin paste with a little water, 1 tbs sugar and 5 fl oz (150ml) each milk and water. Bring liquid and sugar to boil and pour on to arrowroot paste, returning to pan and boiling for 3-4 min while stirring. Remove from heat and add 1 tbs cream sherry.

ASAFOETIDA—*Devil's Dung, Stinking Gum*
Botanical names: *Ferula asafoetida*
Ferula narthex
Family: Umbelliferae

GENERAL
Asafoetida is a famous Asiatic seasoning. It comes from a resinous substance known as gum asafoetida, contained in two varieties of the giant fennels. These are unrelated to the garden and wild fennels though somewhat similar in appearance, and have a dreadful stink due to their content of sulphurous compounds. However, the foetid odour disappears on boiling, for the leaves and stems are still used today as a vegetable in their native Persia and Afghanistan. In ancient times, it was known there as Food-of-the-Gods and the Romans who valued it for medicinal purposes as well as a flavouring for sauces and wines, knew it as Persian Sylphium. Today, it is a popular seasoning in many Indian vegetarian dishes and is sometimes used as a flavouring in France, though generally neglected in other European cooking. All gums obtained from the Ferula genus of plants are reputed to have medicinal values, and several varieties appear in the Chinese *Pentsao* or *Materia Medica* as a plant used in their herbal medicines.

DESCRIPTION AND HABITAT
Ferula asafoetida and *narthex* are tall, evil-smelling perennials with thick roots, stout branched stems bearing long leaves and umbels of greenish-yellow flowers. They grow wild in central and western Asia.

CULTIVATION
These two varieties can be grown from seed in warm climates similar to those of Persia and Afghanistan where they grow into thick forests. The stems are cut to the root and the milky juice which flows out, dries into a resinous mass. A garden variety *F. communis*, said to be poisonous, can be grown in more temperate climates as a decorative border plant for its fine foliage.

FLAVOUR AND HOW TO STORE
The roots and stem contain a strong smelling resinous gum which is sold in solid, wax-like pieces or in powder form for use as a spice. The gum darkens with storing.

USES
Powdered asafoetida can be used in minute quantities as a delicious flavouring for vegetables, and especially for fresh or salted fish. It makes an interesting seasoning for stews, gravies and

sauces, bringing out their flavours. In the orient, the gum is used in their perfumes and as a fixative in pot-pourri.

Medicinally, it is used in pill form to disguise its nauseous taste as a stimulant, antispasmodic and expectorant, and is a useful remedy for children with croup or colic.

RECIPE SUGGESTION
Add a tiny pinch to every kind of fish to give an interesting and unusual taste.

BASIL
Botanical name: *Ocimum basilicum*
Family: Labiatae

GENERAL
An important culinary herb, basil was an ingredient in the famous Fetter Lane sausages. In the past, farmers' wives gave gifts of a pot of basil to their friends both for cooking and for keeping flies away, a practice still continued in France, Italy and Greece. Its Greek name, *Basileus*, means 'king' to indicate its royal position among the herbs. It has a longer history than almost any other culinary herb. It probably came from India to Europe via the Middle East. The Egyptians passed their knowledge on to Arabia, Greece and Rome. Pliny and Dioscorides recorded basil in their works in the first century AD. Later, the monks continued its cultivation. A different kind of basil (*Ocimum sanctum*) is the holy Hindu herb, used in religious ceremonies, but is rarely used in Indian cooking.

DESCRIPTION AND HABITAT
Basil is a low growing annual. It has light green silky leaves and whorls of small, creamy white flowers borne in the angles of the leaves. Grows best in warm climates. Bush or wild basil is inferior to sweet basil, and several good culinary hybrids are being developed.

CULTIVATION
Easily grown from seed, Basil requires a light, well-drained but rich soil or compost. It should be grown in a sunny position outside, sheltered from winds, or in pots placed in a sunny or sheltered spot in the garden. Basil is not easily grown in a temperate climate where the best results are obtained under glass. The authors have given up growing basil commercially out of doors north of London, as only in exceptionally warm summers is the crop sufficient to justify the growing. It cannot stand frost so the seeds should not be sown before May and its season is over by September. Keep nipping off the top shoots to encourage a bushy growth and to prevent flowering. Use the herb when it is about 6 in (18cm) high.

FLAVOUR AND HOW TO STORE

The flavour of the fresh herb is peppery, rather like cloves, with a strong, pungent, sweet smell. The fresh herb can be kept for a short time in polythene bags in the refrigerator or for a long time in the deep freeze, after being blanched quickly in boiling water. A successful way of storing fresh leaves is by placing them in a dry jar with a pinch of salt and covering them with olive oil. The dried herb tastes utterly different, rather like curry.

USES

Use basil sparingly, especially if cooked (which develops the flavour). Basil goes well with tomatoes, and a fresh roll with sliced tomatoes, salt, olive oil and a few leaves of fresh basil will bring words of praise from almost everyone. In spaghetti sauces and rich meat sauces the combination of garlic and basil is far better than either used alone. It also combines well with rosemary, sage and summer savory and with all mushroom recipes. It flavours insipid vegetables and fish, especially red mullet, as well as chicken, eggs and rice dishes. It stimulates the appetite, digestion and nerves. It has been used in the Far East in cough medicines, for kidney trouble and diarrhoea.

RECIPE SUGGESTION

Sprinkle a mixture of chopped fresh basil, parsley and summer savory on to tomato slices, a combination which gives its own peppery flavour. Try a pinch with stewed fruit—or in a tomato juice cocktail.

BAY—*The Sweet Bay Tree*

Botanical name: *Laurus nobilis*
Family: Lauraceae

GENERAL

Although referred to as a herb, bay leaves come from the aromatic sweet bay tree which looks more like a shrub. It is a well known and an important herb and in ancient times it provided wreaths for poets and heroes. Along with other evergreens, it has been used to decorate houses and churches at Christmas. It has an ancient reputation of being beneficial to the health and happiness of man. A native of the Mediterranean countries, the ancient Greeks and Romans dedicated the bay to Apollo and to Aesculapius, the God of Medicine. Later it was believed to have been a protection against the Devil. Throughout history it has been used as a strewing herb for its scent and antiseptic qualities. It was so important as a symbol of success and a protection against all evil, that this gave rise to popular superstition that when bay trees died a great disaster was on the way.

DESCRIPTION AND HABITAT
The sweet bay is an evergreen shrub-like tree with shiny leathery leaves, which are dark green on top and pale yellowish-green on the underneath. The flowers are insignificant and greenish-yellow in colour, followed by dark purple, one-seeded berries. It grows well in Britain, particularly in the shade of some other trees. It will grow very tall.

CULTIVATION
Sweet bay trees can only be bought at general nurseries, and hardly ever at a herb nursery, as it is considered more a tree than a culinary herb plant. It is not choosy about the soil. Sometimes a heavy frost will cause the tree to lose some of its leaves, but generally a new growth will appear on the tree when spring comes. It can be propagated rapidly by planting the cuttings of half-ripened shoots. Small trees can be grown in tubs in moderately rich soil in a sunny position.

FLAVOUR AND HOW TO STORE
Bay leaves have a strong, spicy flavour and a striking aroma which becomes even more apparent when the leaves are shredded or crushed. The leaves can be picked throughout the year although it is better to dry them as then the flavour becomes stronger. They should be dried in the dark and should retain their natural colour and not become brown.

USES
Bay leaves are used as a spicing agent and should be used sparsely. A bay leaf is an important part of a bouquet garni. A leaf should also be added to the stock for boiled fish and in soups. As well as for flavouring, bay leaves have also been used for preserving and marinading. They stimulate the appetite and were recommended by Culpeper as a pain reliever and remedy for skin and ear troubles.

RECIPE SUGGESTION
Bay leaves are a must in herb marinades for fish, meat and poultry, stocks and court bouillon. Always add half or whole leaf to game and liver casseroles, mutton hot-pot, goulash.

BEARBERRY
Botanical name: *Arctostaphylos uva-ursi*
Family: Ericaceae

GENERAL
Bearberry is a medicinal herb used since the thirteenth century when its properties were known to the Welsh 'Physicians of Myddfair'. It was admitted to the *London Pharmacopoeia* in 1763

Bearberry

and is still used in orthodox medicine. In North America and Arctic regions, various Indian tribes use the dried leaves in tobacco mixtures, but the berries are quite inedible.

DESCRIPTION AND HABITAT
Bearberry is a medium-sized shrubby evergreen perennial plant with a woody stem. It has a trailing growth, forming masses of leaves and flowers and a long fibrous root. The leaves are leathery, dark green and glossy on the upper side and light green on the underside with prominent veins. The small flowers appear in May–June before the young leaves. They are white with a red lip and bloom in drooping clusters as many as fifteen together. The berry is bright red, the size of a currant with a tough glossy skin. Bearberry grows on barren highlands and heaths and is common in Scotland. It is found in Europe, Asia and America.

CULTIVATION
Generally not cultivated but found growing wild.

FLAVOUR AND HOW TO STORE
The leaves have a bitter, astringent taste. They are collected in September and October for drying in the usual way at a temperature of 70°–100°F (19°–34°C).

USES
The leaves are used to make an infusion which is taken for diseases of the bladder, kidneys and urinary tracts.

RECIPE SUGGESTION
To make an infusion of the leaves allow 1 teaspoon per person per cup of boiling water; leave to draw for 3 min. Alternatively the leaves can be soaked in brandy—sufficient to cover them —taking 1 teaspoon of the leaves to a cup of boiling water. This drink is taken after the infusion has cooled down.

BELLADONNA—Deadly Nightshade, Dwale (POISONOUS)
Botanical name: Atropa belladonna
Family: Solanacae

GENERAL
All parts of this plant, perhaps better known as Deadly Nightshade, are highly poisonous. Its other name, Dwale, comes from the Danish word for sleep. A drug made from belladonna was used as an anaesthetic during the Middle Ages. Its name is derived from its cosmetic use by Italian ladies to give a sparkle to their eyes. It has grown wild all over Europe for thousands of years.

DESCRIPTION AND HABITAT
Belladonna is a perennial bush plant of medium height. It has dark, dull green oval leaves ending in a sharp point. The drooping, purple bell-shaped flowers bloom in June and July and the whole plant has an unpleasant smell when crushed. It is not a common plant in Britain, but can be found in chalky limestone districts, near old buildings or ruins since it was widely cultivated in the 'physick' gardens for its medicinal value.

CULTIVATION
Grows wild.

USES
The juice of the rootstock and leaves contains the alkaloid drug 'atropine'. Today it is used medically as a narcotic, diuretic and sedative. It is used to relieve spasms as in whooping cough and pain in feverish conditions. Externally it is used to dilate the pupils during eye examinations and for gout and rheumatic inflammations. Owing to the poisonous nature of this plant, even the smallest quantity must not be used except under medical supervision; the mere handling of the plant can be dangerous.

BERGAMOT—Bee Balm
Botanical name: *Monarda didyma*
Monarda fistulosa—Wild bergamot
Family: Labiatae

GENERAL
Bergamot is a herb used mainly medicinally, but its leaves and flowers combine well with salads. Most herb nurseries only stock *Monarda didyma*, the red variety, as the popular tisane made from it is generally preferred. It is sometimes known as Oswego Tea because in the past the Oswego Indians of North America were very fond of this drink, and its other name Bee Balm is appropriate since bees are attracted by the fragrance of the nectar-rich flowers. Both varieties of bergamot are native to North America and were discovered there by European colonists; through them it became known in Britain. At the time of the Boston Tea Party, Americans would drink bergamot tea while boycotting British imported tea. Bergamot's botanical name *Monarda* originates from the Spanish physician Nicholas Monardes who discovered their properties in the sixteenth century.

DESCRIPTION AND HABITAT
Both varieties are widespread in North America but can be successfully grown in Britain.

They are perennial and highly scented. Red bergamot has an orange scent, while the so-called wild bergamot has more of a lemon scent. They grow to medium height, flowering in mid-summer. The flowers of red bergamot are scarlet, the leaves rough and hairy. Wild bergamot has clusters of purple flowers and soft cotton-like foliage.

CULTIVATION
Wild bergamot will succeed in somewhat drier conditions than the red, which must have rich moist soil. Given this condition, red bergamot will spread rapidly and grow in large clumps. It should be dug up at least once every two years, the older roots discarded and the younger replanted. The roots are woody and fibrous and easily broken by hand. The plants die down after flowering and begin to grow tall again with the coming of spring.

FLAVOUR AND HOW TO STORE
The flavour of red bergamot, which is the variety chiefly used, is delicate and a little pungent. The leaves can be dried and stored in the usual way.

USES
As well as the young leaves, the scarlet flowers of the red bergamot are edible. The chopped leaves and flowers will improve the appearance as well as the taste of a salad. The leaves can also be added to cooked dishes, notably pork. A tisane made from the leaves is soothing and sleep inducing. It may be drunk alone or added to wine, soft drinks or other teas.

RECIPE SUGGESTIONS
Bergamot milk makes a good nightcap. Pour 10 fl oz (275ml) boiling milk over 1 tbs of shredded dried leaves. Stand for 5 min before straining. Sweeten if liked with honey, adding a little lemon. For the tea, a tsp of the herb per cup should be simmered in water for 10 min, preferably in a stainless steel or enamel saucepan. This also can be sweetened with honey.

BETONY (WOOD)—*Bishopwort*
Botanical name: *Betonica officinalis*
Family: Labiatae

GENERAL
Betony, a medicinal plant, was considered to have many healing properties and virtues, and was a favourite herb of the Saxons. It was also believed to keep away evil spirits and was cultivated in country churchyards for this purpose, thereby earning the name Bishopwort. It was cultivated in the monastery herb gardens of the Middle Ages when it was thought to be a remedy for all kinds of illnesses.

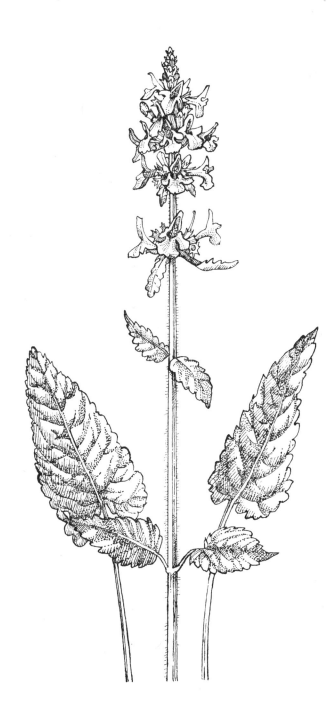

Betony

DESCRIPTION AND HABITAT

A perennial of small to medium height, betony is one of the most common flowers throughout Britain, growing in woods and along hedge banks. The small crimson flowers, which appear from June to August, are densely crowded in the axils of the uppermost pair of leaves and form a spike. The stemmed leaves are hairy and coarsely toothed and the whole plant strongly scented.

CULTIVATION

Grows wild.

FLAVOUR

Betony has a pleasant delicate taste somewhat like a fragrant China tea.

USES

Betony, a healing herb, is aromatic and astringent. It was used as an aperient and a nervine, especially for head and back ache. Its juice was used to heal cuts, sores and ulcers. The old German name for betony was *Zehrkraut* or 'wasting herb' and it was given to children who lost weight for no apparent reason. For this a tea was made, one to two cups being sipped slowly each day and a strong decoction was added to the bath water. It was also recommended for women's ailments and asthmatic attacks when caused by a building up of phlegm. Nowadays it is used by herbalists as an ingredient in medicines for digestive and rheumatic conditions and for varicose veins; also made into an ointment.

RECIPE SUGGESTION

To make the tea: place 1 teaspoon of the herb in a cup and add boiling water. Allow to steep for 5 min, strain and drink.

BILBERRY—*Blueberry, Whortleberry, Buckleberry, Whinberry*
Botanical name: *Vaccinium myrtillus*
Family: Ericaceae

GENERAL

Bilberries, a wild fruit with medicinal properties, are very pleasant to eat for their own sake. Of ancient origin, bilberries are also a favourite food of the Rocky Mountain Indians. Dioscorides recommended them for the treatment of dysentery.

DESCRIPTION AND HABITAT
The bilberry bush is a small wild deciduous shrub, hardly ever cultivated. It has ovate, pointed leaves which are rosy when young, then go yellowish-green and turn red in the autumn. The shrub bears pink flowers in May, and the fruits, which ripen July–August, are blue-black, the size of a blackcurrant, covered with a delicate grey bloom. Bilberries can be found in many parts of northern Asia and Europe, including Britain, in high heathy districts, mainly in deciduous woods, in dry sandy soil.

CULTIVATION
Grows wild.

FLAVOUR AND HOW TO STORE
Bilberries have a slightly acid flavour. They can be excellently preserved as a jelly or jam.

USES
Bilberries can be stewed with a little sugar and made into a tart or eaten with cream. On the Continent they are mostly eaten with sugar and plenty of milk. A tisane can be made from the leaves, which is good for sufferers of diabetes. Bilberries are also good for the treatment of scurvy, urinary complaints and dysentery. The leaves and root bark are useful as a local application to ulcers.

RECIPE SUGGESTION
Bilberry Leaves Tea: Pour 20 fl oz (575ml) boiling water over a teaspoon (5–8g) bilberry leaves. Infuse 10 min, strain and serve with sugar and lemon slices.
Bilberry Muesli: Soak 1 level dessertspoon medium oatmeal in 3 dessertspoons water for 12 hrs. Then mix in juice of ½ lemon, 1 heaped dessertspoon yoghurt, honey to sweeten as desired and 5 oz (140g) bilberries either pressed or put in liquidiser. If berries are not very juicy, thin muesli with a little fresh milk.

BLESSED THISTLE—*Milk Thistle, Holy Thistle*
Botanical name: *Carduus benedictus*
Family: Compositae

GENERAL
Blessed thistle is a famous medicinal herb, introduced into Britain by the Romans who also used it for cooking. It was widely cultivated for centuries as a cure for many diseases and is mentioned in all the great herbals. It was an ingredient in plague medicines and today is used in herbal tonics.

Blessed Thistle

DESCRIPTION AND HABITAT

Mostly grown as an annual, blessed thistle is of medium height. The flower heads are large, solitary and rather drooping with purple florets. The leaves are dark green, deeply lobed and prickly with white veins.

CULTIVATION

Growing in waste places in southern Europe, it can easily be grown from seed. It does well in almost any soil and flowers from June to August.

USES

In Roman times all parts of the plant were used; the root was boiled, the young leaves eaten in salads and the flower heads were eaten like globe artichokes.

Nowadays it is used by herbalists as a tonic and diaphoretic and for female complaints, but it should only be used in a mild dose or it becomes an emetic.

RECIPE SUGGESTION

To make an infusion for a tonic: to a teaspoon of finely chopped leaves and flowers add 20 fl oz (575ml) of boiling water. When cold strain and drink one cupful a day, a large mouthful at a time. To induce perspiration, drink hot.

BORAGE

Botanical name: *Borago officinalis*
Family: Boraginaceae

GENERAL

Borage has an ancient reputation for having a wonderful effect on the mind and body. Pliny believed that it 'makes men merry and joyful'. During the Roman occupation the old Greek proverb 'I, borage, bring always courage' became known and Gerard's herbal repeats this with the words: 'borage gives courage'. Its pretty flowers are greatly favoured by honey bees.

DESCRIPTION AND HABITAT

Borage, a native of the Mediterranean, is a sturdy annual plant of medium height which grows well in any kind of soil, even in stony ground. In rare varieties, the flowers are white or pink but they are usually bright blue with black anthers—very attractive and also edible. The plant has large ovate leaves, grey-green in colour.

CULTIVATION

Borage is an annual grown from seed and the seeds germinate very quickly. The plant reaches maturity in about 5–6 weeks. Borage reseeds itself and when once grown, it has hardly ever to be resown. If more borage is wanted, simply scatter a few more seeds. The plants will continue to flower until the first frost. Borage grows best in loose, stony soil which contains chalk and preferably sand. Sow the first seeds in March, covering them well with soil. They can also be grown in window boxes.

FLAVOUR AND HOW TO STORE
Borage adds a fresh, slightly salty, cucumber flavour to salads. It should always be used fresh since it is difficult to preserve the flavour and colour of this fragile plant when dried.

USES
The flowers and the leaves of borage are edible. The small young leaves should be picked and finely chopped, as otherwise their hairy texture may make them unappetising. The leaves and flowers can be added to lettuce, cucumber or potato salad and this improves the appearance as well as the flavour of the dish. Since ancient times, the borage flower has been added to wine cups and can also be added to non-alcoholic drinks with the same exhilaration and refreshing effect. The flowers can also be candied and eaten as a sweet.

RECIPE SUGGESTION
To candy the flowers, use the same method as for cowslip flowers.

For a refreshing summer drink, place two or three borage flowers and young leaves in a glass jug and pour over chilled, home-made lemonade made from a fresh lemon, 2¼ oz (60g) sugar and 10 fl oz (275ml) water.

BRYONY—White (POISONOUS)
Botanical name: *Bryonia dioica*
Family: Cucurbitaceae

GENERAL
The medicinal value of bryony root has been known since Hippocrates' time. In the four-teenth century, the juice was mixed with deadly nightshade and administered as an anaesthetic.

DESCRIPTION AND HABITAT
White bryony is common in southern England and Europe. It is a perennial plant with a thick tuberous rootstock. The stems climb over hedges and bushes by tendrils which grow from the bases of the leaf stalks. The leaves are rough and deeply divided and the flowers, which bloom in May, are greenish and grow three or four together, in the axils of the leaves. The berries are red or orange.

Buckbean

CULTIVATION
Grows wild. Not advisable to cultivate.

USES
In homeopathic medicine preparations of the root are used for the treatment of whooping cough and also chilblains. A tincture, obtained from a homeopathic chemist, is effective on chilblains and helps to prevent them in the future.

BUCKBEAN—Bogbean, Water Trefoil, Marsh Trefoil, Marsh Clover

Botanical name: *Menyanthes trifoliata*
Family: Gentianaceae

GENERAL
This wild plant of many names is worth while cultivating. It will make a pretty border, growing in or out of the water on the edge of a garden pond. Its botanical name *Menyanthes* denotes that it flowers for a month which is generally June, but sometimes also May and July! Its medicinal value has been well known for centuries; it was important for healing the once-dreaded scurvy.

DESCRIPTION AND HABITAT
Buckbean is a hardy perennial, aquatic plant. It has clusters of lily-shaped, rose coloured flowers which when open, reveal a white fringe. It can be found growing in marshy districts of North America, North Asia and Arctic Europe, including the north of England and Scotland.

CULTIVATION
Buckbean can be successfully cultivated in moist, peaty soils or shallow water. Propagate by division of the creeping roots into lengths of a foot (30cm) each with a terminal bud, and push them into soft mud.

USES
The leaves can be added to wine or an infusion made with boiling water. It is a tonic, beneficial in cases of rheumatism, debility of the liver and skin diseases. External application is good for glandular swellings. In Sweden it is used as a substitute for hops in the brewing of ale, and Laplanders boil the roots as a vegetable.

RECIPE SUGGESTION
To make an infusion: place 1 oz (30g) of the leaves in a jug and add 20 fl oz (575ml) of boiling

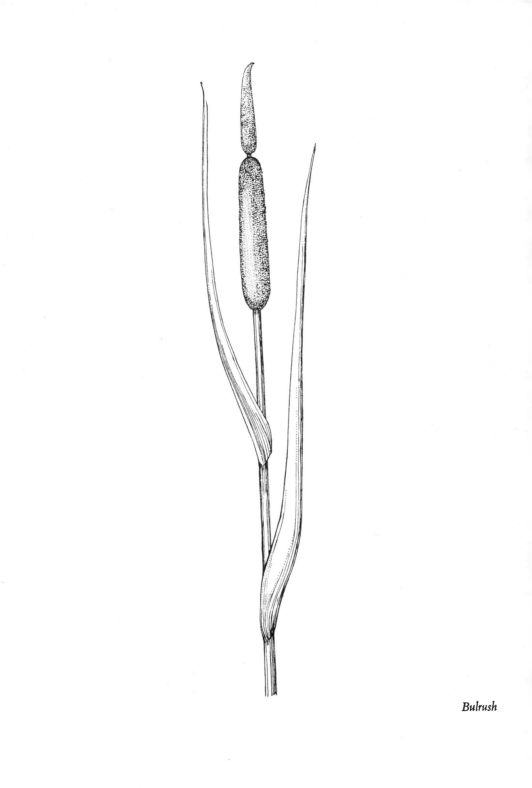

Bulrush

water—cover and leave to get cold. Then stir and strain. A wineglassful is taken 4 times a day.

BULRUSH—*Reedmace*
Botanical name: *Typha latifolia*—Great Reedmace, Cat's Tail
Typha angustifolia—Lesser Reedmace
Family: Typhaceae

GENERAL
The two varieties of the reedmace are useful food plants. They are commonly called bulrush and mistaken for the true bulrush *Scirpus lacustris*—which has little food value. Identification should therefore be made with care. Reedmace, sometime known as 'Cossack asparagus' grows abundantly on the shores of the Don River in Russia. There, the young stems, with outer skin removed, are eaten like asparagus and considered to be a delicacy.

DESCRIPTION AND HABITAT
A tall perennial plant, the common great reedmace grows throughout Europe and North America in marshes and on the margins of lakes, ponds and ditches. It has a short creeping rootstock. The long sword-shaped leaves are linear and nearly flat. Each stout stem carries a dense continuous spike of small flowers—this is the 'mace'. When in flower the upper male part consists of yellow closely packed anthers, whilst the lower female part is a dense mass of soft brownish hairs. The fruit forms in the lower part, the nuts or seeds being enveloped in the rusty brown hairs and the upper part becomes quite bare.

The lesser reedmace differs only in that it is a smaller plant, the leaves are grooved at the base and the male and female spikes are slightly disjointed. It is not such a common plant.

CULTIVATION
A wild plant.

FLAVOUR AND HOW TO STORE
The whole plant has a delicate sweet taste and the seeds, when roasted, have a nutty flavour. These can be gathered when ripe and after removing the down, can be stored in glass screw-top jars.

USES
Roots of the reedmace can be peeled and cooked as a vegetable, or grated and used raw in salads. Flour can be made from the pollen in a survival situation. The insides of the fresh young shoots can be eaten raw or cooked like asparagus. The seeds or nuts should be roasted before eating to bring out the flavour.

Calamint

RECIPE SUGGESTION
Cut tender young shoots, peel off the outer skin carefully and tie in small bundles of equal length. Place in boiling water for about 15–20 min. Eat hot with a butter sauce.

CALAMINT—*Mountain Balm*
Botanical name: *Calamintha officinalis*
Family: Labiatae

GENERAL
The name comes from the Greek words *kale* meaning good, and *minthe*, mint. In the old days the aromatic leaves were often used as a herb tea.

DESCRIPTION AND HABITAT
Calamint is a hairy perennial with a creeping rootstock and long branches growing to medium height. It has pale purple flowers and the stalked leaves are toothed and broadly ovate. Calamint grows in woods, along hedgerows. A fairly common wild plant, found in England and Ireland and on the Continent and in waste places.

CULTIVATION
Grows wild.

FLAVOUR
Calamint has an aromatic taste and a scent of mint.

USES
With its sweet aromatic flavour it makes a pleasant tea. Medicinally it is a diaphoretic and an expectorant and is used in the form of a decoction of syrup. As an infusion it is said to be useful as a tonic and for making a good cordial, stimulating the heart. As a poultice, calamint leaves are helpful for bruises or rheumatic pains.

RECIPE SUGGESTION
Make an infusion by steeping the whole plant in boiling water for about 20 min.

CALAMUS—*Sweet Flag, Sweet Sedge, Myrtle Grass*
Botanical name: *Acorus calamus*
Family: Araceae

GENERAL
Native to central and south America and to southern Asia, calamus has been grown for its

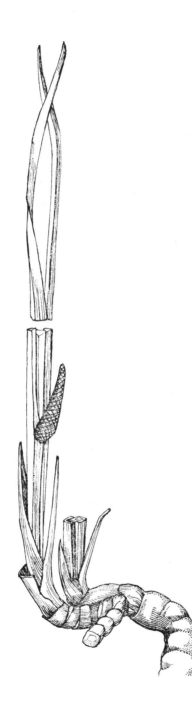

Calamus

rhizomes for thousands of years. It was introduced into Europe in 1557 where it soon became naturalised. It was first brought to Britain in 1796 and grew wild only in Norfolk, where the fragrant leaves were strewn in churches at festival times and the reeds used for thatching. The name calamus is a Greek word for canes. Acorus comes from a Greek word pertaining to the eye and the plant was used for eye complaints. The French cultivate it as an ornamental water plant. Today it is cultivated for the medicinal properties of its root which contains a valuable volatile oil.

DESCRIPTION AND HABITAT
This highly aromatic reed-like plant of the Arum family is a medium-sized hardy evergreen perennial and grows on the edges of lakes and streams. The tall sword-shaped leaves are linear and erect. It has a creeping rootstock and the flowering stems end in dense yellowish-green spikes. It only flowers when growing in water and can be found in nearly all parts of the world.

CULTIVATION
Calamus can be grown successfully in the garden round the edges of ponds, in muddy soil and propagation is by root division in March.

FLAVOUR AND HOW TO STORE
The inner part of the calamus stalk has a sweet taste with an agreeable, slightly orange-like flavour. The fleshy rootstock has a warm, pungent, rather bitter taste. The two- or three-year old rhizomes are gathered in autumn and dried for commercial use. The scent and taste improve after drying, though it does not keep long without deteriorating. Probably difficult to dry at home.

USES
Calamus leaves give a delicious flavour to creams and custards and are used in the same way as a vanilla pod to flavour the milk. The rootstock is candied as a sweetmeat by confectioners. The oil extracted from the plant has been used to flavour beer and is today used in perfumes and medicines. Medicinally, the rhizome is a stimulant and tonic. For indigestion and flatulence, an infusion is made, or the dried root either raw or candied, can be chewed. In Turkey the candied roots are eaten as a protection against disease and for coughs. The oil essence is also added to inhalations.

RECIPE SUGGESTION
For tonic, make an infusion of 1 oz (30g) rhizome to 20 fl oz (575ml) boiling water. Take freely in teacupfuls.

CAPER
Botanical name: *Capparis spinosa*
Family: Caparidaceae

GENERAL
Capers are the unopened flower buds of the caper bush, pickled in wine vinegar and eaten as a condiment. They have been used in this way for hundreds of years. Dioscorides, the Greek physician, recommended the use of the leaves and roots of the caper plant for reducing swellings.

DESCRIPTION AND HABITAT
The caper bush, a native of the tropics and sub-tropics, is an attractive low trailing shrub with large white flowers and small oval-shaped leaves. It blooms from May to August, each flower lasting just for one day.

It grows wild in the Mediterranean region and can be cultivated in warm climates or greenhouses.

CULTIVATION
Capparis spinosa can be grown in a hot house and is propagated by cuttings in sand under a bell-glass.

FLAVOUR AND HOW TO STORE
Capers have a strong aromatic flavour which is due to the presence of capric acid, and only comes out when they are pickled. Capers are always sold in their pickling liquid and it is important that they are not allowed to dry out.

USES
Capers are used in sauces and relishes for flavour and as a garnish on other foods. Traditionally, in England, caper sauce is served with boiled mutton. Capers are an ingredient in Sauce Tartare for fish dishes and seafoods, also in fish curries, and can be added as seasoning to chicken salads and veal stews.

RECIPE SUGGESTION
To 8 fl oz (225ml) seasoned white sauce add 1 tsp tarragon vinegar, 1 tbs cream and 1 tbs capers—a good sauce with boiled chicken.

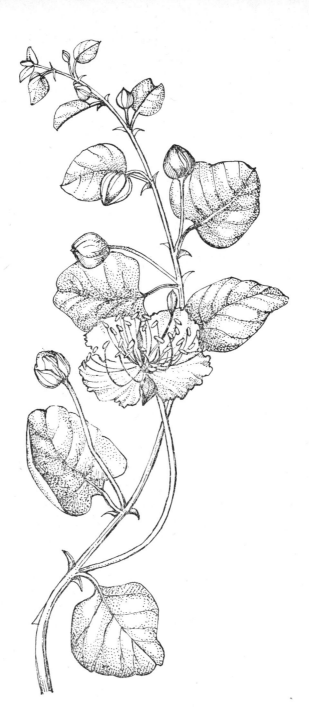

Caper

CAPSICUM—Chili Peppers
Botanical name: *Capsicum annuum*
Family: Solanaceae

GENERAL
The condiments paprika, red pepper and cayenne pepper, as well as chilies and 'bell' peppers, all come from the large Capsicum pepper family, a member of the 'nightshade' group of plants. After their discovery in the New World by the Spanish explorers in the fourteenth and fifteenth centuries, nearly all countries with tropical or sub-tropical climates cultivated the capsicum. In this way, more than a hundred different varieties of the plant have been produced, from the mildest 'sweet' or 'bell' peppers, also used as a vegetable, to the hottest 'chili' peppers which are dried and ground up to make the well-known 'hot' condiments used in kitchens all over the world.

The medicinal uses of capsicum peppers goes back for more than a thousand years when the South American Indians used them as a healing remedy for cramp and diarrhoea. They were of course unaware then of the valuable vitamin C the peppers contained.

DESCRIPTION AND HABITAT
Out of the many species of cultivated capsicum peppers—some annual and some perennial—we describe the five most common varieties. They are indigenous to central and South America and West Indies, but their cultivation has spread to Europe and tropical regions of Africa, Asia and India. Sometimes they are found growing wild in these areas as 'escapes'.

Capsicum annuum: This species includes nearly all sweet peppers and a large number of pungent ones. It is the most widely cultivated and nearly all European and USA varieties belong to it. It is an annual plant, 1–3 ft (30–90cm) high (although some varieties grow taller) bearing white flowers. The fruits vary in length from ½–11 in (1½–27cm) and in colour from yellow to brown, or from purple to bright red. The ripe pods have flat seeds. In shape they may be long and thin, small and round or conical, pointed and more fleshy. Varieties differ in appearance and taste according to location, the colder climates producing the milder peppers. A wild variety, called 'bird pepper' or 'chilitepin', is found in South and Central America and southern USA.

Capsicum frutescens: Perennial, growing up to 6 ft (180cm) tall with woody stems and greenish white flowers. Found mainly in tropical regions, this variety produces the hottest peppers. The colour of the ripe pods varies from red to orange to yellow. They are grown in India, Thailand, Mexico, Japan, Turkey and Africa.

Capsicum chinense: Grown in western hemisphere, tropical South America, Caribbean, south Central America. This species is closely related to *C. frutescens* and produces round, highly pungent fruits. It has large leaves and flowers grow in clusters of three to five.

Capsicum pendulum: This variety is grown in Ecuador, Peru, Bolivia and produces conical pungent fruits. The plant is distinguished by its yellow or brown spotted flowers.

Capsicum pubescens: This small, hairy plant grows in higher regions than other chills in South America, occasionally Mexico and Central America. It has bluish purple flowers, small oblong, pointed, pungent fruits, red or orange in colour with black seeds.

CULTIVATION

All varieties of capsicum require a long, sunny growing season to ripen the fruit. The annual varieties are propagated by seed sown early in spring, if necessary in a hothouse and then transplanted later. They require a warm, well drained sandy or loamy soil and frequent attention during the growing period. Flowering commences about three months after sowing and lasts another three months.

FLAVOUR AND HOW TO STORE

The products from the different capsicum varieties have a range of pungency and flavours. *C. annuum* produce the fleshy varieties which are milder in flavour, sometimes even sweet, and also the fiery hot little bird peppers. *C. frutescens* produces the hottest of all, 'birdseye' or 'devil' peppers. Cayenne pepper, always bought ground, is another very hot product of *C. frutescens*. Red pepper is prepared from larger fruits and is less pungent. Peppers can be bought dried, either whole or ground. The vegetable varieties may be bought fresh. When preparing fresh chili peppers it is advisable to wear gloves to protect the skin from a burning irritation which may be caused by handling them.

USES

The bellshaped, fleshy peppers may be eaten raw or stuffed and cooked, green or ripe, as a vegetable or in salad. The mildest may be candied for sweets. Paprika, a rich source of vitamin C, may be used for flavouring and is a popular garnish to add colour to such foods as eggs cheese, potatoes. Commercially, paprika is used in sausages and it is the principal seasoning of Hungarian goulash. Cayenne peppers should be used in small amounts to flavour fish, pickles, curries and is important for 'devilled' or barbecued dishes. Chili powder is a blend of ground capsicums with other herbs and spices used in Mexican dishes such as chili con carne, hot tamales and as seasoning for eggs, fish and gravies. Hot varieties of *C. annuum* and *C. frutescens* are mixed to make crushed red pepper for use in sausages, spaghetti sauces and pizzas. Tabasco peppers are used in barbecue sauce and the ready-made Tabasco sauce. Whole chilis and chilitepines may be used to flavour vinegar and pickles. All capsicums are used medicinally as carminatives, stimulants and aids to digestion. Also for treatment of dropsy, diarrhoea, toothache and gout.

RECIPE SUGGESTION

For a spicy nibble, add salt and cayenne pepper to hot oil and butter, then sauté blanched almonds until golden brown. Serve cold. Serve chili sauce and pickles at barbecue parties to add a warm, zesty flavour to an outdoor meal.

CARAWAY

Botanical name: *Carum carvi*
Family: Umbelliferae

GENERAL

The caraway seeds we use as a spice come from the fruits of the caraway herb. Caraway is probably one of the most ancient of all herbs and spices, and was surrounded by many superstitions. German folk used to place a dish of caraway under a child's crib as a protection against witchcraft. It is a cousin of anise, dill and fennel. Its flavour is characteristic of German and Austrian cooking; they are the world's largest users. The name comes from the ancient Arabic, karawya, by which name it is still known. Another variety, Roman caraway (*Carminum cyminum*), is cultivated in Mediterranean countries. It is stronger but considered inferior and largely ignored for culinary purposes.

Man has used caraway as a spice and medicine for 5,000 years. Remains of meals containing caraway have been found in dwellings dating from the Stone Age. The Egyptians buried their dead with it and Isaiah, the prophet, wrote about caraway cultivation. In the eighth century AD, the cultivation of caraway spread from North Africa to Europe, where it has been grown ever since. It is mentioned by Shakespeare and, in Victorian times, Prince Albert was so fond of it that he introduced caraway seeds to Britain.

DESCRIPTION AND HABITAT

The caraway plant is a medium sized biennial. It has attractive, feathery foliage and bears umbels of white flowers in June/July. The ripe fruits split into two crescent-shaped seeds which are dark brown with light brown ridges. Wild caraway plants may be found but they are inferior to the cultivated. The best and largest cultivated crop is grown in Holland, but it is also grown commercially in Germany, Russia, Scandinavia and England.

CULTIVATION

Caraway will grow in almost any soil with little attention except for weeding and hoeing and, if the seeds are not collected, it will freely self-sow. If sown in August, a crop will be available the next summer. If sown in April or March, the plants will grow to about 8 in (18cm) during the first summer and should be pruned in the autumn. It will flower and go to seed the following July. The plants should be cut when the seeds are ripe and the sheaves left until thoroughly dry when the seeds can be threshed or shaken out.

FLAVOUR AND HOW TO STORE
The flavour of caraway seeds is pleasant and spicy, but rather sharp. The roots have a similar flavour, while the young leaves have a flavour more like dill. Caraway seeds should be stored in a cool, dry place well away from sunlight.

USES
Caraway is an all-purpose spice and is a valuable seasoning for savoury foods such as cabbage, bread, potato dumplings and meats such as pork, goose and sausages. Like most other spices it helps the digestion. It is added to soups, stews and other vegetables such as carrots, mushrooms, turnips, beets. In some countries it is used to flavour cakes and sweets. The roots may also be eaten boiled as a vegetable, and young leaves may be chopped over a salad or soup. A tisane can be made from the seeds for digestive and bowel complaints, and it is safe to give to children who generally like the flavour. The seeds can be chewed after a meal to dispel dyspepsia and sweeten the breath.

RECIPE SUGGESTION
Caraway cheese flan. Line a medium sized pie plate with short crust pastry. Into this put 2 slices chopped, lightly cooked bacon and 1 medium finely chopped cooked onion. Mix together 3 beaten eggs, 3 tbs cream, ½ tsp caraway seeds and 4 oz (120g) grated cheese; add salt and pepper to taste. Pour this mixture over the bacon and onion in pastry case, sprinkle ½ tsp caraway seed on top and bake in moderate oven at 350°F (gas mark 5) for 30–40 min until firm and golden.

CARDAMOM
Botanical name: *Elletaria cardamomum*
Family: Zingiberaceae

GENERAL
Cardamom seeds, a highly favoured Indian spice, contain volatile and fixed oil, salt of potassium, starch, mucilage, resin and ash. The early Egyptians used the seeds for medicinal purposes and chewed them to keep their teeth white. Nowadays, they grind them and put them in coffee. In Roman times cardamom was used as a popular flavouring and digestive spice. Today, it is an important seasoning in Christmas cooking and in curry mixtures, and is used a great deal in Germany, Russia and Scandinavian countries for flavouring spiced cakes, sweet

pastries and breads. In France and America, its volatile oil is used in perfumery. For thousands of years, as far back as the fourth century BC cardamom seeds have been in use in their native India. They were known to have been traded by the Greeks at that time. They are mentioned in Roman times by Dioscorides in his *Materia Medica*, and by the epicure Apicius.

DESCRIPTION AND HABITAT
Cardamom, a member of the ginger family, is a perennial shrub with a tall leafy stem having shorter flowering stems. When flowering is over they produce small seed capsules; these are irregularly shaped, oblong and light greeny-grey in colour. Each capsule contains three or four dark brown seeds. The fruits, or seed capsules, are gathered before they are ripe. After drying they are usually bleached to a creamy colour before being sold. Cardamom grows abundantly on the Malabar Coast high up in the Cardamom Hills from 2,500 to 5,000 feet above sea level. A longer seeded variety of the shrub is grown in Ceylon, and it is also grown to some extent in central America, Mexico and Guatemala.

CULTIVATION
Cardamom can only be grown in hot climates. It is propagated by seed, or by division of the rhizome. The fruits are picked whilst still growing and dried in the sun. The plants bear fruit for about twelve years, starting in the fourth year.

FLAVOUR AND HOW TO STORE
Cardamom has a delightfully pleasant aroma, faintly reminiscent of eucalyptus, with a strong spicy and agreeable taste. You achieve the best taste if the seeds are removed from the capsules before drying and grinding. It is therefore advisable to buy whole cardamom and to remove the seeds yourself, as commercially, capsule and seed are ground together, slightly impoverishing the flavour. They should be stored, as usual, in closed glass jars.

USES
Cardamom flavours well both sweet and savoury dishes. It is used as an ingredient in curry mixtures and in Continental sausages. It is often used for flavouring fruit salads, grape jellies, baked apples, Christmas and other cakes. Some liqueurs are also flavoured with the addition of cardamom. Medicinally, cardamom as an infusion, helps against flatulence and disorders of the stomach; it stimulates the appetite and is used also to flavour unpleasant tasting medicines. It is an ingredient in some eau-de-colognes.

RECIPE SUGGESTION
For Cardamom Fruit Salad for 4 people: make a syrup by simmering for 5 min 5 fl oz (150ml) each of water and clear honey, juice of ½ a lemon and ¼ tsp ground cardamom. When cool strain over a fruit salad made of 1 grapefruit, 1 orange, 2 bananas and 2 apples, peeled and

sliced; the juice of ½ a lemon and a sprinkling (pinch) of ground cardamom. Allow syrup to permeate for ½ hr before serving chilled.

CELERY and CELERIAC
Botanical name: *Apium graveolens*
Family: Umbelliferae

GENERAL
Several varieties of celery have been developed from the original wild celery called smallage, which has a sharp taste. The naturally white ones are called 'self-blanching' while others are green but have had the sharpness bred out. The turnip-rooted celery, called celeriac, which has an excellent flavour, is a popular vegetable on the Continent.

Celery as we know it today was developed, mainly by the Italians, during the seventeenth century, from the wild celery of European salt marshes. The Ancients associated celery with funerals and thought it an omen of ill luck. It came to be used in Britain during the nineteenth century.

DESCRIPTION AND HABITAT
It is a biennial plant with delicate light-green leaves growing at the top of swollen stems which are white or green, according to the variety. Wild celery can be found in marshlands, particularly near the sea. The stems grow to medium height and bear clusters of white flowers from June to September.

CULTIVATION
Without the aid of a greenhouse, it is difficult to raise celery from seed and it is usually best to buy plants in May and plant them in soil deeply dug and well manured. The leaves may be cut at any time for flavouring. The celery stalks can be earthed up for blanching when about 12 in (30cm) high. The variety grown for its turnip shaped root should be harvested when it has achieved a good size in late summer or early autumn.

FLAVOUR AND HOW TO STORE
The celery flavour is distinctive; the small, green leafy types being sharper than the large white varieties. The flavour of the celery seed is strong and somewhat sharp. The leaves and seeds can be dried and stored.

USES
The celery flavour can be imparted to soups and stews using the leaves or commercially prepared celery seeds and celery salt. Celery stalks, which should be crisp, are eaten raw alone

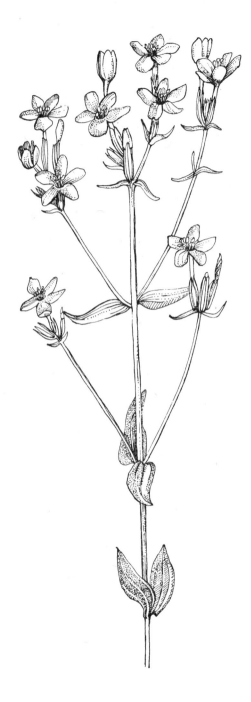

Centaury

or with salads. The French and Swiss favour celery as a braised vegetable rather than raw. Celery is rich in vitamins, mineral salts and active nutritional elements, and is valuable for salt reduced diets. Folk medicine indicates that celery is good for rheumatism, bronchitis and intermittent fevers.

RECIPE SUGGESTION
For cucumber soup: sauté together lightly 1 cucumber cut in small pieces, 1 tbs chives and 1 tbs chopped celery leaves in 1 oz (30g) butter until soft; add 1 oz (30g) flour and cook a little longer. Blend in 20 fl oz (575ml) chicken stock, bring to the boil, season, then simmer gently for 30–35 min. Remove from heat, cool, pass through blender. Serve hot, or add a small carton of cream and chill thoroughly before serving.

CENTAURY
Botanical name: *Centaurium umbellatum*
Family: Gentianaceae

GENERAL
Centaury is a well known medicinal herb. The great English herbalists Gerard and Culpeper give detailed information about its healing capacities. It grows wild in dry pastures and on chalky cliffs. All parts of the plant, including the flowers and seeds containing its bitter substances, are used for intestinal and stomach complaints. Its name is said to have been given to it when it cured a wound in the foot of the Centaur, Chiron.

DESCRIPTION AND HABITAT
Centaury is a low growing annual and belongs to the Gentian family. It has pale green, oval leaves and pink-red funnel-shaped flowers. It is found in temperate and sub-tropical climates.

CULTIVATION
Under favourable conditions, the flowers appear in July and August, but do not remain open after noon. It likes a loamy, warm soil and grows wild in woodland glades. It can be grown in gardens but only in really hot summers will the plant produce flowers and seeds.

FLAVOUR AND HOW TO STORE
No culinary properties. The whole plant can be dried for healing purposes in the usual way. Best harvested just before flowering.

USES
Centaury has a beneficial effect on the digestive system. It is also good as a general tonic and has a cleansing effect on the liver and kidneys. Applied externally, it helps skin troubles and wounds. 'The herbe is so safe that you cannot fail in the using of it . . .', Culpeper.

RECIPE SUGGESTION
Take ½ teaspoon of the dried herb and steep in a cup of cold water for 8 hours. Strain, then warm liquid to make it good to drink. One should take 2 cups a day, sipping slowly, always before meals, never directly after them.

CHAMOMILE

Botanical names: *Matricaria chamomilla* (True or Wild Chamomile)
Anthemis nobilis (Roman or Lawn Chamomile)
Family: Compositae

GENERAL
There are two different plants called chamomile; only their name is the same. They look somewhat similar and can only be distinguished by investigation of the flower head receptacles. Roman chamomile has no value other than its use in forming a lawn, while the *Matricaria chamomilla* which is the true chamomile, is of great medicinal value. It is, however, little known even by nurseries. It has a pleasant scent—when the authors visited the Acropolis in Athens the wonderful scent of the wild chamomile growing all over the ground was overwhelming. This true chamomile is an important healing plant, used for centuries. The hollow green receptacle at the base of the blossom distinguishes it from the Roman chamomile which has a solid receptacle. The chief healing substance of true chamomile is the famous deep blue oil extracted from the fresh flowers. The blue colour releases a hydrocarbon called azulen, and the richer the colour the greater the anti-inflammatory healing power. It is found in plants growing wild or in cereal fields. Chamomile has been grown in Europe for many centuries. It may have been cultivated in Britain even before the Roman occupation.

DESCRIPTION AND HABITAT
True chamomile is an annual, the Roman chamomile a perennial plant. Both varieties are low growing with yellow and white blossoms flowering from May/June until August/September. The flower heads of the true chamomile with their distinctive, single ray-florets which reflex soon after flowering, can be picked during the whole flowering period. Roman chamomile has double, white florets, giving out a pleasant smell when crushed.

The two chamomiles grow like weeds by the wayside, or on arable waste land, commons and in gardens.

CULTIVATION
Roman chamomile should be sown over the area chosen for a chamomile lawn. It should be a sheltered plot to avoid the invasion of too many grass seeds which are a nuisance to have to remove. The ground should be prepared in the usual way for sowing and the seed broadcast.

True chamomile will be best sown in a plot of its own, as this will facilitate picking the flowers. For this purpose it is mainly sown in rows. The seeds germinate easily.

FLAVOUR AND HOW TO STORE

The flowers of true chamomile should be dried either in the heated airing cupboard or in the oven. The dried flowers should be handled carefully as they disintegrate easily. They can be stored in cellophane bags in the dark, as they are a little too bulky for glass jars.

USES

Roman chamomile is used exclusively for lawns. The soothing effect of the minute amount of the blue healing oil contained in the flowers of true chamomile is used for a large number of ailments in the form of a tisane for abdominal pains, nervous upsets, cystitis, dilated veins and rheumatism—it can also be used as a mouth rinse for toothache and inflammation. Infusions can be added to steam baths or as compresses for skin troubles (boils, abscesses, eczema) conjunctivitis, haemorrhoids, earache and cramp. Chamomile oil makes an excellent hair rinse or massage for unhealthy, lifeless hair.

RECIPE SUGGESTIONS

Preparations for the various applications:

a) Tisane: pour 8 fl oz (225ml) boiling water on to 1-2 tsp dried chamomile flowers. Infuse for 3-5 min. Strain through muslin cloth. Do not reboil. Drink hot or cold.

b) Inhalations/steam bath: put small handful of chamomile flowers in pot. Pour on boiling water, inhale the steam, keeping head covered with towel.

c) Bath infusion: for a full bath, take about 11 oz (330g) herb mixture containing equal parts of chamomile, lovage, sage, yarrow, peppermint, rosemary, fennel. Pour on boiling water, infuse 10 min and add to bath water.

d) Hair rinse: equal parts of chamomile, limeflowers, fennel and some sage, rosemary, nettle, horsetail, yarrow. For blonde hair use plenty of chamomile; for dark hair, less chamomile, more rosemary. Place 2 heaped tbs of mixture in a jug, pour on 40 fl oz (1 litre) boiling water. Steep until cooled to right temperature. Strain, use for final rinse of hair wash. Use same mixture of herbs steeped in sunflower oil for hair oil to be massaged into the scalp. Allow the herbs to steep in oil for some weeks, standing in the sun whenever possible. If some herbs (for the mixture), are missing make up with the other herbs.

CHERVIL

Botanical name: *Anthriscus cerifolium*
Family: Umbelliferae

GENERAL

Chervil is an aromatic, slightly sweet herb. It is an essential ingredient in French cooking, almost replacing parsley as a flavouring herb. It is one of the Lenten herbs and chervil soup is

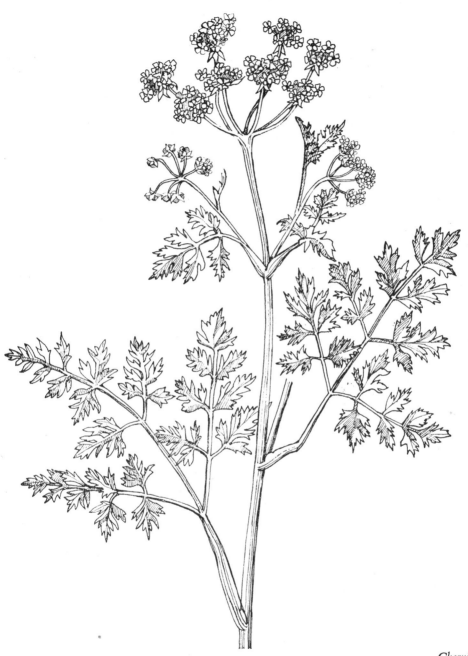

Chervil

traditionally eaten in South Germany on Maundy Thursday. Originally, chervil came from south-east Europe but it is an old seasoning of the North. The Romans brought it to Britain, but today it is mostly cultivated on the Continent. A tuberous-rooted variety is sometimes grown and its carrot-like root eaten as a vegetable.

DESCRIPTION AND HABITAT
Chervil is a small annual herb which does not like too much warmth or direct sunshine. The plant, with its pale green delicate lacy leaves, has a sweet scent. The flowers, which are white and very small, come in June, but the plant should be harvested before they bloom. The root is thin, whitish and smells slightly like aniseed. Chervil is grown in most countries with a warm and temperate climate. It dislikes hot, dry conditions.

CULTIVATION
Because chervil has to be used lavishly, allow sufficient space for a good quantity; best sown in August and September for the late crop and in February and March for the early supply. If sown in June and July it should be regularly watered, and if possible shaded. Chervil prefers relatively light soil, but with care, you can achieve results in medium heavy soil. Sow the seeds in rows approximately 6 in (15cm) apart. The seeds should be sown on top of the soil and slightly pressed in. They will germinate in 2 or 3 weeks but should be kept moist. Chervil is one of the earliest herbs ready for use in spring—it is also a suitable plant for growing indoors or in a window box.

FLAVOUR AND HOW TO STORE
Chervil is a mild, pleasant seasoning of subtle flavour. It has the property of improving a mixture of any herbs. It is not really a suitable herb for drying unless special precautions are taken to preserve its delicate flavour. Drying should be done at a low temperature, if possible in the airing cupboard or a cool oven. The thin, delicate leaves dry down to almost nothing and for domestic use it would be better to use them fresh. Once dried, chervil should be kept in airtight containers in the dark.

USES
Chervil is so popular in France that it is used instead of parsley for nearly every dish, parsley being used for decorative purposes. It will be found in most herb mixtures, fines herbes, and bouquets garnis. Fresh leaves are excellent in salads and salad dressings, with raw vegetables and in herb soups and sauces. It can be used for flavouring chicken and with tarragon, in decorating jellied egg and fish dishes; it makes a useful decorative herb for any dish. Chervil rarely spoils any dish to which it is added, even if a little too much is used. It has a stimulating effect on all functions of the metabolism. It is used finely cut and slightly warmed as a poultice on painful joints.

CHERVIL SOUP

Sauté 3 tbs fresh chopped or dried chervil in 2–3 tbs butter or oil. Stir in 2 tbs flour, smooth with a little cold stock (or water) taken from 20 fl oz (575ml). Heat remaining stock, add to mixture with little salt, and cook for 20 min. Before serving add 1 tbs fresh or sour cream.

CHICKWEED
Botanical name: *Stellaria media*
Family: Caryophyllaceae

GENERAL

Chickweed is mainly considered to be a troublesome garden weed, but it is a nutritional herb with a high copper content and other constituents. It was used medicinally and eaten as a vegetable. Chickweed is known to have been used in Britain in the fourteenth century to reduce swellings and help set broken bones. Small birds eat the seeds and are thus provided with food for most of the year.

DESCRIPTION AND HABITAT

Chickweed is a low branching annual, but it flowers and seeds in such a short time it can be found almost all the year round. The stems are succulent and smooth but for a line of hairs down one side. The leaves are eggshaped with hairs on their short stalks. After rain and dew the hairs on stems and stalks retain water which is absorbed by the upper leaves, the surplus being carried by the hairs down to the next pair of leaves, and so on. The flowers are small and white and the petals each deeply lobed and smaller than the sepals. Chickweed grows throughout Europe, America and Asia in waste and cultivated places, by streams and roadsides and is abundant in Britain.

CULTIVATION

Grows wild.

FLAVOUR AND HOW TO STORE

Chickweed has a pleasantly salty taste but no scent. This herb should only be used when fresh.

USES

The whole plant can be eaten as a vegetable, being cooked like spinach, or used raw as a cress. Medicinally the fresh leaves, bruised, can be used as a poultice on ulcers. Chickweed is cooling and a demulcent and an ointment made by mixing 115g bruised fresh leaves with 225g lard can be used for skin irritations and chilblains. An infusion of the whole herb is said to be helpful in kidney disorders.

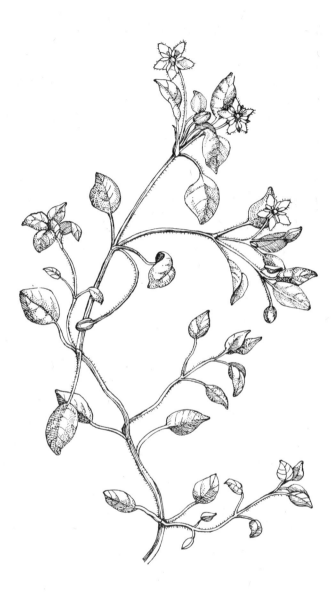

Chickweed

RECIPE SUGGESTION
Infusion: Add 20 fl oz (575ml) of boiling water to 1¼ oz (30g) chickweed; allow to draw for 3-5 min and drink warm, a cupful once or twice a day.

CHICORY
Botanical name: *Cichorium intybus*
Family: Compositae

GENERAL
Chicory, both wild and cultivated, has been used since early times in salads and as a winter vegetable. Its roasted, ground root is a well known additive to coffee, always used on the Continent and believed by the French to counteract the stimulating effect of caffeine. It was used by the ancient Greeks and Egyptians, was known by the Romans as a delicate vegetable and mentioned by Virgil and Pliny.

Chicory contains a bitter principle, inulin and sugar. In France the curly leaved endive (*Cichorium endiva*) is called chicory, whilst the blanched head of the *Cichorium intybus* is their endive, known as Barbe de Capucin.

DESCRIPTION AND HABITAT
Wild chicory is a perennial of medium height with lance-shaped, deeply toothed leaves and hairy stems. The pure blue flowers, the size and shape of a dandelion, grow in clusters in the axils of the upper leaves. Chicory flowers from May to September and grows on limestone hills, roadsides and in waste places throughout Europe and Asia, and has naturalised in North America.

CULTIVATION
The cultivated varieties are treated as annuals and sown from seed in June. Flowers should be removed as soon as they appear to encourage root growth. To force crowns for salad, take up the roots in October/November and plant them in large pots or boxes. Cover with a deep layer of sharp sand. From the root grows a tight head of white leaves for use in winter. If roots only are wanted for roasting or medicinal preparations, they are lifted at the same time.

FLAVOUR AND HOW TO STORE
The root and leaves have a bitter taste and the leaves are mostly used blanched. The green leaves of wild chicory can be dried and stored in the usual way.

USES
The dried root of chicory which grows quite large when cultivated is roasted and then ground to a powder for adding to coffee. The fresh green leaves can be used in salads. The blanched leaves of the cultivated variety are cooked as a vegetable or eaten raw in salads.

Chicory

Chicory is a tonic, diuretic and laxative and this medicinal property is concentrated in the milky juice which comes from the rind of the fresh root. A decoction of this is helpful in cases of jaundice, gout and rheumatic complaints.

RECIPE SUGGESTION
Winter Salad: Wash and slice 2 chicory heads, half each of a red and green pepper, removing seeds. Mix together in an oil and lemon dressing to which is added 1 teaspoon each of the herbs mint, chervil, lemon balm and salad burnet. Allow to permeate.

CHIVES
Botanical name: *Allium schoenoprasum*
Family: Liliaceae

GENERAL
The chive is a well known member of the onion group, cultivated in Britain under the alternative name of rush leek. There is also a large leaved variety known as the giant chive. Other relatives are garlic (*Allium sativum*) (see page 131) and the so called Welsh onion *Allium fistulosum* which is generally used in the same way as the green of spring onions. Stronger in their growth and flavour than chives, their greens are recommended for cooking whereas chives are preferable for fresh salads, raw vegetables or dishes where a delicate onion flavour is required.

The history of the chive goes back nearly 5,000 years to the days of the ancient Chinese. It was introduced to Britain by the Romans.

DESCRIPTION AND HABITAT
Chives are hardy perennial plants belonging to the lily family and will grow in any garden soil. The plants grow from small flat bulbs in clumps and have hollow, thin, grass-like stems. The flowers are delicate purple pompoms and the plants make a decorative edging for a herb bed. The chive plant is native to the cooler parts of Europe including Britain and can occasionally be found wild in dry, rocky places. They may also be found wild in Canada and northern USA.

CULTIVATION
Chives are easy to grow but should be watered during dry spells as the little bulbous roots remain near the surface. Seeds can be sown in spring, or propagation carried out

by dividing the plants which should be planted about 6 in (15cm) apart. If the plants are allowed to seed themselves, they will spread over a wide area. They live for a long time and take a great deal out of the soil, so a good organic fertiliser should be added from time to time, to encourage growth of the green tops. Lack of food results in yellowing of the tips. The flower heads should be nipped off, since chives are grown only for their 'grass'. When cutting the herb for use the 'grass' should be cut to within 2 in (5cm) of the ground. Cutting can continue until the first frosts when the plants die back, reappearing with the warmer weather in February/March. Chives will flourish indoors in pots. Welsh onions, more vigorous even than chives, can be cultivated and propagated in the same way.

FLAVOUR AND HOW TO STORE
Chives have a mild onion flavour. They can be green-dried domestically if first finely chopped and spread out well on a suitable tray, then placed in a low oven (under 100°F) for about an hour. They can also be quick frozen, or alternatively, they will keep fresh for a short while in a polythene bag or screw-top glass jar in the 'fridge. Commercially they have been successfully green-dried, and in the States, methods of freeze-drying are used as the demand for chives increases.

USES
The bright green colour of chives makes them an ideal tasty garnish for fresh salads. Chopped finely, they are excellent in sauces and mashed potato, and for flavouring cream cheese and scrambled eggs. They go well with most cooked vegetables, but their onion flavour may be too distinct for asparagus and very young vegetables such as petit pois. Chives are also a recommended addition to rich fatty dishes.

RECIPE SUGGESTION
Herb Potato Cakes: Mash four medium boiled potatoes, while still hot. Mix well with 2 tbs butter, salt. Reconstitute 1 tbs green-dried chives in 1 tbs warm milk, and add. When cool, add well beaten egg, shape into flat cakes, fry in butter. If fresh chives are used omit the warm milk.

CINNAMON
Botanical name: *Cinnamomum zeylanicum*
Family: Lauraceae

GENERAL
Cinnamon is the dried, fragrant, inner bark of the cinnamon tree which grows in Sri Lanka

(Ceylon)—the 'true' cinnamon and the only one sold in Britain under the name 'cinnamon'. There are other varieties of the cinnamon tree with sweet-smelling spicy barks, one of which we know as cassia. It has been a valued spice since ancient times. In 500 BC Hippocrates wrote of its important medicinal properties. It was probably brought to the Middle East by Phoenician traders. In the Old Testament, the use of cinnamon is mentioned as a perfume and as an ingredient of the holy anointing oil used by Moses in the Tabernacle. Cinnamon has been used in Europe since the ninth century AD but it was, at first, very expensive. Since the last century however, cinnamon has come down in price and is now one of the most popular spices.

DESCRIPTION AND HABITAT
Cinnamon is a bushy evergreen tree which, in its native habitat, may grow very tall. The long, deeply veined, fragrant leaves are dark green and glossy above, lighter underneath. The flowers are small and yellow, and the berries dark purple. The commercially grown variety is a bush of about 6 ft (2m) high and is cut back in order to obtain more branches from which the bark can be cut. True cinnamon, native to Sri Lanka and the Malabar coast of India, is also grown commercially in the Seychelle Islands and other Eastern countries.

CULTIVATION
Cinnamon is propagated in tropical climates by cuttings or by seed planted in groups of four or five. Germination takes about three weeks. Every two or three years the shoots are cut back to the ground, the bark is peeled off the shoots and left for a day. The outer bark is then stripped off and as the inner bark dries, it rolls up resembling a quill about 1 in (2½cm) in diameter and light brown in colour. While they are still damp, the smaller quills are laid inside the large ones and, as the whole dries out, they become tightly curled together.

FLAVOUR AND HOW TO STORE
Cinnamon has a fragrant spicy flavour which is slightly sweet. When ground the flavour becomes stronger. As it very quickly loses its aroma, cinnamon should be carefully stored in glass screw-top jars. The thinnest bark is the best quality cinnamon, having the finest aroma. Cinnamon can be bought ground or as sticks.

USES
Whole cinnamon sticks are used for spicing hot drinks, especially mulled wine and punch; also in fruit punches and fresh or stewed fruit. Add to pickling liquids and, with cloves, vinegar and sugar, to the pan when boiling mutton. Ground cinnamon is used in bakery and sweet dishes; sprinkled on to fruit pies, milk puddings and custards. Can be added to chicken pie, stuffed cabbage and sprinkled over ham and pork chops.

Medicinally cinnamon is astringent and carminative. It is a strong stimulant for the glandular system, and being an antacid is helpful for stomach upsets and diarrhoea. Cinnamon is also good for colds and sore throats. In earlier days it was used as a breath sweetener, as a tonic for the whole system and was given as a sedative to mothers during childbirth.

RECIPE SUGGESTION

An unusual sweet is Cinnamon Ice Cream made with 5 fl oz (150ml) of double cream, 1 egg, 4 oz (120g) sugar, juice of ½ lemon, 2½ tsp ground cinnamon, pinch salt, 10 fl oz (275ml) milk and 2–3 drops cochineal. Beat cream and egg together, then slowly add sugar and remaining ingredients, beating continuously. Freeze in trays for about 4 hr.

CLARY—*Clear Eye*
Botanical name: *Salvia sclarea*
Family: Labiatae

GENERAL

Clary is a herb with culinary and medicinal uses.

The name clary comes from the Latin word 'clarus' meaning clear. In the Middle Ages herbalists used a decoction of the leaves for eye complaints. They also used the seeds for an eyewash, by soaking them in water to form a thick, viscous substance.

DESCRIPTION AND HABITAT

Clary is a small herbaceous biennial which has long spikes of purplish-blue or white flowers. The stem has a reddish tinge and the large leaves are heart-shaped, hairy and irregularly serrated. It flowers from May to September. Clary is native to Italy, France and Switzerland but can be found growing in fields, along roadsides and in waste places in southern Europe, Britain and parts of the United States.

CULTIVATION

Clary plants which are biennial, will flourish in light soil with reasonable drainage. The seeds should be sown in spring and the leaves will be at their best for use during the following winter and spring. The plant will seed and die after its second summer.

FLAVOUR AND HOW TO STORE

Clary is an aromatic herb with a slightly bitter taste. The leaves are dried and stored as any other herb.

USES

Years ago Clary was used to flavour soup and added to wine and ale to make them more potent. Fresh clary leaves, fried in batter, make unusual, original fritters.

Medicinally, the leaves made into a tea have been used for eye complaints, digestive and kidney troubles. Nowadays the highly aromatic oil is extracted and used as a fixative in perfumes.

RECIPE SUGGESTION
Clary Fritters: Dip whole fresh leaves in batter, and fry till golden.
Decoction: Infuse the herb in boiling water and use to bathe eyes.

CLOVE-PINK—Gillyflower
Botanical name: *Dianthus caryophyllus*
Family: Caryophyllaceae

GENERAL
There are many different varieties of Dianthus, but *D. Caryophyllus*, the old-fashioned carnation known as clove-pink, is one of the earliest flowers to be cultivated in Britain. It was grown for decorative, flavouring and medicinal purposes. The Arabs used the petals to add a pleasant flavour to their bitter herb tonics. Chaucer mentioned it in the fourteenth century, and in the seventeenth and eighteenth centuries, clove-pinks were used as a flavouring in vinegars, soups, sauces, wines and liqueurs, and as a decoration in salads.

DESCRIPTION AND HABITAT
The clove-pink is a perennial with narrow, bluish-green leaves. The flowers are deep pink and can be single or double. Mostly a cultivated plant, it sometimes 'escapes' and can be found growing wild.

CULTIVATION
Easy to grow in fairly light, well-drained, limey soil, pinks can be raised from seed sown in spring or by cuttings taken in June. They can also be propagated by pulling clumps apart and re-planting the pieces; they soon root.

FLAVOUR AND USES
The spicy flavour and fragrance is distinctly clove-like. The light-scented taste of the petals can be used to flavour ales and wines and the name carnation comes from the word coronation, as they were regularly used in celebration cups at coronations and weddings. These drinks were believed to have a beneficial effect on the heart. The petals may also be candied for eating as a sweet or used to flavour unpleasant-tasting medicines. Their fragrance is valuable in pot-pourris and herb sachets.

RECIPE SUGGESTION
Clove-pink syrup: Bring 10 fl oz (275ml) water, 4½ oz (120g) sugar and a slice of lemon rind

slowly to the boil and boil steadily for 10 min. Draw pan away from heat, remove lemon rind and add a handful of clove-pink petals. Allow to infuse until cold. Strain and use in fruit salads, stewed pears or apples.

CLOVES

Botanical name: *Eugenia aromatica*
also: *Syzygium aromaticum* and *Eugenia caryophyllata*
Family: Myrtaceae

GENERAL

Cloves are the dried flower buds of the clove tree, one of the myrtle family. An important ingredient in many recipes, the fragrant clove has become an everyday spice. Its name is derived from the Latin *clavus* meaning a nail, which it closely resembles in shape.

Cloves were one of the earliest spices mentioned in ancient Chinese writings. The Greeks and Romans valued cloves for medicinal purposes and by the fourth century they had become a well known spice to Europeans who imported them through the Eastern caravan trade routes. In the fifteenth century, when the Portuguese navigator Vasco da Gama opened up the sea route to East India, clove trees were found in the Molucca Islands. Crops were later established by the French in Zanzibar, Mauritius and other tropical parts of the French Empire.

DESCRIPTION AND HABITAT

The cultivated evergreen clove tree with its brilliant red flowers, grows very tall. The flower buds when dried, turn reddy-brown and are rich in volatile clove oil. Nowadays Zanzibar is the most famous clove island but they also come from Pemba, Madagascar, West Indies and their native habitat, the Molucca Islands.

CULTIVATION

The clove tree flourishes only in tropical climates near the sea. The small seedlings are planted out in the field at two years old and yield their first crop at six to eight years. The flower buds are harvested when they are light red and dried in the sun on grass mats until they turn reddy-brown.

FLAVOUR AND HOW TO STORE

Cloves are strongly aromatic and have a pungent, spicy taste. Good quality cloves should be plump, oily and not easily broken. They can be bought whole or ground and should be stored in glass screw-top jars.

USES

Cloves are used in Christmas baking, spiced cakes, mincemeat and gingerbreads; also in puddings and sweets, in mulled wines and marinades for meat and fish. Whole cloves are used for pickling and to spice mutton, pork and game. They are useful for spicing insipid fruits like pears, and also go well with others such as apples, damsons and cherries. An important ingredient in many sauces such as bread sauce. An orange studded with cloves gives off a lovely aroma in a room and can be used as an insect repellent. Oil of cloves is used in the perfume and soap industries; also as a pain killer, especially for toothache.

RECIPE SUGGESTIONS

Sprinkle freshly ground cloves over a plain junket. When making iced tea, infuse 1 clove per cup of hot tea for 3 min. Strain and pour over crushed ice.

COLTSFOOT—Foalswort, Coughwood
Botanical name: *Tussilago farfara*
Family: Compositae

GENERAL

Coltsfoot is a well known weed and wild plant, and was used by the Romans as an effective remedy for coughs. Its botanical name comes from the Latin word for cough, *tussis*. The soft down of the leaves was used to provide stuffing for pillows and also made tinder for lighting a fire. Two of its varieties are still used today in Chinese herbal treatment for chest complaints. They also use the flowers for an eye bath.

DESCRIPTION AND HABITAT

Coltsfoot is a hardy perennial with a creeping, thick white root. It has yellow flowers blooming from March to May and the leathery, fragrant green leaves follow the flowers. It is a feature of coltsfoot that you will never see the leaves and flowers together. The underside of the leaves is covered in soft down. The flowers also give way to a ball of down, as do dandelions and the seeds are dispersed in the same way, by the wind. It can be found abundantly in Britain and Europe, on waste land and in places where no other plants could grow.

CULTIVATION

Coltsfoot is not generally cultivated, but it will grow in any poor soil.

FLAVOUR AND HOW TO STORE

Coltsfoot has a bitter, somewhat astringent taste. Both the flowers and leaves are dried in the usual way for storage.

USES
It has no culinary uses, although coltsfoot leaves, rich in vitamin C, make a healthy addition when chopped into salads, or drunk as a tisane. It is principally a medicinal herb and an important ingredient in herbal tobacco smoked for chest complaints such as bronchitis, asthma and obstinate coughs. Coltsfoot tea, sweetened with honey, will also help these symptoms and should be taken hot, first thing in the morning before rising. Coltsfoot has a reputation for healing dilated veins, especially thread veins in the face. For this purpose, fresh leaves can be crushed to make a poultice, or the leaves, fresh or dried, made into an infusion into which cotton wool pads are dipped and applied to the affected parts.

RECIPE SUGGESTION
For infusion: 1 tsp fresh chopped or green-dried coltsfoot leaves per cup, pour boiling water over and allow to steep for 10 min. For the 'cough tea' strain, sweeten and drink several cups daily. For application to dilated veins, use when lukewarm.

COMFREY—Knitbone, Boneset, Consound
Botanical name: *Symphytum officinale*
Family: Boraginacae

GENERAL
Comfrey's reputation as an outstanding medicinal plant has endured many centuries. It is also an interesting culinary herb as its leaves and stalk can be used for several wholesome dishes. Research has shown its healing qualities to be largely attributable to the two substances obtained from the root, allantoin and choline which promote healthy proliferation of the red blood cells and the circulation generally. It is a valuable composting plant and often grown for 'ploughing in'.

Comfrey has been a well known natural remedy in England and Europe since the Middle Ages. It was used to aid the repair of broken bones, and as a wound herb. It was sometimes called 'Saracens Consound' as the Turks and Saracens used it for this purpose. Its ability to stop internal bleeding and heal ulcers was also well known.

DESCRIPTION AND HABITAT
A rough, hairy perennial of medium height, comfrey has leaves up to 10 in (25cm) long at the base, decreasing in size up the stem. The flowers, which bloom from early May throughout summer, are bell-shaped and grow in drooping clusters. Their colour may be blue, purple, pink or cream. Comfrey is native to Europe and temperate Asia. It is common in Great Britain

but more frequently in the south, and rarely in Scotland. It grows in damp, shady places, especially in ditches and near streams.

CULTIVATION
Comfrey is easily grown; propagation is by seed or by root division in autumn. The roots should be dug up for use from October to March and the leaves gathered in June and July.

FLAVOUR AND HOW TO STORE
Comfrey leaves are somewhat bitter, but quite edible. They wilt rapidly after picking. The leaves may be dried and powdered or ground before storing in air-tight jars.

USES
Comfrey provides gentle remedies safe for use with delicate children, invalids and old people. The liquid decoction, ointment or poultice made of leaves and/or roots, can be used to treat rheumatism, arthritis, wounds, bruises and swellings. Its alternative names, knitbone and boneset indicate its success in helping the repair of broken bones. In some cases, it has been used successfully for healing malignant tumours and progressive ulceration. The tea brewed from the leaves and root makes a good cough mixture and is used for more severe lung disorders such as pneumonia and tuberculosis. It arrests internal bleeding of the lungs, stomach or bowel and may also be taken for dysentery and internal ulcers. The tea should always be freshly made as it ferments quickly, and taken in wine-glassful doses. The young leaves may be chopped into salads or cooked like spinach. The stalks, if blanched, make a good substitute for asparagus. Dried leaves or flowers may be added to cooked vegetables just before serving. The roots can be used in chutney or to make comfrey wine.

RECIPE SUGGESTIONS
Fresh comfrey leaves, washed and surplus water shaken off, should be cooked without additional water over low heat for 10 min. Serve as a green vegetable. Try comfrey 'au gratin'— lining an ovenproof dish with cooked rice, making alternate layers of cooked comfrey, grated cheese and dabs of butter, finally topping with layer of rice. Add a little milk and bake in hot oven for $\frac{1}{2}$ hr.

CORIANDER
Botanical name: *Coriandrum sativum*
Family: Umbelliferae

GENERAL
The dried aromatic coriander seed is widely used in spice mixtures and curry powders. Sometimes known as Dizzycorn because when freshly crushed and the aroma inhaled, it can reduce dizziness.

A herb mentioned in the Bible, coriander was first introduced into Britain by the Romans. It was used ground with cumin and vinegar, rubbed into meat as a preservative. During the Middle Ages coriander was used in love potions and to cure a spotty face. Later it was an ingredient in the famous eau-de-Carne—a liqueur made in Paris in the seventeenth century, and used as a drink as well as a toilet water.

DESCRIPTION AND HABITAT
Coriander is a medium-sized annual with umbels of pinky-white flowers and feathery, bright green leaves. The whole plant has a disagreeable smell until the fruits ripen, when the characteristic sweet aroma is strong. The dried coriander fruit, generally called seed, is small, round and ridged. Native to southern Europe and Asia, coriander is cultivated throughout temperate regions of the world, to a great extent in India. Having escaped from cultivation, coriander may occasionally be found wild in south-east England.

CULTIVATION
Coriander can be grown in a light, fertile soil in a sunny position. Seed is sown in early spring, and after a hot summer, should be ready for harvesting in August when the fruits have turned from green to grey. The plants should be cut when dew is on the ground, and then left for a few days to complete the ripening. After threshing they must be thoroughly dried before being stored.

FLAVOUR AND HOW TO STORE
Coriander has a distinctive, sweetly aromatic flavour and a spicy scent when crushed. The aroma of coriander actually improves with keeping and it should be stored in glass screw-top jars. It may be bought either whole or ground.

USES
If the leaves are gathered when young, they add an unusual flavour to soups and salads. The ground seed is used in curry powders and spice mixtures, especially in Germany where it goes into the making of sausages and frankfurters. It also flavours stuffings for poultry and game. Used whole and ground a great deal in the making of cakes, bread and pastries, it can be sprinkled on milk puddings and with cooked fruit such as apples and pears. Coriander is particularly good with beetroot dishes and rubbed on to pork and ham before roasting. Nowadays coriander is used only to a small extent in medicine. It is carminative and used to stimulate digestion, and flavour otherwise disagreeable medicines, as a tonic and in cough syrups. The oil contained in the seeds is used in perfumes and to flavour sweets, cocoa, chocolate, tobacco, liqueurs and other alcoholic drinks.

RECIPE SUGGESTION
Try Coriander Celery, an original and delicious vegetable dish. Wash, trim and divide a

head of celery in four. Sprinkle with juice of 1 lemon. Plunge into boiling water and boil for 10 min. Strain and cool under cold running water. In another pan mix 1 tbs olive oil, juice of a lemon, ¼ tsp thyme and 1 bay leaf. Bring slowly to boil, then add 1 oz (30g) coriander seed, salt, pepper and finally the celery. Cook gently for 20 min. Serve celery chilled with strained liquid over, sprinkled with paprika and accompanied by brown bread and butter.

CORNFLOWER
Botanical name: *Centaurea cyanus*
Family: Compositae

GENERAL
Once a familiar cornfield weed, the lovely blue cornflower is now cultivated as a garden plant. Long ago it was called 'hurtsickle' for its tough stems would blunt the sickles used by reapers. The juice from the flowerheads expressed and mixed with alum-water can be used in water-colour paints or to make blue dye or ink.

DESCRIPTION AND HABITAT
Cornflower is a medium-sized hardy annual. The slender stems are ribbed and downy. The lower leaves are usually lobed whilst the upper ones are entire and narrow. Brilliant blue flowers are most common, but there are red, rose-pink and white varieties.

CULTIVATION
The cultivated varieties of cornflower are larger and more robust than the wild species. Seed is best sown from August to October and thinned to 12 in (30cm) apart in spring. They will then produce bushy plants with many flowers throughout the summer. If they are sown in spring, they will flower the same year, but not become bushy.

USES
The flowers have no scent but can be used medicinally as a cordial and tonic. When dried with their colour retained, they may be mixed with other herbs in an infusion for eye-baths or eye compresses. They are also included in herbal facial steams. Their lovely flowers give colour to pot-pourris.

RECIPE SUGGESTION
Infusion of Cornflower for inflammation of the eyes: Place ⅓ oz (8g) cornflower flowerheads

in a teacup; cover with boiling water and infuse for 15 min with a saucer over the cup. When cold use to bathe the eyes.

COSTMARY—*Alecost, Bibleleaf*
Botanical name: *Chrysanthemum balsamita*
Family: Compositae

GENERAL
A highly aromatic plant used medicinally and for spicing food, costmary was brought to Britain by the Romans and has been grown for many hundreds of years in Europe. In the fifteenth century it was so popular it was grown in quantity in Spain for export. The name alecost comes from the days when costmary was added to home-brewed ale to give it a sharper tang; the name bibleleaf comes from an old custom of putting a leaf in the Bible as a book marker.

DESCRIPTION AND HABITAT
Costmary is a medium-sized perennial with a creeping rootstock. The leaves are long and slender and the flowers, which only open when in full sunlight, are white petalled with bright yellow centres.

CULTIVATION
Costmary grows well in almost any soil, preferably in a dry sunny position. Propagation is by root division.

FLAVOUR
The plant has a scent of mint and when used as a tea or in cooking the flavour becomes lemony as well. It is a strong flavour and very little need be used.

USES
In the Middle Ages a medicinal powder was made out of the costmary leaves for the relief of upset stomachs. It was said to cure worms in children and to be good for conditions of ill health where there was a loss of weight and emaciation. It was used for dysentery and the ague; it is also a tonic and makes an agreeable herb tea. Nowadays costmary is used in pot-pourri where it intensifies the scents of other leaves and flowers.

RECIPE SUGGESTION
A fresh young leaf or ¼ tsp dried chopped leaves can be placed in the bottom of a pan when roasting beef, venison or chicken.

Couchgrass

COUCHGRASS—Twitchgrass
Botanical name: *Agropyrum repens*
Family: Gramineae

GENERAL
Couchgrass, such a nuisance in lawns and flower beds, has a special place in the wild larder. Amongst other constituents, it contains vitamins A and B, potassium salts and organic acids. In former times, it was used for all deficiency diseases and for many other ailments. In times of food shortages the starch content of its root was used to eke out the bread dough. In France they make a tisane from couchgrass root which has a soothing effect and is a popular drink.

DESCRIPTION AND HABITAT
A tall perennial grass-like weed. The slender, creeping roots produce several flower stems resembling rye or beardless wheat. The leaves are flat with a long, cleft sheath and are rough to touch. Couchgrass abounds in fields, by the roadsides and in gardens. It spreads rapidly, is very hardy and therefore a difficult weed to eradicate. It can be found mainly all over Europe, America and North Asia.

CULTIVATION
A wild weed.

FLAVOUR AND HOW TO STORE
The root, the only part used, has a sweet taste, not unlike liquorice. It should be collected in spring. All traces of leaves and rootlets should be removed and then cut into very short lengths before drying. Store in the usual way.

USES
Since the sixteenth century it has been known that the root has medicinal qualities for cleansing the blood, rheumatic complaints, diseases of the bladder and as a diuretic. It was much praised by Culpeper who used it for all kidney complaints.

RECIPE SUGGESTION
Make an infusion of 2 tsp of dried chopped root in 20 fl oz (575ml) water and boil for 10 min. Take up to 2 cups a day.

COWSLIP—Paigles
Botanical name: *Primula veris*
Family: Primulaceae

GENERAL
The fragrant cowslip is a familiar wild flower in spring with its lovely yellow blooms. The

medicinal properties of cowslip, like other members of the primrose family, have been used since early times for strengthening the nerves and as a sedative. In country districts cowslip wine was made from the flowers. The well prepared liquor is pleasant in flavour, very intoxicating and is not unlike the sweet wines of the South of France.

Its country name 'paigles' is of Anglo-Saxon origin meaning St Peter, and it was so-called because the hanging flower heads look like a bunch of keys—the emblem of St Peter.

DESCRIPTION AND HABITAT
Cowslip is a small perennial plant with downy leaves growing from the base of the stem, and umbels of stalked creamy-yellow flowers. It grows in woods and moist pastures.

CULTIVATION
Grows wild.

FLAVOUR AND HOW TO STORE
The corollas of the cowslip flowers, which are the only parts used, have a pleasant sweet taste and fragrant smell. They are mostly used fresh, but can be dried and stored in the usual way.

USES
Cowslip flowers were used for wine making and candied for use as an attractive decoration for cakes and sweets; also eaten fresh with cream. The leaves were eaten as a salad or boiled as a green potherb.

Cowslip ointment was believed to remove spots, wrinkles and other blemishes. It is reputed to be sedative, antispasmodic and helpful against vertigo and cramp when drunk as an infusion.

RECIPE SUGGESTION
To preserve cowslips in sugar, put alternate layers of fresh flowers and sugar into an earthenware pot, ending with a thick layer of sugar; cover and seal. 1–3 tsp should be taken daily.

CUMIN
Botanical name: *Cuminum cyminum*
Family: Umbelliferae

GENERAL
Cumin seed is a strong aromatic spice, an essential ingredient in all curry and chili powders. It is widely used in India as a condiment and flavours many Eastern and Mexican dishes.

In Biblical times cumin seeds were valued for their digestive properties and were used for flavouring bread and other dishes during the periods of ceremonial fasting, to make up for the lack of meat. It was a popular condiment in England in the Middle Ages and up to the seventeenth century, but has since largely been replaced by caraway.

DESCRIPTION AND HABITAT

Cumin is a low-growing annual. The slender plant has a branching stem, long, narrow deep green leaves and small umbels of white or rose-coloured flowers. The oblong fruits, or so-called 'seeds' are about ¼ in (½cm) long, yellowish-brown colour, covered with tiny hairs. Originally cumin was grown in Upper Egypt, Arabia and India, but nowadays most cumin is grown in Iran, Sicily and Malta.

CULTIVATION

Cumin is grown from seed in rich loam soil in a well-drained sunny position. It takes three or four months to mature and needs an equable climate—it cannot survive very hot dry tempera-tures. It may be grown in England (provided the English summer is not too short) if sown in pots, planted in a hot bed and later transferred to a warm bed of rich soil.

FLAVOUR AND HOW TO STORE

Cumin has a strong, aromatic, spicy taste, even a little bitter, but pleasantly so. It can be bought whole or ground and should be kept in screw-top jars.

USES

Apart from the important use of cumin in curry powder, it is used a great deal commercially to flavour meats, pickles, chutneys and cheeses—there is a Dutch Edam flavoured with cumin and the German Munster cheese. It is a good seasoning for soups and stews and can be ground from a pepper mill for this purpose. In Mexico cumin flavours a number of national dishes and in oriental cookery it is used whole with fish, game, meats, poultry, sauces and vegetables. It goes well with cabbage, devilled eggs, rice and sauerkraut.

RECIPE SUGGESTIONS

Add 1 tsp cumin seed to the water in which shredded cabbage is to be cooked. When cooked, drain and toss the cabbage and cumin with a little salad oil before serving.
Sprinkle whole seeds on top of plain or sugar cookies before baking.
Mix ⅛ tsp ground cumin into egg yolk and other ingredients for devilled eggs.

DANDELION

Botanical name: *Taraxacum officinale*
Family: Compositae

GENERAL

This plant, despised as a troublesome weed, is nature's greatest healing aid, and is a medicine chest in itself. It contains the active substances of vitamins, sugar, proteins, fat, mucilage, saponins, choline, wax and rubber; mineral salts of potassium, calcium, manganese, sodium, sulphur and silicic acid; as well as the bitter principles of alkaloids, glycosides and tannins. The dandelion is therefore a wholesome food plant whose leaves can be eaten raw or cooked, the roots made into coffee and its juice used for a tisane. The name dandelion comes from the French *dent de lion*, referring to the tooth-shaped edges of the leaves. Arabian physicians recommended its great healing power in the tenth and eleventh centuries, and Gerard in his famous herbal, describes the numerous uses of this herb.

DESCRIPTION AND HABITAT
The dandelion, a hardy perennial, grows wild nearly everywhere. In France it is cultivated and sold in the markets as a vegetable. It has a fleshy root and a straight stem up to 8 in (20cm) tall topped by a bright golden-yellow flower—a collection of tiny florets each one providing a ripe seed in time. This makes it rich in nectar and a popular plant with bees. Its flowering period is from early spring until late autumn; when the blooms die they are replaced by the familiar fluffy ball of seeds; a mass of down easily dispersed by the wind, spreading the seeds over a wide area. The whole plant including the root, contains a milky juice.

CULTIVATION
When a crop of dandelion is required, it is very easy to propagate either by sowing seed or by division of the roots. If re-seeding is not required, the flower heads should be removed immediately after appearing.

FLAVOUR AND HOW TO STORE
The flavour of dandelion is somewhat bitter. This bitterness increases with age but the younger plants are quite palatable. The leaves and roots can be dried and stored in the usual way, although it is recommended that long roots be first cut into lengths of about 4–6 in (10–15cm).

USES
Tender young dandelion leaves, which can be blanched if liked, are useful additions to spring salads. The young leaves may also be boiled as a vegetable similar to spinach, although they will be bitter for many tastes. The dried leaves are used in dandelion and burdock drink, and the flowers for dandelion wine which is considered good for the blood. The roots, cleaned, chopped, roasted and then ground, make dandelion coffee which is a natural beverage without the side effects of coffee such as insomnia or digestive trouble.

Dandelion is recommended for diabetics since its sugar substances do not burden the metabolism. The juice of the plant has a general fortifying effect on the body systems and is said to be a cure for various ailments such as eczema, blood diseases, loss of appetite and dropsy. The juice, when mixed with agrimony and made into a tea, has proved to be a relief for rheumatism and arthritis sufferers. Dandelion's bitter principles are said to strengthen the stomach, improve digestion and have a beneficial effect on the liver, kidneys and gall bladder.

RECIPE SUGGESTION
Italian Dandelion Salad: Rub salad bowl with cut clove of garlic and shred into it 8 oz (225g) young dandelion leaves. Cover with dressing of 2 tbs sunflower oil, 1 tbs lemon juice, 1 tsp each fresh chopped or green-dried tarragon, chervil and salad burnet. Toss salad, adding a little salt and if liked, ripe black olives. Serve with herb bread or hot garlic bread.

DILL

Botanical name: *Peucedanum graveolens* or *Anethum graveolens*
Family: Umbelliferae

GENERAL
Dill is a fragrant, decorative plant of the parsley family with a long history of medicinal and culinary value. It has a special place in the kitchen, for its delicate flavour cannot be matched by any other herb. On the Continent it is the custom to use dill in all fish dishes, which adds to their flavour and makes them easier to digest.

Dill is mentioned in old Egyptian texts and was recommended by Roman and Greek physicians. Its use gradually spread throughout Europe and it is known to have been cultivated in England about 1570.

DESCRIPTION AND HABITAT
A fragrant annual of medium height, dill has a smooth, dark green stem with pale stripes and faint blue specks. It has feathery bluish-green leaves and bears umbels of yellow, flat flowers from June to the end of August. Dill can be found growing wild in the warm countries of southern Europe but has to be cultivated further north.

CULTIVATION
Seeds should be sown in shallow drills from April to June. They are delicate plants and have to be weeded and the soil kept moist. In dry weather, young dill plants are inclined to go to seed suddenly in which case they have to be re-sown.

Dill leaves may be cut for use at any time, but they are at their best just before flowering. The roots of dill are weak and do not usually stand transplanting. Take care not to grow dill close to fennel, to avoid cross pollination or overpowering the more delicate flavour of the dill.

FLAVOUR AND HOW TO STORE
The green leaves of dill have a subtle piquant flavour, whilst the seeds are sharper and somewhat bitter. Leaves for drying should be harvested before flowering but they dry down to almost nothing and a large number of plants are needed to make drying worthwhile. If seeds are required, the fruits should be allowed to ripen on the plant. The seeds can then be shaken out for drying and storing in the usual way.

USES
Chopped leaves will enhance the natural flavours of cucumbers, salads, any green vegetable, potatoes, soups and stews of meat or poultry, and most of all, fish. Its subtle flavour tends to 'cook away' so the leaves are best added to dishes just before they are removed from the heat. Dill seed as well as the plant can be steeped in wine vinegar to make dill vinegar, pickles, and particularly cucumbers which are called Dill Pickles. It makes a useful seasoning for salt-free diets. It has an ancient reputation for settling indigestion and curing stomach aches, for inducing sleep and stimulating the appetite and milk production in nursing mothers. For these purposes dill leaves and seeds may be infused in water or wine.

RECIPE SUGGESTION
Mix 1 tbs dill with 2 oz (60g) butter and ½ tsp lemon juice; refrigerate. Use as required on grilled steaks, new potatoes and carrots, hot French bread.

ELDER
Botanical name: *Sambucus nigra*
Family: Caprifoliaceae

GENERAL
The elder, so well known for its white flowers and dark berries, grows abundantly in the countryside. It has wonderful properties for cooking, baking, wine-making and also for medicinal and cosmetic purposes. All parts of the elder are rich in salts and vitamins. Even its wood was appreciated for making musical instruments. These valuable properties have been well known since ancient Greek and Roman times, and described in the famous old English herbals.

DESCRIPTION AND HABITAT
The elder grows into a bush or tree 9–30 ft (3–10m) tall. The bark is rough, changing in colour from brown to grey-white. The branches grow out from low down on the bush. The

leaves are dark green with finely jagged edges and the flowers, which bloom in June and July, are yellowish-white, growing in clusters. They are followed by berries which are plump and jet black when ripe. The elder grows in many countries, mainly in hedgerows, in clearings, in woods and on waste land, particularly near human dwellings. The bush has quite a strong, not too pleasant smell.

CULTIVATION
Elders do not require special attention but thrive best in a fertile, damp soil in a sunny place. Propagation is by division of the roots or by taking cuttings of bare shoots in the autumn. The bushes should be pruned in late autumn or early spring. When harvesting the flowers, care should be taken in handling them as they bruise easily and will turn black before they can be used or dried. All the flowers on the sprig should be out when they are picked. The berries may be gathered during September and October when they are fully ripe, and should be stripped from their stalks with a fork.

FLAVOUR AND HOW TO STORE
The taste of the flowers, leaves and bark is spicy and rather bitter. The berries have their own sharp taste which can be made delicious in various ways. The flowers and leaves can be spread out over nylon netting and allowed to dry in a cool circulation of air.

USES
Elderberries are used for making pies, jelly, jam and syrup. They combine well with apples or crab apples. They are preserved by bottling them in jars or they can be dried and used as an alternative to currants in cakes and other sweets. The juice from the berries is boiled to make a refreshing drink, but they should never be eaten raw. Elderberry wine is well known to every countryman and woman, and in Portugal the berries help to colour port. Elderflowers make delightful sweet fritters, described in the recipe. The berries contain a high content of vitamin B and are good for oedema and neuralgia. They make a good general tonic, stimulating the appetite and dispelling insomnia. A tea made from the young leaves in spring is diuretic and suitable for diabetics. Elderflowers and berries infused in water are a good medicine for a heavy cold since it will induce perspiration. For toothache, this infusion should be held in the mouth for a few minutes. Elderflower water is a pleasant bath additive and lotion for the skin and eyes. The centre of the bark and the roots work as a laxative taken in small doses.

RECIPE SUGGESTION
Elderflower Fritters: a 'wild' sweet, popular in many Continental countries. Pick small sprigs of elderflowers and wash gently, Make a batter with a mixture of 7¼ oz (210g) plain and wholemeal flour and 2 tbs soya flour. Add 1 egg yolk and 1 tbs oil. Mix until smooth with 10 fl oz (275ml) milk, beat well and leave covered in a cool place for ½ hr. Whisk egg white until

Elecampane

stiff and fold into batter. Dip elderflower sprigs in batter and fry in deep hot fat until golden brown. Drain and serve hot with sugar or vanilla sauce.

ELECAMPANE
Botanical name: *Inula helenium*
Family: Compositae

GENERAL
Elecampane is a medicinal herb little used in Europe and America nowadays. Varieties of it are grown in north China, Mongolia, Manchuria, Korea and Japan where the flowers are still used in herbal medicines as tonics, carminatives and laxatives. The virtues of elecampane's medicinal properties were celebrated by the Greek physician Dioscorides in the first century AD. In medieval Britain, the roots were candied and eaten as sweetmeats, as well as used in medicines for eye complaints.

DESCRIPTION AND HABITAT
A medium-sized perennial, elecampane has large yellow flowers from June to August. The stem is thick and hairy whilst the oblong leaves are rather fleshy with soft hairs on the undersides. Its value lies in the root which contains inulin and is harvested in August. It is native to many countries of the world.

CULTIVATION
An easy plant to grow in most soils, propagation is by root division in the autumn, or seeds sown in spring.

FLAVOUR AND HOW TO STORE
It has an aromatic slightly bitter taste but is not used today for flavouring.

USES
Elecampane root is used in tonic medicines as a gentle stimulant for the digestion, and to counteract acidity of the stomach. Pieces of the root covered with sugar can also be eaten to relieve these symptoms.

RECIPE SUGGESTION
For a decoction: Steep 1 heaped tsp of chopped root in 10 fl oz (275ml) boiling water for $\frac{1}{2}$ hr. Leave until cold and drink 1–2 cupfuls a day.

EYEBRIGHT

Botanical name: *Euphrasia officinalis*
Family: Scrophulariaceae

GENERAL
Eyebright is exclusively a medicinal herb. We do not know whether it was used in ancient times, but it is first documented in the fourteenth century by an Italian physician, Matthaeus Sylvaticus of Mantua, as an effective remedy for all eye disorders. It was also used as a kind of ale in Elizabethan times. In France it was known as *casse-lunette*, and in Germany as *Augentrost* which shows its general use in Europe in these times. It is still used today as a recognised remedy for eye troubles.

DESCRIPTION AND HABITAT
Eyebright is a small, hardy annual, wild plant. The more fertile the soil, the taller it grows. It has wiry, branched, erect stems, jagged leaves and tiny flowers, white or lilac in colour with yellow centres, which bloom throughout the summer. Eyebright can be found on heaths and dry pastures in Europe and north and west Asia.

CULTIVATION
Eyebright is a semi-parasite, partly relying on the roots of other plants for its nourishment. Therefore it will not grow readily in a garden unless surrounded by grass or other plants upon which it can prey. Plants for use should be gathered by cutting just above the ground during July and August when in full flower.

USES
The juice pressed from a fresh plant may be used or the herb infused in milk or water to make a lotion which may be used either warm or cold to bathe the infected eye three or four times daily. This lotion cleanses the eye and soothes inflammation. Eyebright tea may also be drunk as a digestive tonic or as a remedy for a headcold or hayfever.

RECIPE SUGGESTION
Eyebath: Mix together in equal proportions, the herbs eyebright, chamomile, fennel, marigold petals, horsetail, lady's mantle and yarrow. Using 1 heaped tsp of this mixture per cup, pour on boiling water and allow to steep 5 min. Strain and use as an eye-bath or for eye compresses.

Fat Hen   *Good King Henry*

FAT HEN
Botanical name: *Chenopodium album*
Family: Chenopodiaceae

GENERAL

Fat hen, one of the goosefoot family, which also includes beetroot and spinach, is a common weed today, but as far back as the Neolithic Age, early man has cultivated and eaten it as a nutritious green vegetable. He was undoubtedly unaware of the large quantity of iron, protein, vitamin B1 and calcium contained in it, more even than in cabbage and spinach. It is still grown in America today where certain Indian tribes eat it as a vegetable and grind the seeds for flour to make their bread and gruel. Fat hen is often confused with its relative Good King Henry (*Chenopodium bonus henricus*) which was once widely cultivated in English gardens as a potherb, and recognised for its antiscorbutic properties. Its young shoots can be eaten like asparagus and both varieties should not be neglected in the garden, for not only are they nutritious substitutes for spinach, but fat hen is known to benefit neighbouring plants by raising the mineral nutrients in the soil.

DESCRIPTION AND HABITAT

Fat hen is a medium-sized annual with green or reddish stained stems and alternate branches. The stalked leaves vary in shape and size and both stem and leaf are covered with a whitish powder, giving rise to its botanical name *album*. The masses of minute pale green flowers grow on short spikes in the axils of the upper leaves. It is found growing wild in all temperate climates of the world, particularly on soil rich in nitrogen, and abundantly on the seashore. Good King Henry is a perennial, very similar in appearance and habits.

CULTIVATION

Fat hen can be grown from seed sown thinly in March or April. The rows should be thinned out and treated like spinach. Good King Henry can also be raised from seed, or by division in autumn.

FLAVOUR AND HOW TO STORE

Both varieties have a pleasant taste—a tangy salty flavour when raw and bland when cooked. The leaves can be dried for use in winter salads, otherwise always use fresh.

USES

The young leaves of both varieties can be cooked like spinach, or used raw in salads. It makes a pleasant vegetable with a mild taste, and the leaves also make a good green soup. In spring, the plants can be earthed up and blanched shoots eaten like asparagus.

RECIPE SUGGESTION

Thoroughly wash 1 lb (½ kilo) fat hen or Good King Henry, removing the stalks. Cook in the same way as spinach, then drain and chop. Put ½ oz (15g) butter in pan, cook until a light brown, add the greens, mixing well. Remove from heat and stir in 2 fl oz (50ml) thick cream. Season and serve.

FENNEL

Botanical name: *Foeniculum vulgare*
F. dulce—Sweet Fennel or Carosella
F. piperitum—Florence Fennel
F. azoricum—Finocchio
Family: Umbelliferae

GENERAL

Fennel has been grown for thousands of years as a culinary herb all over the world. This has led to several different varieties being developed, and both the green part and the seeds of the plants are used for flavouring. Italians are fond of vegetable fennel, 'carosella', which are the young stems of sweet fennel, and 'finocchio' or Florence fennel, which is grown for its bulbous stalk bases.

Fennel was known to the old civilisations of China, India, Egypt. In ancient Greece it was a symbol of success and called 'Marathon' in reference to their great victory at that place over the Persians in 490 BC. The Romans ate the young shoots of fennel as a vegetable. Pliny recommended it for the eyesight, a belief also held by medieval herbalists. Fennel root was a principle ingredient in sack, a popular drink in Shakespeare's England, and Culpeper recommends it as an antidote against poisonous herbs and mushrooms and for snake bites.

DESCRIPTION AND HABITAT

A tall hardy perennial, fennel has delicate, bright green foliage and bears umbels of yellow flowers during July and August. It has a faint anise fragrance. It is native to southern Europe especially near the sea, but can also be found growing wild in temperate parts of Europe including Britain, where it is most common in Devon and Cornwall. It is cultivated for seed production in France, Germany, Italy, India, Japan and America.

CULTIVATION

Fennel thrives in well-drained, loam soil in a sunny position. Propagation may be by seeds sown in early spring or division of established root stock. Seeds are sown in drills 2 in (5cm) deep and 14 in (35cm) apart. Pieces of root, lifted in March, should be replanted 12 in (30cm) apart. It should not be planted near to dill as they are closely related and cross pollination may occur and the flavours may mingle. In autumn the plants should be cut down to about 4 in (10cm) above ground. The green foliage is cut for use from just before flowering time until the first frost comes. The seeds ripen from September to the end of October and are harvested when grey-green in colour. Fennel is a suitable herb for town gardens and window boxes.

FLAVOUR AND HOW TO STORE
The flavour of fennel is slightly reminiscent of anise. It is related to dill but its flavour is less pungent and more sweet and aromatic. It should be used cautiously as it contains a hidden tang. Sweet Fennel is less bitter with a stronger taste of anise. Finocchio fennel is used raw in salads. Fennel seeds may be dried at a low temperature, taking care to move them frequently or they may turn black or mouldy. The green foliage used in cooking is not suitable for domestic drying, but it is done commercially and the dried herb can be bought in jars.

USES
Traditionally fennel is used with fish in accompanying sauce or stuffing since its digestive qualities can counteract the richness of oily fish. It is also used with pork or veal and in marinades for other meats; in soups, sauces and salads, and to flavour pastry and cakes. It is a helpful herb for slimmers as it is supposed to accelerate the digestion of fatty foods. The thickened base of Florence fennel is boiled or braised like celery, and the young stalks are eaten raw in a salad or with cheese. Fennel seed may be added to apple pies and is a good digestive spice often added to babies' gripe water, or chewed as a breath sweetener. It is helpful medicinally for earache, toothache, coughs and asthma. The seeds are good for the eyes and may be infused in water to make a soothing eye lotion.

RECIPE SUGGESTION
A good fish sauce is made by adding chopped fennel green into 2 oz (60g) melted butter or a plain white sauce.

FENUGREEK—Bird's Foot, Greek Hay-seed
Botanical name: *Trigonella foenum graecum*
Family: Leguminosae

GENERAL
Fenugreek is a member of the bean family cultivated for its seed and one of the oldest culinary and medicinal plants. It is one of the few herbs whose cultivation for medicinal purposes is currently increasing, since its potential in the fields of birth control and feeding the hungry

nations of the world has recently been recognised. Experiments are being carried out on the seeds which contain diosgenin, an important substance in the synthesis of oral contraceptives and sex hormones. Fenugreek is a nourishing, body-building herb and its consumption is encouraged in such countries as India where it can be cultivated easily and where food shortage is a serious problem.

Evidence from the Pyramids indicates that the Egyptians used fenugreek as food, medicine and embalming agent. The Greeks and Romans cultivated it for food and medicine, and as fodder for their cattle. Medicinally, they used it to cure mouth ulcers, chapped lips and stomach complaints.

DESCRIPTION AND HABITAT
Fenugreek is a hardy, erect annual of medium size. Each leaf has three distinct leaflets and the richly scented, creamy flowers bloom from June to August, followed by long compressed pods each containing about sixteen seeds. Indigenous to Mediterranean shores, fenugreek is also cultivated in India, Africa, Egypt, Morocco, United States and occasionally Britain.

CULTIVATION
Fenugreek grows in mild climates in most well-drained soils. Grown from seed, the plants take about four months to mature, after which they are uprooted and dried. The seeds can then be threshed out for further drying and storage. Seeds may also be planted in boxes and allowed to sprout until a few weeks old, when the green shoots can be cut and used.

FLAVOUR AND HOW TO STORE
Fenugreek's flavour is somewhat bitter, reminiscent of lovage or celery, with a similar odour. The dried seeds may be stored in the usual way.

USES
Ground fenugreek seed is an ingredient in curry powder and the Jewish sweet dish Halva. Mango pickles and chutney contain the whole seeds, whilst extract of the seed is used in making imitation maple syrup. Young shoots are chopped and added to salads. Seeds soaked in water may be made into a paste for application to abscesses, boils, corns. A strong tea made from the seeds is helpful for digestive ailments. For fever, a soothing remedy is made from the tea with the addition of lemon juice and honey. Cosmetically, fenugreek is said to improve the complexion and the condition of the hair. For these purposes the seeds should be infused in water for bathing the face, or crushed and mixed with oil for rubbing into the scalp. Horses who eat it will be blessed with a glossy coat!

RECIPE SUGGESTION
Fenugreek seed tea: 1 tsp of seeds per pint of boiling water. Allow to stand for 6 min. For full nutritional value, do not strain—take the seeds too.

Flax

FLAX—Linseed
Botanical name: *Linum usitatissimum*
Family: Linaceae

GENERAL
Common flax has always provided the fibres for the linen trade. The seeds have various medicinal values. The seed-oil is well known for its use in furniture polish and also as an ingredient of printers' ink.

Evidence of flax plants has been found in ancient Egyptian tombs. It is mentioned in the Bible and throughout European history in connection with its medicinal and fibre qualities.

DESCRIPTION AND HABITAT
Flax is a hardy annual of medium height with small, pointed, pale-green leaves. The flowers are a beautiful deep blue and bloom from June to July, followed by the seeds which contain the well known linseed oil, rich in protein. The husk contains valuable mucilage used medicinally. It is generally cultivated but it freely self-seeds and may escape to grow wild in surrounding pastures.

CULTIVATION
Flax may be cultivated in any tropical or temperate region. Flax crops are seldom raised in Britain now as they quickly exhaust the soil. It requires a deep, moist loam soil. The seeds are sown in March and April and the crop harvested in August. The plants are stacked and the seeds allowed to ripen.

FLAVOUR AND HOW TO STORE
At present it has no culinary use.

USES
Fibre from the plant is used in the making of linen. The oil-bearing seeds are used for medicinal purposes, having a lubricating effect on intestinal membranes, good for constipation, sore throats and tonsillitis. Their properties enrich the blood and strengthen the nerves. For external use, crushed seeds are made into poultices for applying to all inflammatory swellings.

RECIPE SUGGESTION
For bronchial catarrh, steep 1 dsp crushed seeds in 1 cup cold water for ½ hr. Remove the viscous extract and drink the residue. For poultice, make a mash of linseed flour and spread on linen cloth, folded over and apply as hot as possible.

Foxglove

FOXGLOVE—(POISONOUS)
Botanical name: *Digitalis purpurea*
Family: Scrophulariaceae

GENERAL

Although the foxglove is a familiar plant, it is not so well known that its leaves contain the extremely poisonous 'digitalis' the important medicinal drug for cardiac diseases. However, its appearance is unlikely to be confused with any non-poisonous plant and the unpleasant taste and obnoxious odour of the leaves when bruised discourage tasting. You will never see animals browsing on foxgloves. It is valuable in treating many symptoms and conditions as well as heart diseases, but should only be administered under strict medical supervision. The botanical name, *digitalis* means thimble, in reference to the shape of the flower.

It was not mentioned by the Ancients as one of their healing plants, but old English herbals of the sixteenth and seventeenth centuries recommend it for many ills which bear no relation to its modern use.

DESCRIPTION AND HABITAT

The foxglove is a biennial plant but sometimes the roots are sufficiently vigorous to keep it alive for several years. In the first year it will grow only a rosette of leaves. The second year it will produce one or more tall flowering stems. It will flower the second summer, usually during July. The flowers grow from the main stems, drooping crimson, purple or white bells, highly favoured by bees, and offering shelter from inclement weather to other smaller insects. The somewhat hairy leaves diminish in size from the bottom of the stems upwards. It can be grown in almost any soil and is found wild in Europe, including Britain, particularly the west of England, North Africa and the Azores.

CULTIVATION

Foxglove is grown as a tall, decorative garden plant, though its poisonous character is not without danger to children. It is also grown commercially for pharmaceutical purposes. It is grown from seed sown in April or May and will flourish in light, well-drained soil, with some slight shade. It is freely self-seeding. The true medicinal variety will produce flowers of dull pink or magenta colour. The leaves are collected while the plant is in flower and sent to manufacturing druggists.

USES

It produces a valuable drug in the treatment of valvular diseases of the heart and high blood pressure, since it slows and strengthens the heart beat. It is not safe for heart disorders where the heart is already labouring, nor should it be administered over a long period since it may upset the stomach or overact on the heart, lowering the blood pressure to a dangerous level. In cases of pneumonia or other infections of the lungs it is swift in strengthening the heart beat and improving the nervous structure of the pulmonary organs. Digitalis also acts on urinary functions of the body, being a remedy for dropsy.

GARLIC

Botanical name: *Allium sativum*
Family: Liliaceae

GENERAL

Garlic is an all-round flavouring and medicinal herb. It is so strong that it can only be used in very small amounts. Medicinally, its essential volatile oil has antiseptic properties which prevent the formation of bacteria as well as healing infections in the intestines, and is a cure for many ailments and symptoms. In countries where typhus and cholera are endemic, nearly the whole population add small doses of garlic to their food as a preventative measure. These properties of garlic have been known since time immemorial and it was cultivated in the Mediterranean countries, in Egypt, China and India. It was a common food of the Egyptian labourers when building the pyramids, and later of the Roman labourer and soldier, but rejected by the upper class for its strong smell. Both Hippocrates and Dioscorides mentioned its importance for medicine. It was certainly known in Britain in the sixteenth century and is mentioned in Shakespeare's plays, but it was probably grown here long before.

DESCRIPTION AND HABITAT

Garlic is a hardy perennial with long flat, solid leaves. The flower stalk grows erect from the bulb and the flowers are whitish, tinged with purple. The bulb consists of several small egg-shaped bulblets or cloves, enclosed in a white membrane. The characteristic odour is present in the whole plant but is strongest in the bulb. Garlic has been cultivated for so many centuries that it is doubtful whether any true garlic can be found growing wild, other than those 'escapes', but the plant is believed to have originated in the deserts of Central Asia. Garlic has several wild relatives growing in England, all with a similar odour but of little medicinal or culinary value.

CULTIVATION

The cloves should be planted in well dug ground at the end of February in rows 9 in (20cm) apart with 12 in (30cm) between the rows. Garlic prefers sunny positions in light, well drained soils. The bulbs can be dug up when the foliage has died down in late summer and they should be hung up to dry under cover in a light shady place. The dried leaves will then be easily removed. Cloves may also be planted in autumn for a supply of garlic early the next year.

FLAVOUR AND HOW TO STORE
Garlic has a strong pungent flavour which does not resemble any other herb. The strong odour which accompanies garlic and lingers on the breath may be disguised by peppermint, or is said to be removed if parsley is eaten at the same time. The dried bulbs may be stored in a cool, dry place.

USES
For subtle flavour, rub the cooking dish or joint of meat with a cut clove of garlic. For stronger flavour, the clove may be crushed or chopped and added to the dish. If the outer skin is not peeled off, it may be used whole and removed before serving. As well as flavouring meat, vegetables, fish and salads, it is also used in garlic butter, garlic oil, vinegar and mayonnaise. It helps to bring out the flavour of mushrooms. Dehydrated garlic powder and salt have increased the popularity of garlic flavouring since they are easy to store and have little odour. Crushed cloves may be infused in water or milk and taken for all disorders of the digestion, and will keep high blood pressure down. It has an antiseptic effect good for infectious diseases and inflammations of the stomach and intestine. Taken for persistent bronchitis, it will expel catarrh. It may be used in the treatment of gall bladder and liver troubles, headaches, fits, faintness and skin blemishes. The reason for these effects is found in the volatile oil which contains sulphur and traces of iodine and fruit sugar.

RECIPE SUGGESTION
Mix 1 clove of garlic, finely chopped, into 4¼ oz (120g) fresh butter. Spread thickly on to French bread; wrap in foil and heat in moderate oven for 10 min.
A cosmetic hint: for bringing pimples and boils to a head, dab on the expressed juice of a clove of garlic.

GENTIAN
Botanical name: *Gentiana lutea*
Family: Gentianaceae

GENERAL
One of the oldest healing plants, Gentian is named after Gentius, King of Ilyria in 180 BC, who is said to have discovered its medicinal value.

Gentian

DESCRIPTION AND HABITAT
This variety of gentian is found only on the Continent, growing in abundance on the Pyrenees and Alps. It is a medium-sized perennial with bright, pale green oblong leaves. The flowers are bright yellow and grow in clusters around the stem in the axils of the leaves. The root, which is the part used, often grows to about 3 ft (90cm) long. These gentians should not be confused with the brilliant blue of the rockery plant gentian, the *Gentiana acaulis*.

CULTIVATION
Wild plant on the Continent and America, not in Britain.

FLAVOUR AND HOW TO STORE
Used only medicinally.

USES
Gentiana lutea is a popular tonic medicine. The bitter principle contained in the root is helpful for the digestion and all ailments concerning the digestive organs. Gentian schnapps is made from the roots which is good for a weak stomach, for dispersing blood clots and as a preventative against influenza. It also fortifies, very quickly, those feeling exhausted, hungry or cold, when only one mouthful will stimulate the stomach and the muscles. Gentian improves the blood by stimulating the increase of blood corpuscles in the correct proportion, so it is effective in cases of anaemia, weakness of heart or nerves and brings down fever.

At all times gentian should only be taken under medical supervision because it cannot be given to those with high blood pressure or to women in early pregnancy; also it must be taken at least one hour before a meal otherwise it has an adverse effect on the digestion.

GINGER

Botanical name: *Zingiber officinale*
Family: Zingiberaceae

GENERAL
The ginger plant has been cultivated for its rhizomes since very early times in India and southeast Asia, where it is still considered to be essential in the daily diet as protection against diseases and an aid to digestion. There is also a wild variety found in Japan called Zimioga. Nowadays ground ginger is used in the traditional Christmas gingerbread, cakes and biscuits and in Britain a great deal is used in the making of ginger beer.

The pleasant properties of ginger have been appreciated throughout the centuries and were mentioned by the Chinese philosopher Confucius (551–479 BC) and by the Greek physician Dioscorides, and in the Koran, the sacred book of the Mohammedans. Originally from south-east Asia and China, ginger was one of the first true spices to come to Europe through the Arab traders. It was widely used by the Greeks and later the Romans who brought the spice to England.

Ginger is grown today in other tropical countries, West Indies (reputed to produce the best 'dried' ginger), West Africa, Japan and Brazil.

DESCRIPTION AND HABITAT
Ginger is a tall perennial reed-like plant, with thick underground stems or rhizomes which are the parts used. When harvested early, while still green, the ginger is candied, crystallised and preserved in syrup. When allowed fully to ripen it is used for the ground ginger spice. For dried ginger the rhizome is thoroughly cleaned, boiled, carefully peeled and then dried in the sun for a week.

CULTIVATION
Ginger is grown only in countries with a constant, hot, humid climate and a heavy rainfall. It is propagated by division of the rhizome and the plant is ready to harvest after nine months to a year.

FLAVOUR AND HOW TO STORE
Ginger has a highly aromatic scent and a sweet, hot flavour. It is available crystallised, preserved in syrup, dried whole and ground. For storing the whole dried ginger is best in an airtight container, and the ground ginger in a glass screw-top jar.

USES
Ginger is an essential ingredient of all curry powders; it is used to spice meat stews, poultry, chutney and pickles, vegetable soups and cheese dishes. Ginger adds a delicious flavour to stewed and preserved fruit and puddings, and in bakery for spiced cakes, gingerbread and biscuits.

Ginger has always been used medicinally to stimulate the digestion and ease flatulence. It has antiseptic qualities and is also useful as an expectorant when combined with other remedies; on its own it is helpful for colds and spasms.

RECIPE SUGGESTION
Ginger Pancakes: Mix 3½ oz (100g) flour, pinch of salt and 1 tsp ground ginger together. Add one whole egg and one egg yolk, then 8 fl oz (225ml) milk and 3 tsp rum, stirring until smooth. Leave covered for ½ hr. Fold in a beaten egg white and cook pancakes in the usual way.

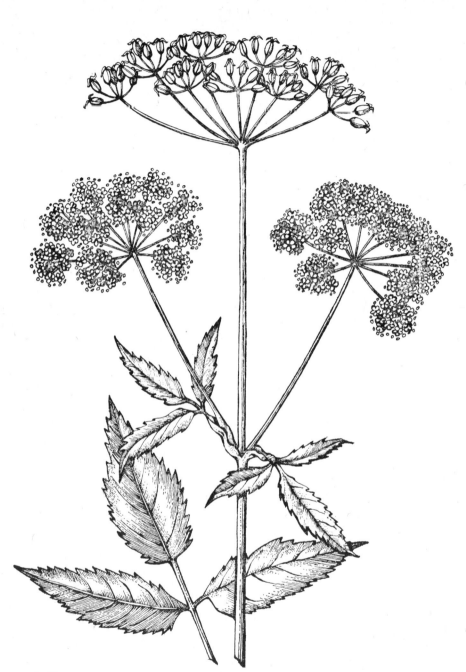

Ground Elder

GROUND ELDER—*Goutweed, Goatsfoot, Herb Gerard Bishops Elder*

Botanical name: *Aegopodium podagraria*

Family: Umbelliferae

GENERAL

Ground elder is one of the weeds we consider to be a great nuisance in the garden. It is hard to believe that it contains valuable properties and was used in former times medicinally and as a potherb. In the Middle Ages, it was cultivated in the monastery gardens, and dedicated to St Gerard, the patron of the gouty. The English herbalists Gerard and Culpeper sang its praises and today it is still used by herbalists for aching joints, especially for the pain of sciatica. In Sweden and Switzerland the leaves were once used as a vegetable and spring salad.

DESCRIPTION AND HABITAT

A relative of parsley, ground elder is an erect perennial of medium height having a hollow, furrowed stem. The leaves are large with ovate, sharply-toothed lobes, and the flat umbrella-like flowerheads bear umbels of white flowers. They bloom from June to August and are followed by flattened seed vessels which are jerked open when ripe and scattered by the wind for considerable distances. The stout root system spreads rapidly underground, smothering other plants.

CULTIVATION

Grows wild.

FLAVOUR AND HOW TO STORE

The young fresh leaves when cooked, have a tangy, aromatic flavour, somewhat like spinach. The leaves can be dried like other herbs and should be stored in the same way for making a medicinal tea.

USES

The leaves make a wholesome green vegetable. Medicinally, a tea is made of the leaves and taken in conjunction with hot fomentations of the root and leaves applied to the painful joint.

RECIPE SUGGESTION

For the tea, pour 10 fl oz (275ml) boiling water on to a handful of ground elder leaves, or 1 level tsp dried leaves. Cover and leave to infuse for a short time, and take undiluted in a wineglass several times a day.

Fomentation: boil together fresh roots and leaves and apply directly on to joint as hot as can be borne.

Ground Ivy

GROUND IVY—Alehoof, Creeping Jenny
Botanical name: *Nepeta glechoma* or *N. lederacea*
Family: Labiatae

GENERAL
The country folk of Britain and Europe have known ground ivy for many centuries as a common, creeping, wild herb which provides a potent tonic and general stimulant when taken as a tisane. The colonists took it to America where its country name was changed to Creeping Charlie.

Evidence found on glacial river beds indicates that ground ivy has been native to Britain since the Ice Age. It has, for many centuries, been employed as a healing herb. Until the use of hops was permitted in Britain in the fifteenth century, ground ivy was one of the principal herbs used in brewing beer to clear and flavour the liquid; hence its other country name, alehoof.

DESCRIPTION AND HABITAT
A perennial evergreen, ground ivy has trailing stems which frequently give off root fibres into the soil. The plant rapidly carpets the ground with its heart-shaped dark green leaves, which become stained crimson or purple in sunlight. The flowers vary in colour from blue to purple, occasionally white. They open in April and continue to bloom for the greater part of summer and autumn. Ground ivy will be found creeping over the ground by the roadside, in hedgerows and woods, especially oak. It grows in most parts of Britain, south Europe, Asia and Japan.

CULTIVATION
A cutting of wild ground ivy will take root if transplanted into the garden, provided the soil is not too light and sandy, but it is generally considered too invasive to plant on cultivated ground. It is most suitable for growing in hanging baskets or window boxes.

FLAVOUR AND HOW TO STORE
Ground ivy has an aromatic, bitter taste. The whole herb should be gathered in May when the flowers are still fresh, and the leaves dried and stored in the usual way.

USES
A tea made from a large handful of leaves to 2 cups of hot water can be taken for coughs, tuberculosis, kidney complaints and as a digestive tonic. For women, it will also bring on menstruation and help to expel a retained afterbirth. Externally, ground ivy mixed with the flowers of yarrow and chamomile, can be used effectively as a poultice for abscesses, boils, ulcers and rashes. The fresh juice from the leaves sniffed up the nose relieves congestion and

headache. In China, preparations of ground ivy are used as anodynes for all fevers and pain, including toothache and earache.

RECIPE SUGGESTION

To make an infusion, pour 20 fl oz (575ml) boiling water over 1¼ oz (30g) ground ivy leaves and allow to steep for not more than 3 min. Strain, sweeten and cool before drinking.

HAWTHORN—May, Quickset, White Thorn
Botanical name: *Crataegus oxyacantha*
Family: Rosaceae

GENERAL

Hawthorn's beautiful flowers which appear in the country hedges in May, are familiar to all. Less well known is hawthorn's healing capacity as an effective, non-toxic remedy for various heart conditions such as valvular insufficiency, rapid and feeble heart action and general weakness of the heart. Hawthorn's alternative name, Quickset, comes from its historical use in Britain as a hardy hedge plant.

DESCRIPTION AND HABITAT

The hawthorn, or may, grows abundantly in Britain. It is a shrubby, deciduous spring tree which can grow very tall. The flowers bloom in masses during May and have a strong smell. They are commonly white but can be pink. The crimson berries, known as 'haws', ripen in September.

CULTIVATION

Can be grown from seed which usually germinates during the second spring.

FLAVOUR

The leaf buds have a pleasant nutty flavour, whilst the haws are sweetish and rather dry.

USES

The green leaf buds of hawthorn can be eaten in the spring in potato salads or between bread and butter. The flowers can be used for liqueur and the ripe haws for a delicious jelly preserve.

The liquid extract from the haws is used as a cardiac tonic.

RECIPE SUGGESTION

To make the jelly: Allow 10–15 fl oz (275–425ml) water for every 1 lb (450g) of fruit. Simmer gently till soft. Strain through jelly bag. Make up in the usual way, allowing 1 lb (450g) preserving sugar for every 20 fl oz (575ml) of juice.

A medicinal tea is made with 1–2 tsp dried haws per cup of water, infused for 20 min. Drink hot.

HEMLOCK—(POISONOUS)
Botanical name: *Conium maculatum*
Family: Umbelliferae

GENERAL
Hemlock, a common wild plant, belongs to the large umbelliferae family and is very poisonous. It is easy and dangerous to confuse hemlock with other umbelliferaes similar in appearance to herbs such as parsley, carrot, fennel and cow parsley. Every part of the plant contains a volatile, oily alkali called 'coniine' which is highly narcotic. Hemlock is mentioned in the old Greek legend that the god Prometheus brought fire to mortals in a hemlock stalk. Socrates, the Greek philosopher, chose to drink a cup of hemlock juice rather than renounce his teachings.

Identification of wild plants for survival should always be made with great care, especially this group of poisonous wild plants which includes hemlock, cowbane or water hemlock, water dropwort, fool's parsley, water parsnip and wild carrot. Hemlock and water hemlock are particularly dangerous, for if only a small amount of the juice is swallowed it can produce vomiting and paralysis and even prove fatal.

DESCRIPTION AND HABITAT
Hemlock is a tall annual or biennial plant with hollow, smooth stems marked with purplish blotches, and it has a long tapering root. The leaves are divided like a feather and the leaflets deeply lobed. The flowers are white and grow in large umbels, and the egg-shaped fruits have wavy ridges. Hemlock grows abundantly in Britain and throughout the temperate regions of the northern hemisphere in damp places, along roadsides and ditches and in open woods.

Water hemlock or cowbane, *Cicuta virosa*, is a perennial plant of medium height. Its short thick root somewhat resembles a parsnip and it grows in ditches and along the margins of rivers and lakes.

CULTIVATION
A wild plant.

FLAVOUR
Hemlock has an unpleasant bitter taste and a disagreeable smell of mice which all parts of the plant give off when bruised or crushed.

USES
Hemlock was used in former times as a sedative medicine for nervous spasms, epileptic attacks and whooping cough. It was one of the plants in a mixture of herbs used as an anaesthetic.

Externally a compress of hemlock leaves was said to reduce palpitations of the heart and to heal open sores and ulcers. It is not much used in medicine today.

HENBANE—Hogbean (POISONOUS)
Botanical name: *Hyoscyamus niger*
Family: Solanaceae

GENERAL

Henbane is a highly poisonous plant of no particular value except for its medicinal, narcotic properties. In ancient times it was used for sleeplessness and as a pain reliever. The poisonous character of the plant is dangerous to fowls.

DESCRIPTION AND HABITAT

There are two types of henbane, the annual and biennial. They come from the same seed but the annual form from the weaker, later developed seeds, and this is the smaller variety. It flowers in July/August and the biennial flowers in May/June. The flowers are yellow with purple veins. Henbane grows to medium height and has divided grey-green leaves which are, like the stem, hairy and sticky to touch. The whole plant has an unpleasant odour and acrid taste. It grows wild from Britain to India.

CULTIVATION

A wild poisonous plant.

FLAVOUR

Slightly acrid taste with unpleasant smell. No culinary use.

USES

The alkaloid drug hyoscyamine is obtained from the leaves and the flowering tops, and it is used for treating all nervous complaints. It has an antispasmodic effect and is helpful in cases of whooping cough. It can be a substitute for opium in medicines for children. Infusions of henbane leaves are used in drops for earache, but all uses must be applied only under medical supervision.

HIBISCUS—*Roselle, Karkadé, Jamaica Sorrel, African Mallow*
Botanical name: *Hibiscus sabdariffa*
Family: Malvaceae

GENERAL
The lovely flowers of this species of hibiscus are well known throughout the tropics for their flavouring qualities. In Africa the plant gives its name, Karkadé, to the thirst-quenching drink made from its flowers. It has become a custom in southern Germany to drink rose hip tea with hibiscus flowers which gives the tea a lemon flavour and beautiful colour. The botanical name *Hibiscus* was the one Dioscorides gave the mallow.

DESCRIPTION AND HABITAT
A tall bushy annual with reddish stems and red flowers, it is found in tropical Asia, Africa, India, Central America and southern USA.

CULTIVATION
It is a tender tropical plant which can be grown in temperate climates in hot houses. Propagation is by seed or cuttings taken in spring.

FLAVOUR AND HOW TO STORE
The flowers give a slightly acid, lemony flavour to drinks. They are dried and stored in the usual way.

USES
The flowers are used to make a ruby-coloured tisane which is refreshing and may be drunk either hot or iced. They can also be added to punches or fruit cups and to make a jelly or sauce similar to cranberry. The rose hip and hibiscus flower drink, so popular on the Continent, can be bought there ready-mixed at health food and drug stores.

RECIPE SUGGESTION
For Hibiscus Punch, which can be served hot or cold: make an infusion of 2 heaped tsp hibiscus flowers, 2 or 3 cloves, ½ stick cinnamon and a small piece of vanilla pod per pint of boiling water, and allow to draw for 5–10 min. Strain and sweeten with honey. If liked, half the liquid can be red wine.

Hops

HOPS
Botanical name: *Humulus lupulus*
Family: Moraceae

GENERAL
An aromatic bitter, the best hops are cultivated in Kent, England, where they have been used for brewing beer since the sixteenth century. The female flowers, or catkins, are the parts used, and years ago, were considered important to the housewife in the making of simples to stimulate the appetite and calm the nerves. Its medicinal uses as a calmative are well known.

DESCRIPTION AND HABITAT
A decorative perennial with long twining stems, hops climb high over bushes and small trees. The flowers are small and yellowish green; the male flowers are in loose bunches and the female are contained in small cone-like catkins which become enlarged after flowering and are the brewer's hops. The small fruits contained in the 'cones' have resinous glands which provide the bitter substance, lupulin.

It is cultivated in the southern counties of England and can sometimes be found growing wild in hedges and thickets, when it is probably an 'escape'. Hops also grow in Europe and were introduced to the USA and Australia.

CULTIVATION
Hops grow well in town gardens and will quickly cover fences or walls. They prefer a sunny position but need to be frequently watered and mulched in dry weather. They should be cut well back in October.

FLAVOUR AND HOW TO STORE
It has a bitter, aromatic flavour and is usually used fresh.

USES
Most hops are used commercially in brewing beer, but they also have other uses.

The young shoots, plucked in May, are similar to asparagus tips and can be cooked and eaten as a vegetable. Cooked hop shoots can be chopped and added to butter sauce to serve with fish and boiled mutton.

Medicinally, hops are tonic, diuretic and anodyne. They are helpful for nervous irritation and sleeplessness; a pillow filled with hops is said to be good for this. Warm hop tea may be drunk to induce sleep. To prepare this pour boiling water on to 3 tsp hop cones per cup. Hop tea is also a good general tonic, helps digestion and promotes appetite.

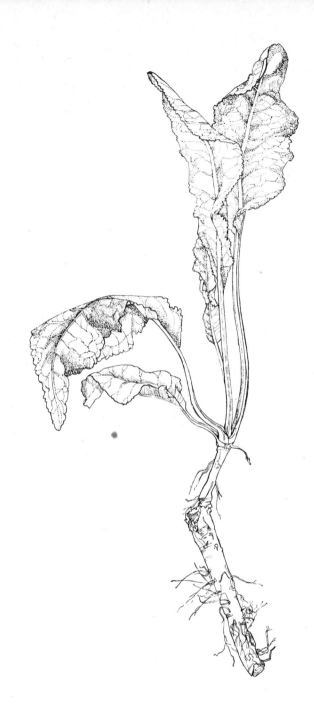

Horseradish

RECIPE SUGGESTION
Hop shoots can be added raw to a thick pea soup and cooked until tender with a little onion and seasoning, adding some milk just before serving.

HORSERADISH
Botanical name: *Cochlearia armoracia*
Family: Cruciferae

GENERAL
Horseradish is grown for its edible roots which when bruised, emit a strong pungent odour. It is a versatile, invaluable condiment for various uses, but its medicinal properties should not be overlooked. It has a high vitamin C content and antibiotic qualities which protect the intestinal tract from harmful bacteria.

It was introduced to Western Europe from its native Eastern Europe during the thirteenth century and was used by the Germans and Danes as a medicine, flavouring and vegetable. It was introduced to England during the sixteenth century and became naturalised here under the name 'red cole'.

DESCRIPTION AND HABITAT
A hardy perennial of the mustard family, it produces white fleshy roots and a tall erect stem with white aromatic flowers and large, dark green, shiny leaves. It bears rounded seed pods which rarely ripen in Britain. It is usually cultivated in central and northern Europe and America but can 'escape' and be found growing wild as a vigorous weed by the wayside and in fields.

CULTIVATION
Horseradish prefers a fairly rich soil which should be kept well free of weeds to allow the roots to develop their full strength. As the seed pods rarely ripen, propagation is by division of the roots. Cold weather improves the flavour of horseradish and the roots should be dug up in October/November when they are 8–14 in (20–35cm) long. The larger ones may be used for flavouring and the smaller ones stored in damp sand or ashes for dividing and replanting the following spring. Small slivers of root should be planted in well dug ground in trenches 2–3 ft (60–90cm) deep with an addition of plenty of manure or compost. If ripe seed is available it should be sown in early spring and the plants subsequently thinned out to every 12 in (30cm).

FLAVOUR AND HOW TO STORE
The flavour of the raw horseradish is hot and biting but with a pungency which makes it refreshing, and somehow cooling. Fresh horseradish roots should not be exposed to the light

or they will turn green, but should be stored in a damp, dark place. It may be bought as a prepared relish, or in dehydrated flakes to be reconstituted in water for use and in this form it is easily stored in air-tight jars.

USES
Horseradish root is usually used raw as it loses its pungency when cooked. Use grated or cut into strips mixed with cream or vinegar in salad dressings, fish sauces or in a filling for avocado pear. Its most well known use is with roast or boiled beef, but it is also delicious with sausages, ham and eggs. During summer the young leaves may be chopped to mix with green salad. Taken raw on bread before meals, it stimulates the appetite and the liver function and has a strong diuretic effect. Horseradish also stimulates circulation and breathing, is said to be a good external remedy for insect bites, stings, burns and cuts as well as chilblains, and has been used in vinegar, cosmetically, for freckles and acne.

RECIPE SUGGESTION
Horseradish Cream for Avocado Pear: Melt 1 tbs butter in pan and fry together until golden brown: ½ stick peeled grated horseradish with an equal quantity of fresh breadcrumbs. Remove from heat, add one apple peeled and grated, 1 dsp yoghurt, 1 tsp lemon juice, pinch salt and sugar and ½ tsp each fresh or dried tarragon and dill. Allow to permeate till cold, leaving uncovered if horseradish is very hot, then chill in refrigerator. Shortly before filling pears, fold in 3–4 tbs whipped cream.

HORSETAIL—Equisetum
Botanical name: Equisetum arvense
Family: Equisetaceae

GENERAL
There are more than twenty different species of equisetum, of which some are edible, though rarely used in cookery nowadays, but the variety E. arvense is well known for its medicinal properties. It contains a high quantity of silicic and other acids, minerals, vitamins, salts and bitter substances. In China it is an astringent remedy for a variety of ailments. Its Latin name, equi a horse and setum a tail, reflects its common name. Fossil remains of giant varieties of Equisetum in the carboniferous period, indicate that our modern dwarf varieties originated at that time.

DESCRIPTION AND HABITAT
Horsetail is a non-flowering, fern-like plant with no affinity to any other group of plants. The green spiky shoots give the plant the appearance of a tiny Christmas tree, and having no

leaves, they contain no chlorophyll. The root is a creeping rhizome sending up erect, hollow, jointed stems which end in cone-like catkins. The young horsetails develop from spores in much the same way as ferns. Horsetail grows everywhere as a troublesome weed in cultivated areas and is widespread on waste land and dunes, usually near water.

CULTIVATION
As it is such a hardy weed it is not generally cultivated. It does not grow well on chalky soil, but flourishes everywhere else. The stems should be harvested during June and July.

FLAVOUR AND HOW TO STORE
The flavour is slightly salty and bitter. For drying, the picked stems should be handled carefully, avoiding bruising or breaking. They should be dried in the usual way and stored in airtight containers in the dark.

USES
Horsetail or equisetum Tea is a remedy for all chest complaints and is even successful in some cases of chronic bronchitis and tuberculosis. Its high content of silicic acid enriches the blood, encouraging the formation of blood corpuscles and is helpful for anaemia, loss of blood and diseases of the kidneys and bladder. For ulcers in the mouth, the fresh juice or tea should be held in the mouth for a minute before swallowing. Due to its astringent qualities, it can stop the bleeding of wounds and helps to dry and heal them. In its various forms, it is recommended for nosebleeds, inflamed tonsils and glandular swellings. One variety, *E. hyemale*, contains so much silica that country folk have used the whole plant to clean and polish fine metals. Today in China it is used for polishing wood. Its content of cobalt, calcium and silica make it an effective fungicide for black spot and mildew on garden plants.

RECIPE SUGGESTION
Horsetail Tea: Soak 1 tsp horsetail per cup of water for 1–2 hr; simmer gently in this water for 10 min; allow to stand for a further 10 min. Strain and drink lukewarm, 1 or 2 cupfuls per day.
For Juice: Take 1 dsp freshly crushed shoots 3–4 times daily.

HYSSOP
Botanical name: *Hyssopus officinalis*
Family: Labiatae

GENERAL
Hyssop is a highly aromatic herb which has provided a culinary seasoning for many centuries,

Hyssop

but it is strong and has to be used sparingly. It has also been used as a cough remedy, and the pulverised leaves were used as a dusting powder for spots and swellings. There is some doubt that the hyssop mentioned in the Bible is *H. officinalis*. However hyssop has been used in Mediterranean countries since before the time of Christ for medicinal purposes. Having deodorant properties, it was one of the herbs used in the cleansing of holy temples. The name hyssop is of Greek origin, derived from the name of a holy herb *azob*.

DESCRIPTION AND HABITAT
Hyssop is a decorative, partially evergreen, shrubby herb which grows to medium height. It has dark green slender leaves and the flowers are blue and bloom from June to September, but there are also pink and white varieties. The leaves contain a volatile yellow oil and sulphur, and the foliage emits a strong fragrance. It is indigenous to south Europe, Near East and south Russia. It is grown in Britain, and is found wild on the walls of old Cistercian monasteries, and also in the USA.

CULTIVATION
Hyssop is fairly hardy and undemanding of soil conditions. Propagation is by seed, cuttings or division of the roots. Cuttings should be taken in spring or autumn; the seeds sown in April. When the seedlings or cuttings are large enough they should be planted out with a good space between them, and well watered. Once thus established, they require little attention. The herb is harvested just as flowering begins.

FLAVOUR AND HOW TO STORE
The taste is slightly bitter and minty. The flowers and young green tops may be dried and stored in the usual way.

USES
Hyssop aids the digestion of fat and is recommended for use with greasy meat and fish such as pork and eel. The flowers and young green shoots may also be chopped and added to salads, game and soups. It may be sprinkled on to fruit such as apricots, in pies. It is an important ingredient in liqueurs, notably Chartreuse. Bees make delicious honey from the blue hyssop flowers. Hyssop tea made from the flowers, is taken for all complaints of the throat and lungs and it will help to relieve bronchial catarrh. It may also be taken for irregular blood pressure, nervous disorders and fits, and used as a lotion to treat ear, eye and throat infections, also insect bites and stings.

RECIPE SUGGESTION
For digestive upsets when travelling abroad, try the authors' own disinfectant 'mixture for abroad'—a blend of herbs which can be added to unfamiliar food. The herbs to use are:

hyssop, ground fennel herb or seed; basil, mugwort, dill, tarragon, lovage, marjoram, rosemary, sage, celery leaves and thyme. These are the essential ones. Of lesser importance, but can be added if available are: borage, nettle, salad burnet, nasturtium and grated horseradish.

ICELAND MOSS—*Cetraria, Iceland Lichen*
Botanical name: *Cetraria icelandica*
Family: Lichenes

GENERAL
There are approximately 2,000 different species of lichen in Britain. They are composite plants consisting of algae in partnership with fungi, and this partnership is called lichen. Unlike ordinary plants, lichens take their food from the soil, the air and inorganic substances of rocks and other mineral salts. Some varieties are parasitic plants living on other growing organisms such as leaves and branches. Iceland moss, one of the many lichens found covering roofs, rocks, trees and soil with its persistent, slow growth has medical properties only and is not a herb for the kitchen.

DESCRIPTION AND HABITAT
Iceland moss is a low creeping plant, brown or grey in colour. Its texture is dry and it eventually dries down to an ash-like substance. It can be found in pure air in northern countries or mountainous regions of warmer countries, often in places where no other vegetation survives. In Britain it can be found on barren, stony moors and heaths.

CULTIVATION
It is seldom cultivated as it smothers every living organism over which it grows. It may cover rocks or stone walls, but it will not grow in towns, as it needs pure country air.

FLAVOUR AND HOW TO STORE
Its virtues are ascribed to a substance called cetarin which has a bitter taste. The dry lichen may be stored in the usual way. When this is boiled in water it swells rapidly and then cools to a jelly.

USES
The tea is taken for all pulmonary complaints including bronchial catarrh and tuberculosis.

It is also recommended for soothing the intestinal tract and for the treatment of dysentery. It is suitable for children, invalids and the aged.

RECIPE SUGGESTION
Tea: 1 tsp stirred into 1 cup of water just off boil. Sweeten with honey or flavour with cinnamon. Drink warm for cough medicine, cool for digestive tonic.

JUNIPER
Botanical name: *Juniperus communis*
Family: Pinaceae

GENERAL
Juniper is a useful medicinal plant, its berries containing numerous beneficial substances such as tannins, resins and organic acids. The berries have a wide range of uses in cookery. Of the many varieties *J. communis* is a good one.

Since Biblical days juniper has been considered a magic plant. It often figured in legends concerning evil spirits and in holy stories. Its aromatic scent made it popular as a strewing herb to sweeten stale air in overcrowded or sick rooms. It was believed to be a protection against epidemics. In Switzerland it was burnt with the fuel in schoolrooms to fumigate them when it was too cold to open the windows.

DESCRIPTION AND HABITAT
J. communis is an evergreen shrub or small tree. In poor, shallow soil it will have spreading growth but in fertile soil it will grow to a good height. It has reddish stems with needle-like leaves. Small yellow flowers bloom May–June. To be certain of obtaining berries from the female shrubs, plant male shrubs with them. The berries take three years to ripen and are first green, then bluish and finally black. Each ripe berry contains three seeds. The whole plant has a strong aroma of pine. It is found in Britain on chalky downs, heaths, in woods and in warm and cool areas of Europe, North America and Asia.

CULTIVATION
Juniper is hardy and suitable for growing in all soils. Propagation is by seeds, which are slow to germinate, or by cuttings of the young shoots planted in a cold frame in spring. The berries should be gathered when ripe during autumn.

FLAVOUR AND HOW TO STORE

Juniper berries are aromatic, spicy and taste slightly of pine. When black the berries are dried, spread out on a tray until shrivelled, then stored in a dry place.

USES

Juniper berries add a piquant flavour to roasts and casseroles of beef, venison, poultry; meat sauces and marinades. Cooked with game, they remove some of its rich 'gamey' flavour which some people dislike. They blend well with other herbs and flavourings and may be crushed before adding to the dish. A conserve or jam for serving with cold meat may be made from the berries. Commercially, oil of juniper is used in distilling gin and other spirits. Juniper berries stimulate the appetite and have a diuretic effect. They are used for urine infections and as a precaution against kidney stones. Their germicidal qualities make them suitable remedies for stomach and lung infections. They may be eaten raw or infused in liquid.

RECIPE SUGGESTION

Juniper Conserve is made by cooking the berries in water till soft, without breaking them, pressing out the pulp and mixing it with 3 times its weight of sugar, beating it all together. Juniper Berry Tea: Use 12–18 crushed berries per cup of water. Bring to boil and boil for 15 min. Good for liver and kidney ailments but not recommended for acute conditions.

LADY'S BEDSTRAW
Botanical name: *Galium verum*
Family: Rubiaceae

GENERAL

Lady's bedstraw is an unusual plant in that it has the property of acting like rennet in curdling milk. It was used long ago in Tuscany to give sheep and goat's cheese a sweeter taste. In Britain it was used in the making of the famous Cheshire cheese, and said to be the reason for the superior quality of the cheese. In the sixteenth century the herb was called 'cheese renning'and the name *Galium* comes from the Greek word *gala* meaning milk. The English name comes from its use as bedding in former times. One of the Madder family of plants, lady's bedstraw roots were once used to procure a red dye.

DESCRIPTION AND HABITAT

Lady's bedstraw is a perennial of medium height with a slightly creeping woody rootstock. The leaves are very narrow and grow in whorls of six to eight. The small bright yellow flowers are sweetly scented and grow in panicles at the ends of the stalks. They flower almost continuously throughout the summer and grow in clumps on banks and pastures all over Europe and

America. It grows abundantly in Britain.

CULTIVATION
It is a wild plant everywhere.

USES
The stems and the leaves of lady's bedstraw are the parts used to curdle milk for cheese. The crushed yellow flowers can be used to give colour to the cheese and also butter. The flowering tops, distilled in water, were used to make a refreshing summer drink.

A decoction made from the plant provides a soothing foot bath. Medicinally it is good for gravel stones and can be used as a laxative, an infusion being made of the leaves.

RECIPE SUGGESTION
Pour 20 fl oz (575ml) boiling water over a handful of leaves. Allow to stand 10 min; strain.

LADY'S MANTLE—*Lion's foot, Bear's foot, Nine Hooks*
Botanical name: *Alchemilla vulgaris*
Family: Rosaceae

GENERAL
Lady's mantle was originally used as a wound herb to promote healing and stop bleeding. Now, however, the plant is most widely known as 'woman's best friend'. Its name is shortened from 'The mantle of our Lady', as its lobed leaves resemble the scalloped edges of a mantle.

It was one of many herbs used by the Arabs as a healing plant. Its anti-inflammatory effects have been well known for many centuries.

DESCRIPTION AND HABITAT
A rapidly spreading, slender, perennial with a stout black rootstock, lady's mantle is covered with soft hairs. It is a low to medium growing herb and bears tiny flowers of yellowish-green with no petals, from June to August. The large, kidney-shaped leaves grow on long stalks at the base of the stem and short stalks higher up. It may be found on grassland and woodland in Asia, Greenland, Labrador and Europe. In Britain it is more common in the north than the south and east, and it can also be found at high altitudes and in cold northern climates.

CULTIVATION
Lady's mantle may be easily grown from seed and will spread rapidly. The leaves should be cut when the flowers are in bloom.

FLAVOUR AND HOW TO STORE
Lady's mantle, with its slightly bitter taste, is used for a medicinal tea. Choose large leaves which are dried and store in the usual way.

USES
Tea made from the leaves may be taken to heal disorders of the female organs and to help restore a normal menstrual cycle. It is recommended during pregnancy, especially just before the birth. It is also a heart tonic which tones the blood and fortifies arteries. Applied as a lotion or as freshly pressed juice, it will help to heal skin troubles, especially acne and freckles. Added to the bath water, it will promote the healing of wounds.

RECIPE SUGGESTION
Lady's Mantle Tea: Use 1–2 tsp of the dried herb to each cup of boiling water and steep for 10 min. Drink 1 or 2 cups a day.

LADY'S SMOCK—*Meadow Bittercress, Cuckooflower*
Botanical name: *Cardamine pratensis*
Family: Cruciferae

GENERAL
Lady's smock is a common wild flower found in most temperate zones. It was once cultivated in French gardens and used as water cress which it resembles, though it has a distinctly bitter taste. It can be eaten raw or cooked and has the same medicinal reputation as watercress against scurvy. Up to the eighteenth century infusions of the flowering tops were used as a remedy for nervous disorders, epilepsy, indigestion and to stimulate a poor appetite.

DESCRIPTION AND HABITAT
Lady's smock is a small perennial with a short rootstock. The feathery leaves at the base of the plant have broader leaflets than those further up the stem. The flowers, which are large and a pale lilac colour, grow in corymbs and these become elongated as the lower flowers grow into fruits; the fruit pods are about 1 in (2½cm) long and contain a single row of seeds. The plant grows in damp places along small streams and in most meadows and is abundant in Britain and other temperate climates, flowering throughout May.

CULTIVATION
Grows as a wild plant.

Lady's Smock

FLAVOUR AND HOW TO STORE
Lady's smock has a bitter pungent flavour somewhat similar to watercress.

USES
Remember its other name, bittercress, but it can be eaten raw in a salad or boiled as a green vegetable, and also made into soup.

RECIPE SUGGESTION
Make an infusion of the flowering tops to stimulate the appetite.

LAVENDER

Botanical names: *Lavandula vera* (Old English Lavender)
L. spica
L. dentata (French Lavender)
Family: Labiatae

GENERAL

Since the sixteenth century lavender has become a popular scented garden shrub and many varieties of different heights and colour have developed. The original Old English lavender (*L. vera*) has the finest aroma. *L. spica* is grown just as frequently nowadays and is very similar in appearance and fragrance. Dutch lavender is also similar but smaller, as is French lavender (*L. dentata*) which has less fragrance and flowers of more delicate colour.

The ancient Greeks and Romans knew several varieties. The Libyans and Romans used it to add to their bath water and its English name probably came from the Latin *lavare*, to wash. Throughout its history lavender has been used for its scent as a strewing herb, and for placing among linen and clothes. It was known in Elizabethan Britain, the first record of its cultivation here being in 1568. It rapidly became a favourite and the Pilgrim Fathers took it with them to America.

DESCRIPTION AND HABITAT

L. spica and *L. vera* grow into fairly tall bushy shrubs. The leaves are narrow and greyish-green in colour. Bluish-purple flowers grow close together in spikes. French lavender has pale mauve flowers and there is also a rare white flowered variety (*L. alba*). All parts of the plant retain the scent when dried, but it is strongest in the flowers, which contain the aromatic oil. All varieties of lavender are favourite haunts of bees. Lavender originated in mountainous regions of Mediterranean countries but has been widely cultivated with success in Britain, France, Italy, Norway and has more recently been introduced to Australia.

CULTIVATION
Lavender prefers an open, sunny position in the garden. It may be grown from seed but is generally propagated by cuttings taken in autumn, kept in sandy compost under cover during winter and planted out the following spring. After flowering, the plant should be pruned to encourage bushy growth.

FLAVOUR AND HOW TO STORE
Lavender has a sweet aromatic taste which will give scent and flavour to whatever it is added. Flowering sprigs are easily dried after cutting and tied into bundles or muslin bags. When dry, the flowers can be stripped from the stems for enclosing in sachets or pot-pourris.

USES
Lavender has a tranquillising effect; even inhaling its scent will calm troubled nerves and depressed spirits. The leaves and flowers are used to make a tea taken for heart palpitations, headaches, fainting, convulsions, migraine, giddiness and insomnia. For headache and faintness, a cold lavender compress may be applied to the temples. Lavender oil may be used in the treatment of wounds, ulcers and sores. Dried flowers or sprigs will keep moths away from stored linen and clothes, and are a principal ingredient in pot-pourri. Added to other herbs in a facial steam bath, lavender will improve the complexion.

RECIPE SUGGESTION
Herb pot-pourris and herb cushions can be made from a choice of more than twenty sweet scented herbs and half a dozen spices. One of the most important ingredients is lavender flowers.

LEMON BALM—*Balm, Melissa*
Botanical name: *Melissa officinalis*
Family: Labiatae

GENERAL
Lemon balm is an easily grown herb popular for its fragrance. Its Greek botanical name, Melissa, means honeybee and a relaxing tisane made from its leaves is generally called Melissa Tea.

It originated in the Middle East but soon found its way to the Mediterranean countries. It was introduced to Britain by the Romans and was an important herb in the monastic apothecary garden, but has also always been grown for its lemon-scented flavour and aroma.

DESCRIPTION AND HABITAT
It is a perennial plant of medium height. It has light green, heart-shaped leaves, wrinkled and

Lemon Balm

deeply veined. It has whitish, yellowish flowers which will bloom all through the summer. Like many savoury herbs used for cooking, it should never be allowed to flower. It is a native of southern Europe and Asia and is easily cultivated.

CULTIVATION
Lemon balm starts to grow early in the spring. It can be grown from seeds or cuttings. Young plants need plenty of space to allow for the development of the lower leaves and the bed must be kept free from weeds. It spreads freely. In winter some people cover the roots with strawy manure, or a thick layer of peat to protect them from frost.

FLAVOUR AND HOW TO STORE
It has a lemon-scented flavour, honey-sweet. The leaves can be harvested twice or three times a season but the leaves are large and at their best at the first cutting. If wanted for drying, use only the first cut. You can cut all the leaves in one go in spring and you will have another harvest six weeks later, but with smaller leaves.

USES
In cooking, use lemon balm in fish and poultry dishes and add it to herb sauces and marinades. It also adds a lemony flavour to jams, jellies, fruit juices, custards, fruit salads and other desserts. The fresh leaves can be eaten with salads and every kind of vegetable. Lemon balm is a herb which can be used generously.

Melissa tea or tisane helps promote relaxation and good sleep. It is also a natural remedy for feverish complaints and against vomiting. Its effects are very mild and therefore it is safe to use over a long period for delicate patients. It is also used in perfumes and toilet waters; in liqueurs and in furniture polish oils.

RECIPE SUGGESTIONS
Add finely chopped lemon balm leaves to an orange mousse.
Stuffed apples: Wash and core apples, fill each centre with a mixture of 2 tsp ground almonds or baked white breadcrumbs, 1 tsp chopped lemon balm, 1 tsp brown sugar and a nut of butter. Bake in a moderate oven 350°F (mark 5).

LESSER CELANDINE—Pilewort
Botanical name: *Ranunculus ficaria*
Family: Ranunculaceae

GENERAL
The lesser celandine is a familiar wild plant which has some culinary and medicinal properties.

Lesser Celandine

Its golden yellow flowers are among the earliest to appear in spring and it blooms right through until May. Wordsworth's favourite flower, the lesser celandine is perpetuated in his verses and its flower carved on his tombstone. It is not related to the greater celandine and bears no resemblance to it—the confusion probably having arisen at the time of Gerard, because both plants bloomed in his garden at the same time.

DESCRIPTION AND HABITAT
A perennial plant of low growth, lesser celandine spreads rapidly. Numerous small tubers grow in clusters round the fig-shaped roots and each of these produces a new plant. The leaves are heart-shaped and a glossy green. The bright, star like, yellow flowers have a varying number of petals and only open in sunny weather. Lesser celandine grows in abundance along roadsides, banks and in damp places throughout Europe and Western Asia.

CULTIVATION
A wild plant.

FLAVOUR AND HOW TO STORE
Lesser celandine has no scent, the leaves are slightly acrid to taste and the roots are bitterly pungent. March is the best time to gather the whole herb for drying and storing in the usual way. The plant must be treated with care, for the sap contains an irritant which can produce sores and ulcers on sensitive skin.

USES
Lesser celandine is milder than others of the Ranunculaceae family and the fresh young leaves are sometimes finely chopped and used sparingly in raw salads.
Medicinally lesser celandine is an astringent for varicose veins and piles—hence its common name pilewort. For this complaint the affected part is bathed with a decoction made from the herb. An infusion is made from a teaspoon of lesser celandine to a teacupful of boiling water and left to steep five to ten minutes then strained. This can be taken internally once a day in small doses. Pilewort ointment is also helpful and should be applied twice a day.

RECIPE SUGGESTION
Pilewort ointment: Melt 4 oz (120g) Vaseline, add 1 oz (30g) dried lesser celandine and stir well. Cover and simmer gently for 45–60 min. Strain, then cool before using.

LIME—Linden

Botanical names: *Tilia europaea* or *vulgaris* (Common Lime)
T. cordata (Small-leaved Lime)
T. platyphyllos (Large-leaved Lime)
Family: Tiliaceae

GENERAL
There are over thirty varieties of lime, all beautiful, decorative trees. For medicinal purposes however, it is best to select one of the three mentioned types; the common lime is a hybrid of the other two. Their flowers make a delicious tisane. They contain, among other substances, tannins, sugar and an aromatic volatile oil. In France this tisane, *tilleuil*, is well known as an after-dinner drink to aid digestion and give a good night's rest. In the USA the equivalent tree is basswood, *T. americana*.

DESCRIPTION AND HABITAT
Lime trees grow very tall and have smooth bark, widely spreading branches and roundish-shaped leaves. The three varieties mentioned have strongly fragrant, yellowish flowers which grow in clusters of four or more with a long bract joined to the stalk. On common and large-leaved lime trees the clusters hang downwards. Large-leaved lime flowers in June, one month earlier than the other two. Bees are greatly attracted to all limeflowers. The fruits are nut-like, the size of a pea, containing one to three seeds. Lime trees may be found wild, especially in ash woods, and are widely cultivated in parks, gardens and suburban streets.

CULTIVATION
Limes prefer a moist loam soil. They are generally propagated by layering, but it will be some time before they bear flowers. Limes are frequently cultivated to form avenues or hedges. One of the most famous and beautiful hedges is the lime tree hedge, of enormous height at Shönbrunn, once the summer residence of Austrian Emperors, some miles outside Vienna. If lime flowers are wanted the trees should not be pruned or topped.

FLAVOUR AND HOW TO STORE
Limeflower tea has a mild aromatic taste. The flower clusters should be gathered fresh during June and July, complete with bracts, and spread out to dry in the dark. They require careful handling and should not be heaped up or pressed down.

USES
To make the tea, the flowers and bracts should be left whole and boiling water poured on to them. The tea may be drunk hot or cold, sweetened with brown sugar or honey, for kidney disorders, bronchial infection or catarrh in the lungs or air passages. It will induce perspiration

and is taken for colds and flu, and should be added to steam inhalations. It is also recommended for cramps of the abdomen or limbs, anaemia and applied as a lotion to cure mouth ulcers and burns. Added to bath water, limeflower infusion will soothe rheumatic pains and aid relaxation. Lime charcoal from the wood of the tree, powdered and mixed with milk or water, will assimilate poisonous substances in the digestive system. It can be taken, followed by a laxative, in cases of accidental or food poisoning, intestinal infection, migraine. The charcoal will also absorb toxins from festering wounds and cancerous growths if sprinkled over and washed off ten minutes later.

RECIPE SUGGESTION
The well known limeflower tea as used in France and Germany is made in a teapot (a glass one if possible to show the beautiful flowers) allowing a tsp of flowers with bracts, per cup with 1 extra for the pot. Pour boiling water on to them and allow to steep for 3–5 min. Strain and drink hot or iced, sweetened with honey if liked.

LIQUORICE
Botanical name: *Glycyrrhiza glabra*
Family: Leguminosae

GENERAL
Liquorice has been used medicinally for centuries and was known to the ancient Egyptians, Greeks and Romans for its beneficial effect on coughs, colds and chills. Its name *Glycyrrhiza* is derived from the Greek meaning 'sweet root' and in the third century BC, Theophrastus the famous Greek botanist and physician wrote that 'liquorice has the property of quenching thirst if held in the mouth'. The root contains a special kind of sugar which is safe for diabetics.

The liquorice plant originally came from the East and has grown since early times in China, Persia, Turkey and the Mediterranean countries. Other wild varieties *G. lepidota*, *G. asperrima* and *G. echinata* are found in North America, Russia, Central Asia, southern Europe and the Orient. Liquorice first came to England in the Middle Ages and soon became popular as a medicine. In the early sixteenth century liquorice plants began to be cultivated in the monastery gardens at Pontefract, which later became the centre of the liquorice confectionery industry.

DESCRIPTION AND HABITAT
Liquorice is a medium to tall perennial plant with leaves divided into several pairs of leaflets. The flowers are racemes of bluish-purple colour. The part used is the stout rootstock which divides immediately below the crown, forming branches growing through the soil to a depth of about 4 ft (120cm) or more. It is a greyish-brown outside with transverse scars, and inside yellow and fibrous.

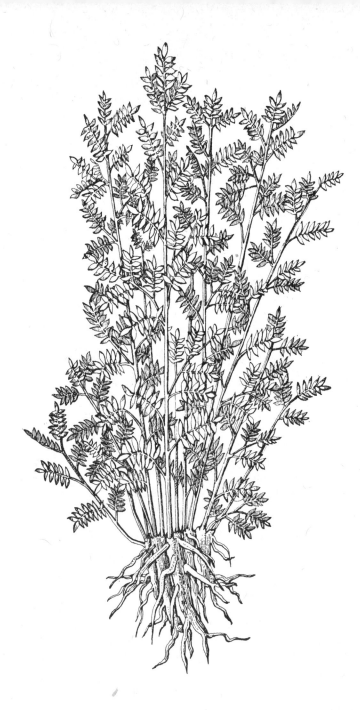

Liquorice

CULTIVATION
Liquorice has grown successfully in Pontefract, Yorkshire, in England on soil consisting of a layer of limestone on a layer of sandstone. Liquorice is planted in a well-manured soil, free of stones, in March or early April and harvested in the autumn, when the leaves have dropped. After the roots have been severed the woody crowns and the suckers are stored in clamps during the winter for planting out in spring. The old crowns produce roots immediately and suckers by the second year, and they are planted in groups of three at intervals of 12 in (30cm) covered with about 3 in (7cm) of soil. After harvesting, the roots are dried before being processed for use.

FLAVOUR AND HOW TO STORE
Liquorice has a sweetish taste with a characteristic scent. The English-grown roots have a better flavour than those from the Continent.

USES
Pontefract cakes, good for coughs and colds, are sold in chemists as well as sweet shops. Liquorice also helps to sweeten bitter medicines.

Mainly used for cough mixtures, liquorice besides being an expectorant, is a demulcent, soothing and protecting the alimentary canal; it is also a gentle laxative. Recent research has discovered that liquorice juice has a pain-killing effect on stomach ulcers. Liquorice tea should be drunk cold.

RECIPE SUGGESTIONS
To make liquorice juice: dissolve 1 oz (30g) liquorice stick in a glass of warm water. Take a few sips throughout the day after meals for 4–6 weeks.
For the tea: add 1 tsp dried root per cup of boiling water. Allow to cool, strain and drink cold.

LOVAGE
Botanical name: *Ligusticum scoticum*
Family: Umbelliferae

GENERAL
Lovage is one of the most useful herbs. It gives a slight spicy taste to every dish and soup. The name lovage, as well as its German equivalent, *Liebstöckel*, refers to love. Because of its great therapeutic qualities, it has been known as the 'All Healing Plant'. Its sharp but pleasant scent can overcome unpleasant odours.

The origin of lovage goes back thousands of years to the Greeks and Romans and it may have come from the Phoenicians. It was one of the most common herbs in ancient times, used for culinary, medicinal and cosmetic purposes. It was cultivated in Britain in the fourteenth century, but it is little known today. It is still widely used in Europe, especially in Italy and Czechoslovakia.

DESCRIPTION AND HABITAT

It is a very tall perennial plant, one plant being sufficient for one family. It has dark green shiny leaves which grow from the straight, hollow stems. The stems are terminated in flower-heads of clusters of yellow flowers which come out in July and August. It has strong fleshy roots which can also be eaten. The roots like to grow deep into the soil, preferably relatively damp. The climate is not important. It is often found in cottage gardens in the north of England and all over the Continent, since in former times, the cottagers would have grown it as a remedy for their sick cattle.

CULTIVATION

Propagation can be done by division in the spring, or sowing seeds in the autumn. The seeds lose their germinating power very quickly and should be sown as soon as possible after ripening. They like low temperatures and darkness for germination. After sprouting, they can be transplanted into a prepared bed, which should be forked over and organically fertilised a little. The plants should be spaced approximately 1½ ft (45cm) either way and take about four years to reach full size, when they will need more space. It is a useful plant for protecting the other herbs from wind and cold weather.

FLAVOUR AND HOW TO STORE

The flavour of lovage is strong and similar to yeast. Under cellophane, fresh lovage can be kept for approximately one week in the refrigerator, but for use during the winter it has to be dried. The drying is not easy since the leaves are thick and contain a fair amount of liquid. Put the leaves on a tray of nylon netting in the heated airing cupboard. Drying will take at least four to five days.

USES

Lovage is a versatile flavouring herb—on its own it makes an especially good soup. The leaves and young stalks can be used in salads, in cooking vegetables, meat and fish, and added to most savoury foods.

Medicinally lovage has a cleansing effect on the system, is antiseptic and can be applied externally to wounds. It was once widely used as a deodorant and makes a refreshing addition to bath water. Lovage is a strong herb and should be used with care at all times.

An infusion of chopped lovage leaves, fresh or dried, makes a tea which stimulates the digestive organs.

RECIPE SUGGESTIONS

Add 1 tsp fresh or dried chopped lovage to a pint of soup such as pea soup and potato soup. Add in the same proportions to meat casseroles, sauces, ham spreads.

Lovage soup: Sauté 2 onions, sliced, in ½ oz (15g) butter until soft. Add and sauté 2 tbs fresh or dried chopped lovage, then ½ oz (15g) flour and cook few min. Gradually blend in 20 fl oz (575ml) stock, a little salt, and simmer for 20 min. Add 10 fl oz (275ml) milk and put through sieve or blender. Reheat and serve sprinkled with chopped parsley.

MACE and NUTMEG

Botanical name: *Myristica fragrans*
Family: Myristicaceae

GENERAL

Mace and nutmeg are the fruit of the nutmeg tree which is a native of the Moluccas and other islands in the East Indies. The earliest records of the use of nutmeg and mace have been in the first century AD when Pliny described a tree with a fragrant nut and two kinds of perfume. The Arabs imported large quantities of both spices in the sixth century, and by the end of the twelfth century they were well known all over Europe. In England in the fourteenth century mace was greatly valued and one of the most expensive of the imported oriental spices.

DESCRIPTION AND HABITAT

The fruit of the nutmeg tree, large and fleshy like an apricot, splits open when ripe to reveal the kernel wrapped in its bright red, net-like mace. The kernels each contain one glossy brown oily seed which is the nutmeg, oval-shaped and about 1½ in (4cm) long and ¾ in (2cm) wide. They are extracted from the dried kernel, the mace carefully separated and both are dried for commercial use. During drying, the mace exudes its characteristic pungent aroma and becomes brittle and horny, turning from red to yellowish-brown. Ground nutmeg is a tan colour. Today nutmeg trees are grown in Indonesia, Granada in the West Indies and in Sri Lanka.

CULTIVATION

The evergreen nutmeg tree grows in a moist hot tropical climate close to the sea, where there is high average rainfall, and where it is said the powerful aroma intoxicates the birds of the air. Propagation is by planting fresh seed and it takes about five or six weeks to germinate. The young plants are moved to their flowering position, preferably a shady one, after six months. The tree grows slowly and cannot be harvested for seven years; they give the highest yields after about twenty years. After harvesting the nutmeg and mace are carefully parted and dried.

FLAVOUR AND HOW TO STORE

Mace has a sweet strongly aromatic and pungent flavour and scent. It can be bought ground or whole, when it is called 'blades of mace'. Maces can be bought bearing the names of the districts in which they were grown, eg Granada mace: Amboina mace etc.

Nutmeg has a sweet warm highly spicy taste and is not so pungent as mace. The aroma of freshly grated nutmeg is strong and fragrant and it is sold whole or ground. Both spices should be stored in glass screw-top jars.

USES

Mace is used sparingly in the making of cakes, biscuits and preserves. It is in many spice mixtures and blends, and an ingredient in a number of seasonings and bottled sauces. Mace can be added to baked fish and béchamel sauce. Both nutmeg and mace are used in cream sauces for fish and meat, in meat loaf, beef stews and pies, and can be sprinkled lightly over soups just before serving. Use as a seasoning on vegetables such as carrots, cauliflower, spinach and potatoes after cooking. They can be added to apple or chocolate puddings and custards. Nutmeg is used to flavour egg or chocolate drinks and mulled wines.

Medicinally nutmeg is carminative and is helpful against flatulence and vomiting, and it helps the digestion generally. In severe cases of diarrhoea grate half a nutmeg and take in a dessertspoon of rum. In small doses nutmeg is a tonic, but can be harmful if too much is taken at once because of its content of myristicin—an alkaloid with narcotic effects which can also produce unpleasant symptoms.

RECIPE SUGGESTIONS

Spiced Roast Beef: Before roasting a joint of beef, rub well with ground mace all over the joint. Add a pinch as well in making the gravy.

Fish Rice with Egg: Mix together 12½ oz (360g) cooked, flaked fish, 11 oz (300g) cooked rice, salt, ½ tsp each ground nutmeg and curry powder. Sauté rice until golden in 1 oz (30g) margarine or butter. Add 3 beaten eggs and scramble all together until eggs set.

MARIGOLD
Botanical name: *Calendula officinalis*
Family: Compositae

GENERAL

Marigold is a vivid garden flower which has culinary, cosmetic and medicinal uses. The flowers contain bitter principles, the colouring substance calendulin, and small quantities of volatile oil. The flowers open only during the day, and according to German folklore, it is an indication of rain if the flowers remain closed after seven o'clock in the morning.

Believed to have come originally from India, marigold's medicinal qualities have been well known in Europe since the twelfth century. The Romans used it as a substitute for saffron, and the Arabs fed it to their fine horses as they believed it increased the strength of their blood vessels.

DESCRIPTION AND HABITAT
Annual, with pale green oval leaves, marigolds are of small height. The flowers have many petals of bright colour, ranging from light yellow to orange-red. Flowering commences in June and will continue to the end of the season if the dead flowerheads are picked off. Marigolds are native to southern Europe and Asia but are hardy enough to be grown in temperate and cool climates. They are found growing wild in cultivated fields, especially vineyards.

CULTIVATION
Marigolds will grow in any soil, preferring a sunny position. Seeds should be sown in March or April and if the flowers go to seed, the plant will freely self-sow.

FLAVOUR AND HOW TO STORE
Marigold petals impart a delicate aromatic bitterness and a strong colour to dishes. They may be used fresh or dried. They should be spread out in thin layers to dry, with adequate ventilation to ensure they do not lose the colour on which their flavour depends. The fresh leaves have a bitter, salty taste.

USES
Used as a substitute for saffron with rice, marigold petals will give the same colour but a different flavour. For colour and flavour they are added to salads, omelettes and cheese. For buns and cakes the petals are soaked in a cup of warm milk which is used for baking when cool. Fresh young marigold leaves are sometimes added to salads. Soaked in oil or ointment, marigold has a reputation for healing old wounds or scars and as a general tonic for the complexion. The petals are made into a tea, or added to other herbal teas such as limeflower or marjoram, and taken for the complexion or for stomach ulcers and digestive troubles.

RECIPE SUGGESTION
Marigold Rice is appreciated for the taste and colour the marigold petals give to it. Simply sauté 8 oz (225g) rice with a chopped onion in some oil, add 20 fl oz (575ml) vegetable stock, a little chopped rosemary and salt. Cook until tender, then add 2–3 tsp marigold petals, first dissolved in hot stock. Serve sprinkled with grated cheese and dots of butter.

MARJORAM

Botanical names: *Origanum majorana*—Sweet or Knotted Marjoram
O. onites—Pot Marjoram
O. vulgare—Wild Marjoram or Oregano
Family: Labiatae

GENERAL

There are three types of marjoram which have different histories and uses. Sweet or knotted marjoram, an annual, is generally preferred for flavouring purposes especially for meat dishes, frequently blended with thyme. Pot marjoram has less delicacy of flavour but is a perennial plant of vigorous growth. Wild marjoram, known as oregano, has the strongest flavour.

Marjoram has a long history as a preserving and disinfectant herb. Sweet marjoram was used extensively by the Greeks who gave it its name which means 'joy of the mountains'. The Romans introduced it to Britain at the time of their conquest. Pot marjoram is reputed to have originated in Sicily and was introduced to Britain in 1759. Wild marjoram was used in ancient Rome as a culinary and medicinal herb, and was considered a symbol of peace and happiness.

DESCRIPTION AND HABITAT

Sweet marjoram is an annual whose seeds rarely ripen out of doors in cool climates, but it will survive in climates where there is no winter frost. A low growing plant, it has a strong aromatic scent and a bushy appearance. It has small grey-green leaves on tough, woody stems and the knotted flowerheads bloom into pale mauve or white flowers from June to September. Pot marjoram is a perennial with a creeping growth sending roots into the ground at intervals, and flowering stems which grow to medium height up and away from the plant. The stems and leaves have a reddish tinge and it has whitish flowers in August. Wild marjoram, also a perennial, grows as a leafy bush with creeping roots, small dark green leaves and red-brown stems. Purple or pink flowers are a great attraction for bees from July to September. It has a scent reminiscent of thyme. Occasionally a variety with green stems and white flowers may be found. Wild marjoram grows in chalky soils on hedgebanks and fields. The aroma is stronger in warmer climates.

CULTIVATION

Sweet marjoram seeds can be sown under cover in March and the seedlings planted out in a sunny place in May. They need frequent watering and protection during sudden cold snaps. Pot and wild marjoram may be propagated by cuttings taken early in summer, by division of roots in April or autumn, or by seed sown in spring. Pot marjoram will require autumn trimming to prevent it growing out of control. The seeds ripen in September/October. Pot marjoram makes an excellent house-plant.

FLAVOUR AND HOW TO STORE

The flavour of knotted marjoram is sweet and spicy. The flavour of pot marjoram is slightly bitter and not nearly so sweet and delicate. Wild marjoram has the spiciest flavour of all when grown in warm climates, though is less peppery in cool countries. The leaves and flowers should be collected for drying during the flowering period and cut just as the flowers are about to break open. They should be carefully dried in the dark to keep their colour and aroma.

USES

Sweet marjoram has the most delicate flavour and is recommended for rubbing into roasting joints of meat, game or poultry. Pot marjoram's flavour will endure longer cooking especially if mixed with other strong flavours like onions or chilis. Marjoram is used in stuffings, forcemeats and sausages and other preserved meats. The French use it fresh or dried with delicate vegetables such as cucumber, salsify and carrots. Sweet marjoram blends well with thyme, and wild marjoram blends with basil, and is used to flavour tomatoes and tomato dishes such as pizza and spaghetti. Marjoram has antiseptic qualities and is made into a tisane taken for the common cold and sore throat. Dried and powdered, it is used as a snuff to clear nasal congestion. It has a reputation for increasing white blood corpuscles and improving circulation.

RECIPE SUGGESTION

Marjoram Liver Dumplings is an economical, traditional dish from German-speaking countries. Form dumplings from a mixture of 8 oz (225g) liver (dipped in boiling water, simmered 2 min, then minced), 2 tbs butter or 1 of suet, ½ tsp marjoram, 1 minced clove of garlic, salt and pepper and about 1 cup of flour gradually worked in. Cook them for 10 min in boiling consommé or bouillon.

MARSH MALLOW—*Mallards*

Botanical name: *Althea officinalis*
Family: Malvaceae

GENERAL

Marsh mallow is a healing and feeding plant and was once considered to have wide curative powers. Its botanical name comes from the Greek word 'to cure'. The whole plant, but mainly the root, contains a large amount of mucilage which is soothing, healing and demulcent and is used in various medicinal preparations.

The plant, formerly called Hock Herb, was first brought to this country from China. Pythagoras and Plato wrote of it, the Romans considered it a delicacy at their tables and

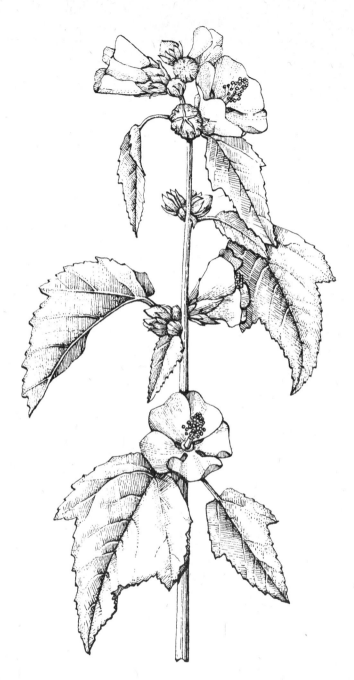

Marsh Mallow

Cicero and Horace both mentioned its laxative properties. An uncommon wild plant, marsh mallow should not be confused with common mallow which is larger, untidy in its growth and has mauve flowers with red veins.

DESCRIPTION AND HABITAT
A perennial plant of medium height, marsh mallow grows wild in marshy areas near the coast in England, Ireland and Europe. The large, oval greyish-green leaves have coarsely toothed edges and are thick and velvety, being covered in stellate hairs. The flowers are pink and grow in clusters in the leaf axils, appearing August/September. The roots are thick and fleshy.

CULTIVATION
The marsh mallow plant, usually found wild, can be grown by splitting off pieces from the crowns of old plants which mature quicker than plants grown from seed. They should be spaced apart. The roots which are greyish-white outside and white and fibrous inside, are scraped and then dried.

FLAVOUR AND HOW TO STORE
The roots which have a sickly, sweet flavour, should be stored in a dry place. The flowers and seeds, as well as the leaves, which must be picked later after flowering time, can also be dried for medicinal use.

USES
The young leaves and tops of marsh mallow are edible and can be chopped and added to salads or cooked as a green vegetable. It has many medicinal uses. The dried root is used to make a tea which can also be added to a mixed herb tea, taken for all chest complaints. The tea is also good for cystitis, incontinence and painful urination; helpful too for colitis, diarrhoea and vomiting, especially in children. An ointment made from marsh mallow root is useful for burns, and poultices made of it will reduce inflammations and help to heal boils and carbuncles. The poultice is prepared by mixing finely grated root with sufficient honey to make a paste, spreading the mixture on a cloth; heat by laying on a plate over a pan of hot water and apply to the affected part as hot as is bearable; renew every two to three hours.

RECIPE SUGGESTION
To prepare the tea: It is important to remember that marsh mallow is only effective when steeped in COLD water. Place 3 tsp of finely chopped root in a cup of cold water. Steep for 8 hr then strain and heat to lukewarm before using. The tea can be made with the leaves and seeds in the same way, when 1 to 2 tsp should be allowed per cup.

MEADOW SWEET—*Queen of the Meadows*
Botanical name: *Spiraea ulmaria*
Family: Rosaceae

GENERAL
Meadow sweet is a common wild plant in Europe and northern Asia. In former times it was one of the fragrant plants used as a strewing herb—its sweet smell filling the room. It was one of the ingredients in herb beer and the flowers boiled in wine were said to make a heady drink.

DESCRIPTION AND HABITAT
Meadow sweet is a medium-sized perennial with square reddish stems. The leaves have serrated edges, are dark green above and white and downy on the underside. The highly scented flowers are small and creamy-white, growing in large dense cymes. Meadow sweet can be found in moist meadows and on the edges of streams and rivers in Asia, America and Europe including Britain, flowering from June to August.

CULTIVATION
A wild plant, rarely cultivated.

FLAVOUR
Meadow sweet has a delicate taste slightly astringent and aromatic.

USES
Meadow sweet tea is diuretic and therefore helpful in ridding the body of excess fluid. It is also used for digestive troubles and for feverish colds. It is an especially good remedy for diarrhoea in children.

RECIPE SUGGESTION
To make the tea: Infuse 1 oz (30g) of leaves in 20 fl oz (575ml) of boiling water for 5 min. Strain and drink.

MELILOT
Botanical name: *Melilotus officinalis*—Common Yellow Melilot
Melilotus alba—White Melilot
Family: Papilionaceae

GENERAL
A fragrant wild herb with flavouring and medicinal properties melilot is one of the clover

Meadow Sweet

Melilot

family and was once widely grown for cattle fodder. On the Continent it was used as a flavouring and in Switzerland the flowers and seeds were mixed with the curd in the making of Gruyère cheese. Today it is used dried for flavouring stews and in stuffings for rabbit meat. Also for marinades. Melilot is sweetly scented due to the active substance coumarin, and highly attractive to bees.

DESCRIPTION AND HABITAT

Melilot is a tall branching annual, or sometimes biennial plant. Each long stalked leaf is divided into three narrow, egg-shaped, light green leaflets with serrated edges. The small yellow flowers grow in one-sided clusters and all the petals are the same length. The hairy seedpod is net-veined and contains two seeds, black when ripe. The plant grows in waste places, by the roadside and hedgerows, throughout Europe and adjoining Asia. All species of melilot are closely related to each other—*Melilotus alba* being the only variety with white flowers which grows mostly in England.

CULTIVATION

A wild plant.

FLAVOUR AND HOW TO STORE

The flavour and scent of melilot is rather like hay and this is more concentrated when the plant is dried. The leaves can be easily dried and should be stored in the usual way.

USES

The aromatic flowers of melilot are sometimes used as a perfume in sachets and pot-pourris mixtures and for flavouring home-made cheeses. The leaves can be applied externally as a fomentation or poultice for inflammation, cuts and abrasions. The herb is a mild expectorant and when made into a tea relieves catarrh. Also carminative melilot is helpful for flatulence and digestive troubles.

RECIPE SUGGESTION

Melilot Tea: 1 tsp of whole herb per cup of boiling water. Allow to steep for 5–10 min. Strain and drink warm.
Fomentation: Use 1 dsp of the finely chopped dried herb to 20 fl oz (575ml) water; simmer for 15–20 min, then wring out pieces of lint in the solution and lay on affected part.

THE MINTS

Botanical names: *Mentha viridis* or *spicata*—Spearmint
M. piperita—Peppermint
M. rotundifolia—Bowles or Apple Mint
M. citrata—Eau de Cologne Mint
M. aquatica—Water Mint
M. pulegium—Pennyroyal
M. arvensis, var *piperascens*—Japanese Mint
Family: Labiatae

GENERAL

Mint is a popular and well known herb all over the world and there are a great many varieties and hybrids. The three most common ones are spearmint, which is sometimes called common mint as it is the one most frequently found growing in gardens; apple mint which is the well known Bowles variety of the round-leafed mints and considered superior to spearmint; and peppermint which has the greatest content of menthol responsible for its cooling, characteristic flavour. It is generally known that mint is beloved by the English with their tradition of mint sauce with roast lamb, and few English gardens are without a patch of mint.

Mint is believed to have come originally from the East and introduced to Europe by way of North Africa. For centuries the Arabs have taken mint tea as a stimulant to their virility and as a social drink. Spearmint was an important herb for the ancient Egyptians, Greeks and Romans. It was frequently mentioned by Dioscorides, Hippocrates and Pliny as a highly valued medicinal and strewing herb and also for flavourings and perfumes. The Greeks scoured their dining tables with it before a meal and added it to their bath water. The Romans used it to flavour sauces, stimulate the appetite and they introduced mint into Britain. Records show that mint sauce was being made as early as the third century, and by the sixth century mint was being used in teeth-cleaning preparations. Peppermint was first named as a separate species during the seventeenth century and recommended as a herbal medicine for diarrhoea in 1696. Pennyroyal was the mint used by sailors on long voyages to purify their drinking water.

DESCRIPTION AND HABITAT

All mints are perennial, have white, lilac or purple flowers and spread rapidly if not carefully restricted. Spearmint grows to a medium height and has a stiff upright stem with long, narrow pointed leaves. Pinky lilac flowers grow in-terminal clusters and are succeeded by tiny brown seeds. Bowles mint, called Apple mint by some nurseries, is taller with similar but stronger fragrance, and has large round leaves with a woolly texture. Eau de Cologne mint has branched stems with smooth, dull green leaves, edged with purple. The name comes from its special fragrance. Peppermint is thought to be a hybrid of spearmint and water mint. It grows to a good height with a slender, erect, deep red stem. The longish leaves are stalked and blushed with red, their undersides covered with fine hairs. Clusters of purple flowers are borne in the axils of the top leaves and rarely produce seed. Water mint is a medium-sized plant with erect, hairy stems of a reddish tinge and oval, hairy leaves. Purple flowers grow in terminal spikes. It is found in wet woods, marshland and the banks of lakes and streams. Pennyroyal is a small old-fashioned variety not so commonly found now. Japanese mint is an important variety in Japan, Taiwan, Brazil, Australia and the USA. It is a peppermint variety with a very high content of menthol.

CULTIVATION
In order to prevent mint from spreading too much, push pieces of slate vertically into the soil. Mints are easy to grow and propagation may be done any time by division of runners, but preferably in spring or autumn. The greatest hazard with mint growing is the possibility of rust developing on the foliage. This is more likely to happen in climates where the temperature is subject to sudden changes, but may be discouraged if the beds are regularly renewed. After an attack some gardeners burn straw over the bed to destroy the spores present in the top soil. If it occurs, the mint should be cut and used immediately and the crop replanted in a fresh bed. Peppermint and spearmint varieties should be kept well apart in the herb garden to prevent the mingling of flavours. Mint may be grown indoors in pots or in a window box. The plants should not be allowed to grow too tall.

FLAVOUR AND HOW TO STORE
All mints have a distinctive flavour and refreshing aroma. Peppermint has the stronger cooling effect. Bowles or apple mint combines the flavour of spearmint and apples. Eau de Cologne mint has its own characteristic scent. Mint is dried and stored in the usual way.

USES
Spearmint is mostly used for the mint sauce or jelly which accompanies roast lamb. Bowles mint makes an even better sauce with its stronger finer flavour. A sauce made with cider or wine vinegar and a mixture of the two kinds of mint has the best flavour of all. Mint adds a distinctive flavour to boiled vegetables like carrots, new potatoes and peas. Its refreshing effect improves fruit and green salads and fruit drinks. Leaves of mint may be rubbed on to any joint of roast meat or poultry. Mints add fragrance to pot-pourris, especially the Eau de Cologne mint which is also a useful garnish for fruit drinks. Peppermint oil is an important flavouring in liqueurs, candies, cordials and medicine. Peppermint tea, a well known French tisane, has a great reputation as a tonic for indigestion, an antispasmodic and for settling the stomach after vomiting. An infusion of spearmint used as a lotion is good for skin troubles and generally improves the complexion. Fresh leaves will bring relief rubbed on to rheumatic joints or an aching head. Pennyroyal infusion has a reputation as a help for bronchial troubles and where there is obstructed menstruation.

RECIPE SUGGESTION
Mint Julep—a refreshing whisky-based summer drink: In each glass start with a little crushed ice, add 1–4 tsp sugar syrup (equal parts sugar and water), 1 fl oz (25ml) whisky and 3–4 fresh mint leaves. Stir well, crushing mint, then top up with crushed ice and slowly fill with whisky. Decorate with sprigs of mint and serve when glass starts to frost.

MISTLETOE
Botanical name: *Viscum album*
Family: Loranthaceae

GENERAL
For many centuries mistletoe has been connected with legends and mysteries, regarded as a holy herb and a good luck plant. This was probably due partly to its power over mental disorders of which people had little understanding, and partly to its peculiar habit of growing out of its 'host' tree.

The ancient Druids greatly revered mistletoe as a holy herb and considered it an ill omen if some fell from its tree. They gathered it for their new year celebrations, which is probably the origin of our custom of decorating the house with mistletoe at Christmas time. It is not only appreciated for its attractive appearance but it has also been used medicinally, though not for cooking. It contains mucilage, sugar, resin, a fixed oil, tannin and various salts.

DESCRIPTION AND HABITAT
Mistletoe is an evergreen parasitic plant, preferring soft barked trees such as apple, and deriving its food from the 'host' tree. Bunches of its stiff stems hang down from high boughs. The leaves and stem are yellowish, the leaves thick and leathery. The flowers grow in threes and are followed by the white berries ripening in December. The berries are very popular with birds who eat the flesh and wipe off the sticky seeds on to branches of other trees, thereby spreading the mistletoe. It is found throughout Europe and southern England and northern Asia. The American mistletoe is a different plant (*Phoradendron flarescens*) with only the name in common.

CULTIVATION
Mistletoe greatly weakens the tree on which it grows, but is generally easy to establish on a 'host' tree if required. The sticky berry should be adhered to a branch or inserted in a crevice of the bark. The seeds send roots penetrating into the bark to establish the plant.

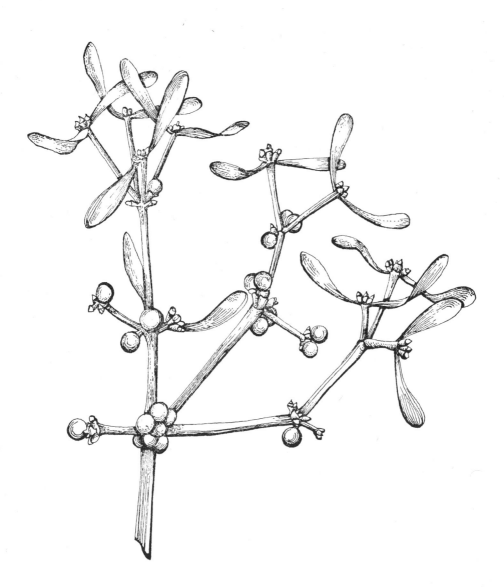

Mistletoe

USES

An infusion of mistletoe is made by steeping chopped leaves and young twigs in cold water. This is taken for treatment of nervous disorders, including epilepsy for which it has been known as a successful remedy for centuries. It also has a regulating effect on other functions: stimulating sluggish digestion, regulating blood pressure and menstruation. Alternative to the tea, 3 or 4 berries may be taken daily, crushed with a spoonful of honey, but children should generally be discouraged from eating the berries as too many may aggravate a nervous condition and cause convulsions.

MUGWORT—St John's Plant
Botanical name: *Artemisia vulgaris*
Family: Compositae

GENERAL

Mugwort, a common wild herb, was probably so-called because it was used for flavouring beer before hops were introduced. Today it is little known that this herb contains valuable bitter substances and volatile oil, and is an important culinary seasoning.

It has been used in Europe since ancient times when Greek and Roman doctors considered it to be an antidote for pain and used it in gynaecological treatment. St John the Baptist is said to have worn a garland of mugwort in the wilderness.

DESCRIPTION AND HABITAT

Mugwort is a perennial herb which grows to a medium height and has an aromatic scent. The leaves are dark green on top with a white down underneath and the stalks are sturdy with a tinge of purple. It bears small purple or yellow flowers of flat oval heads like buttons from July to September. Mugwort is found growing wild in hedges and waste places.

CULTIVATION

Mugwort is a vigorous spreading plant and cultivation is possible in any kind of soil. Propagation is best done by taking cuttings or by root division in the spring.

FLAVOUR AND HOW TO STORE

The flavour of mugwort is somewhat bitter. Fully developed flower buds should be picked from the high flowering shoots before they open, then dried and used whole or carefully picked apart. No attempt should be made to shred them by rubbing as they tend to roll into woolly masses. The leaves can also be dried and stored in the usual way.

Mugwort

USES

Mugwort has a neutralising effect on fat and should be used to season goose, duck and meats and fish rich in fat, such as eel, to prevent indigestion. It has been used as an ingredient in Vermouth and Absinthe and is a recommended seasoning for diabetics. It has an ancient reputation for keeping moths away, and added to the water in a footbath, it is said to ease tired and aching feet. A tea made of mugwort was used as a remedy for rheumatism, nervous disorders and fevers.

RECIPE SUGGESTIONS

Use a pinch of mugwort rubbed over meat when roasting and in all stuffings for poultry, meat and fish such as recommended. Add a light sprinkling of mugwort onto raw salads or mix into the salad dressing. Use sparingly.

MUSTARD

Botanical name: *Brassica nigra* and *B. alba*
Family: Cruciferae

GENERAL

The bright yellow flowers of the mustard plant are a familiar sight, for mustard is one of the most commonly used condiments of today and is grown commercially on a very wide scale.

There are many varieties of mustard but the two usually grown are *Brassica nigra*, producing reddish-brown or black seed and the *Brassica alba* with pale yellow or white seed.

Medicinally the white mustard seed has therapeutic and prophylactic qualities and, though it has been used since the days of Hippocrates, its value has perhaps not yet been fully realised. It has a stimulative action on all the functions of the body and produces a feeling of well-being. The black mustard seed, the more pungent of the two, is used in external medicinal applications.

Mention should be made of the Indian mustard (*Brassica ramosa*), which is extensively grown in India and the Far East. A very pungent variety, it is used as a vegetable, a medicine and the oil from the seeds as a linament.

Originally from southern Europe and the eastern Mediterranean region, mustard has been a cultivated plant for many centuries. From the beginning mustard was an important seasoning and medicinal spice and the young greens cooked like spinach were eaten as a vegetable.

The condiment mustard of the ancient Greeks was made up of the ground seeds mixed with 'must', unfermented grape juice—thus it became known as mustard.

In the Middle Ages mustard was grown in the monastery gardens throughout Europe for use in medicines and for the preservation of food—for mustard mixed with foods halts the deterimental action of the bacteria. It was also considered a good accompaniment to salt meats and fish, for it added flavour and helped in the digestion of these dull winter foods.

DESCRIPTION AND HABITAT
Both varieties of mustard are annual plants with clusters of small bright yellow flowers. Black mustard is the larger plant with smooth narrow pods each containing one row of tiny seeds; white mustard is a smaller plant and the pods are hairy, containing slightly larger seeds.

Mustard is grown throughout the temperate regions of the world, the finest white seed coming from England and Holland, and the finest black seed from Italy and California.

CULTIVATION
The mustards are grown from seed planted in the spring, the black being sown a week or two earlier than the white. The white mustard grows best on a heavy sandy soil where there is a light rainfall, whilst the black prefers a light soil and plenty of moisture; both require a sunny position. As the pods burst open when ripe, scattering the seeds everywhere, they are harvested when fully developed but not quite ripe. The pods are then dried and the seeds threshed out.

FLAVOUR AND HOW TO STORE
White mustard seeds have a pleasant nutty flavour whilst the black seeds are far more pungent; neither variety has an aroma. The flavour is due to hot-tasting volatile oils which the seeds contain. Mustard powder is a mixture of the ground black and white seeds plus turmeric or saffron which add flavour and give it the brilliant yellow colour. Prepared mustard is ready to use, and the mustard seeds are mixed with salt, other spices and vinegar. Vinegar is an acid and this acts as a fixative so the mustard retains its strength and flavour. Mixtures vary in pungency from the mild French mustard to the English which can be very hot and peppery. Mustard powder should be stored in airtight containers and the seed in closed jars.

USES
Use whole white mustard seed in pickling onions, red cabbage, mustard pickles and in preserving meats and fish; as a garnish on vegetable salads and to add flavour to boiled cabbage. The young leaves can be used raw in salads and as garnish; the leaves of the white mustard are used together with cress as a sandwich filling. Dry mustard powder can be added to innumerable dishes and when used sparingly gives an excellent flavour.

Medicinally mustard is chiefly used externally nowadays as a poultice to relieve congestion in bronchitis and pneumonia. A mustard bath helps relieve rheumatic and muscular pains and a footbath eases tired and aching feet. Mustard oil is a valuable embrocation.

RECIPE SUGGESTION
Mustard Sauce: to 5 fl oz (150ml) béchamel sauce, add 1 tsp mixed French and English prepared mustard. Good with grilled herrings.

MYRTLE
Botanical name: *Myrtus communis*
Family: Myrtaceae

GENERAL
Sweet-smelling myrtle, a spice with culinary, medicinal and cosmetic properties, was in regular use in ancient times. In the Orient, dried and powdered myrtle leaves were used as an astringent dusting powder for babies when they were wrapped in swaddling clothes. The Greeks and Romans considered it to be sacred to Venus and myrtle was worn by the winners of Olympic games. The berries were used for dyeing hair in those days and were also eaten to sweeten the breath. The oil extracted from the plant was used in perfumery as well as medicinally. At the feast of the Tabernacle the Jews today decorate their booths with myrtle and in Greece it is a symbol of love and immortality.

DESCRIPTION AND HABITAT
Myrtle is a tall aromatic evergreen shrub. The leaves are ovate and glossy, with pinnate veins and are highly scented when crushed. The creamy white flowers grow singly or in small clusters in the axils of the leaves. It blooms from May to August and the fruit is a blue-black berry when ripe, containing the kidney-shaped seeds. Myrtle is native to southern Europe and the Orient but can also be cultivated with some care in temperate climates.

CULTIVATION
Myrtle requires a sheltered position against a wall where there is good drainage and protection from cold drying winds. It needs to be well watered and the soil round it should be kept compacted. Propagation is by layering in July and when roots have formed they are cut and planted out.

FLAVOUR AND HOW TO STORE
Myrtle has a sweet fragrant smell due to the volatile oil it contains. The leaves and flowers can be dried and then stored in glass screw-top jars.

USES
In former times the inhabitants of Athens used to eat fresh myrtle berries, and the dried berries and flowerbuds were used as a spice, a custom which may still be in use in Tuscany.

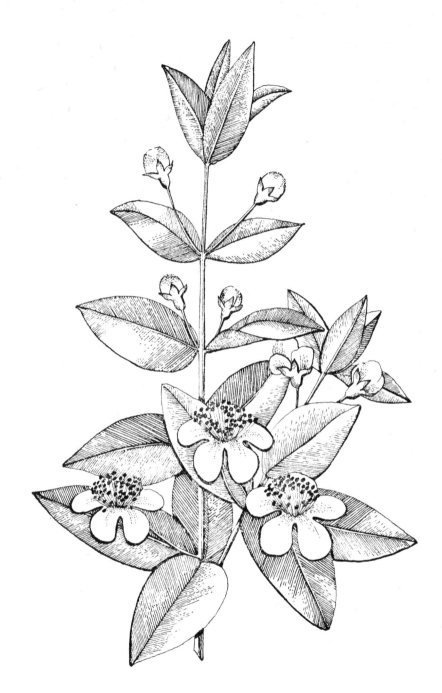

Myrtle

The oil extracted from the bark, leaves and flowers is used in perfumery and the leaves and flowers are used in pot-pourris and sachets. A drink made from the fermented berries of myrtle is called 'Eau d'Agnes'. Medicinally myrtle is carminative and expectorant, helpful in all cases of chest complaint and for this purpose the leaves are made into a tea.

RECIPE SUGGESTIONS
Add dried myrtle flowers to pot-pourris and herb sachets.
Myrtle infusion: On to ½ oz (15g) myrtle leaves pour 20 fl oz (575ml) boiling water and infuse 5–10 min; strain and add a little honey if liked.

NASTURTIUM—Indian Cress
Botanical name: *Tropaeolum majus* or *minus*
Family: Cruciferae

GENERAL
Nasturtium is a decorative plant with some culinary and medicinal uses. The pungent essence secreted by nasturtiums is offensive to root lice and other plant pests. The essence secreted into the soil from the roots is absorbed by nearby plants, improving their resistance to pests.

Nasturtiums originally came from Peru and the custom of using the petals in salads and teas came from the Orient. First introduced to Europe about 1574 when seeds were brought to Spain from the Indies. Gerard mentions receiving seeds from France in 1597.

DESCRIPTION AND HABITAT
The nasturtium is a favourite creeping, climbing, annual garden plant. It has bright green umbrella-like leaves and flowers of brilliant red, orange or yellow. It is a strong growing plant although the more recently developed dwarf variety (*T. minus*) does not climb. Nasturtiums have a high vitamin C content, strongest in the leaves just before flowering in July. They may be found growing wild as 'escapes'.

CULTIVATION
Nasturtiums are easy to grow and once established, seed themselves prolifically. Seeds are sown in spring.

FLAVOUR AND HOW TO STORE
The leaves, petals and seeds have a hot, pungent, peppery taste. The flowers should be used fresh, but the leaves may be dried after chopping, or dried whole and then crumbled.

USES

Nasturtium provides a valuable seasoning for people whose diet restricts their intake of pepper and salt. Leaves and flowers may be chopped and added to salads, sandwiches or mixed with cream cheese just before serving, and the seeds added to pickles or used as a substitute for capers. Medicinally, nasturtium, which is anti-scorbutic, provides an antiseptic and tonic treatment for the blood and digestive organs, for nervous depression, for constipation and to help clear the skin and eyes. As with many herbs, small amounts daily are better than too much. A hot poultice for abscesses or other skin eruptions is made from crushed seeds spread on a soft cloth.

RECIPE SUGGESTION

For mock capers, gather seeds when green, leave in a brine solution for 2 days, then pour over hot spiced vinegar, simmered for 2–3 min. Cover and allow to cool before bottling.

NETTLE—Stinging Nettle
Botanical name: *Urtica dioica*
Family: Urticaceae

GENERAL

It is a pity that the stinging nettle is condemned as a troublesome weed because of its stubborn tenacity to live in the most unwelcome places. Nevertheless it possesses many valuable nutritional and medicinal properties—vitamins, iron, protein, silicic acid, nitrogen, chlorophyll and other trace elements. The Dead or White nettle (*Lamium album*) is not related to the stinging nettle although its appearance is similar; it is entirely stingless and has no curative properties.

Stinging nettles have been present in temperate regions of the world for many centuries; Pliny (AD 23–79) wrote of their sting and medicinal qualities. Country people have used young nettles as a kind of spinach, and in days gone by, would take bundles of nettles to market to sell to the townspeople for their 'spring cleaning diet'. Fibre from nettles was also used to make cloth and considered very durable. This use was revived during World War I when there was a shortage of cotton.

DESCRIPTION AND HABITAT

Stinging nettles are perennial plants of medium height with tough creeping roots, dull green stems and leaves covered with stinging hairs. Tiny greenish flowers grow in catkin formations from June to September, male and female flowers generally on separate plants. Pollen is carried from one to the other by the wind. Nettles thrive on rubbish tips and compost heaps and

Nettle

may be found in waste places and on river banks in temperate regions of Europe, Asia, South Africa, Australia, America and Japan. Their presence indicates the soil is rich in nitrogen.

CULTIVATION
Nettles are strong growing weeds and will thrive anywhere; valuable in the garden as they stimulate the growth of other plants, make them more resistant to disease and improve the quality of root vegetables and tomatoes. The cut stems and leaves rot down into excellent humus. A bucketful of nettles covered with water and left to soak for 6–10 days can be used as a valuable concentrated nitrogen fertiliser, but it should be diluted in the proportion of 1 to 10.

FLAVOUR AND HOW TO STORE
Nettles give a salty, tangy flavour to vegetables and salads. The young leaves and shoots should be gathered while wearing gloves, and the sting is destroyed by drying or boiling them. After drying, they may be rubbed or stored whole in airtight containers.

USES
Nettles are valuable in salt-reduced diets since they supply minerals and natural salts which do not burden the system. They may be chopped and sprinkled over salads and vegetable dishes, or boiled and eaten as a green vegetable. They contain vitamins A and C which discourage colds, and nettle tea is a comforting gargle for sore throats. A cup of nettle tea taken night and morning will improve the function of the liver, gall bladder and intestines.

RECIPE SUGGESTION
A purée from nettles will provide an alternative to spinach purée and may be mixed with lettuce or sorrel, or a mixed vegetable soup.

NIPPLEWORT
Botanical name: *Lapsana communis*
Family: Compositae

GENERAL
Nipplewort is a common wild plant belonging to the dandelion family. It is now naturalised in America and eaten in Istanbul as a tasty salad herb. In England the somewhat bitter tasting leaves were cooked and eaten as a green vegetable. Its generic name *Lapsana* is Greek in origin and was used by Dioscorides.

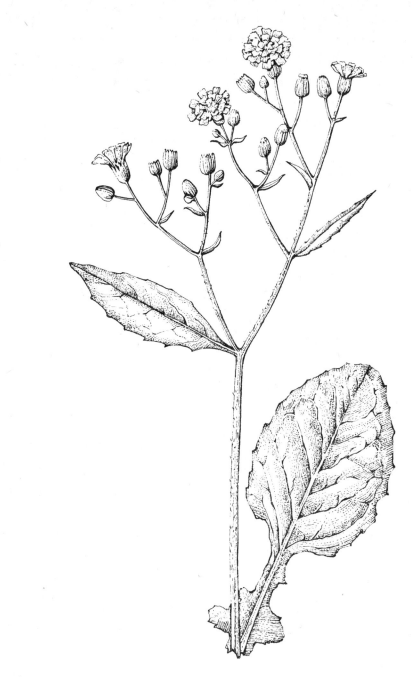

Nipplewort

DESCRIPTION AND HABITAT
Nipplewort is an annual and it first appears in spring as a ring of leaves lying near the ground. The thin egg-shaped leaves are hairy and coarsely toothed, with distinctive smaller lobes growing along the leaf stalk. The flower stems grow fairly tall and branch at the top into a loose irregularly spreading cluster of small bright yellow flower heads; these remain closed in bad weather. It flowers from July to September. Nipplewort can be found growing throughout Europe, Eastern and Western Asia and America.

CULTIVATION
A wild plant.

FLAVOUR AND HOW TO STORE
The leaves of nipplewort taste somewhat like radishes, hot and sharp. They can be gathered in the spring and used fresh.

USES
The fresh young leaves can be finely chopped and sprinkled over green salads. An infusion made from the dried leaves and used warm was used in former times as a soothing remedy for sore nipples.

RECIPE SUGGESTION
The chopped leaves should be dressed with oil and lemon juice with the addition of some other herb such as lemon balm, parsley or chervil.

ONION
Botanical name: *Allium cepa* (also Tree Onion or Egyptian Onion)
Allium fistulosum—Welsh Onion
Allium ascalonicum—Shallot
Family: Liliacea

GENERAL
The onion is unique for its many uses and properties. It is a perfect vegetable and flavouring as well as a kind of condiment, but perhaps less well known are its medicinal qualities. It contains a glycocide similar to mustard oil, a pungent volatile oil, a plant hormone like insulin as well as a large amount of vitamin C and other vitamins, mineral salts and trace elements. All varieties contain these active substances. Onions were one of the earliest plants to be cultivated and were grown in the ancient civilisations of India, China and Egypt. The Romans

brought them to the north over the Alps and their doctors and herbalists used them extensively. Over the centuries many different varieties have been developed which differ in size, colour and pungency of flavour and aroma.

Shallots are said to come from Ascalon, a town in Syria. They are milder and used for seasoning soups, stews and raw salads. Welsh onion got its name from the German word *walsch* meaning foreign. It is grown for its green leaves (onion green) which provide a milder onion flavouring for many dishes. These leaves continue to grow from spring to autumn however often they are cut. The tree onion or Egyptian onion, a strange, rather attractive looking plant, is a variety of the *allium cepa*.

DESCRIPTION AND HABITAT

The onion, *allium cepa*, is truly a biennial plant although it does complete its life cycle in one growing season in many countries where the days are long and warm. From a single small bulb or 'set', grows one or more erect leafless stalks—the height differing with the variety—each topped with a cluster of small greenish flowers.

Shallots have compound bulbs consisting of a cluster of small bulblets or cloves.

Welsh onions are hardy perennials with long, tapering roots and strong fibres. The long, green leaves are round, wide and hollow.

The tree onion, also a perennial, produces a cluster of bulbs with leaves at the top of a tall hollow stem.

Onions are cultivated all over the world and a few varieties may be found growing wild.

CULTIVATION

Onions are propagated by seed, by transplants or by specially grown small bulbs known as 'sets'. The bulb is developed as the leaf bases swell. They grow best in a sunny position in fairly rich well-drained soil. For early crops onions can be sown in late August in a sheltered place for transplanting out in March to April; or sow in March and thin out later. Bend the foliage tops over in mid-July/August to hasten the ripening, which is usually achieved after two or three weeks. Shallots are propagated by bulbs planted in February pressing them into the earth so they are nearly covered. When the leaves turn yellow the clumps are ready to be lifted and dried, usually about the end of July. Welsh onions are propagated by division of the roots, and tree onions by bulbs.

FLAVOUR AND HOW TO STORE

The pungent flavour and aroma of the onion is familiar to everyone. Shallots have a more subtle taste. Welsh onion green has the same characteristic flavour but is milder. After lifting and drying the bulbs, they should be tied in bundles and hung, bulbs down, in a cool ventilated place such as an open garden shed.

The green tops of the welsh onion can be dried and stored in the same way as chives after cutting into small pieces. To prepare a quantity of chopped onion for use the next day, cook them in a little butter first before storing in the refrigerator.

USES
All types of onions from the small white onions to the big Spanish ones, are indispensable in cooking. They are used in sauces, ragouts, broths and stews of meat and poultry. They can be boiled or baked as a vegetable, puréed or stuffed and are particularly good served with a sprinkling of oregano (wild marjoram). Shallots lend their subtle flavour to cold salad dressings, and cooked they are the basis of many famous sauces such as béarnaise, beurre blanc and sauce bercy. Welsh onion is generally used as a delicate seasoning. Chopped, it can be added to salads, cream cheese, eggs and in bread and butter. The smaller varieties are delicious raw and pickled.

Medicinally onions have antiseptic, diuretic, expectorant, detoxicant, anthalmintic and antispasmodic qualities. They should be included in the daily diet to discourage common coughs and colds. Onion is irritating to the skin and stimulates the circulation of blood in the mucous membrane. It helps in reducing blood pressure, cleansing the blood generally and in kidney troubles. It also promotes digestion while stimulating the appetite and fortifies the nerves, heart and glands. Raw onion juice rubbed on to arthritic and rheumatic joints is believed to relieve the pain. Brittle finger or toenails can be improved by rubbing in the juice several times a day. For mental workers, a daily intake of onions with their content of phosphorous, helps lucid thinking, creativity, concentration and memory. It is also a herb to be used for diabetics. In spite of its virtues the onion is not tolerated by everyone, especially those who suffer from flatulence. It is said that the surface of a cut onion attracts germs from the air, and for this reason onions should be used up immediately and not left for another day. If stung by a wasp or bee, an onion cut near the root and put on the sting for a short time, will draw out the poison, thus avoiding swelling and pain.

RECIPE SUGGESTION
Mix equal amounts of onion juice and honey and take 3 or 4 tsp a day for hoarseness, sore throat, coughs and bronchial catarrh. A common dish in Spain is onions cut into small slices poured generously over with olive oil and eaten with bread and a glass of sherry.

PANSY—Heartsease
Botanical name: *Viola tricolor*
Family: Violaceae

GENERAL
The pretty wild pansy, one of the violet family, is a medicinal herb which contains tannins,

alkaloids, saponins and glucosides, as well as various salts and acids. During the Middle Ages it was valued as a purifying tea. It was made into a cordial and believed to be helpful in heart disease—hence its common name heartsease. It is sometimes known as Heart of Trinity, so called because of the three colours in each flower.

One of the oldest flowers in cultivation, the wild pansy is the ancestor of today's garden varieties. Many Elizabethan writers and herbalists sing its praises for its beauty and usefulness.

DESCRIPTION AND HABITAT
Heartsease can be readily distinguished from other species of the family by the colours in the flower which are a mixture of white purple and yellow. Also the two upper petals of each flower are erect instead of leaning forward. It has a many-branching stem with large leafy, deeply divided stipules. The leaves are spoon-shaped with crenate edges and are stalked. Heartsease grows abundantly on hedge banks and waste ground and can be found at the edges of cornfields and often in the garden. It blooms throughout the summer months in Britain, Europe and other temperate countries.

CULTIVATION
A wild plant, it can also be grown as a garden plant.

FLAVOUR AND HOW TO STORE
Heartsease has very little taste or scent. Both flowers and leaves are dried for medicinal use and should be stored in glass screw-top jars.

USES
Dried pulverised leaves of heartsease can be sprinkled on a wound; if mixed with honey it makes a healing ointment. For skin infections the affected part can be treated with compresses of gauze soaked in an infusion of the plant. The infusion can also be taken to help blood disorders, weak nerves, exhaustion, nervous heart complaints and for jaundice, as it stimulates the metabolism.

RECIPE SUGGESTION
Infusion: Allow 1 tsp of the dried herb per teacup of hot water—infuse for 3 min. If made with cold water allow 8 hr to infuse. For cleansing the blood and strengthening the nerves add a teaspoon of honey per cup and drink 3 cups daily for 1 or 2 weeks.

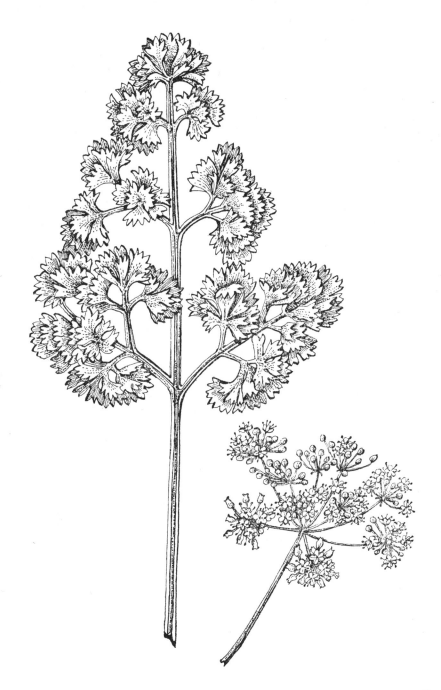

Parsley

PARSLEY

Botanical name: *Petroselinum crispum* (Curly Parsley)
Petroselinum sativum (Hamburg Parsley)
Family: Umbelliferae

GENERAL

Parsley is one of the most popular of herbs and a rich source of vitamins, proteins, iodine, iron, magnesium and other minerals. As it is so valuable and versatile, it is a good habit to include some parsley in your daily diet. It has a reputation for dispelling the odour of onions and garlic from the breath. The curly variety is the most popular as a seasoning and a garnish. Hamburg parsley is grown for its parnsip-like roots which are popular as a vegetable on the Continent, as well as its foliage.

The ancient Greeks did not eat parsley but regarded it as a symbol of death and used it in funeral rites. The Romans however, did eat it and wore garlands of it at feasts to absorb wine fumes and prevent intoxication. The curly forms of parsley became popular in medieval England and were associated with many stories of black magic and superstitions, most of which seem to be connected with its reputation for slow germination. The seed was believed to have to go to the Devil and back seven times before the plant would grow; it would only grow successfully where the woman was master of the household; and that to transplant it would bring ill luck to the gardener. Hamburg parsley was introduced to Britain in 1727 and became popular during Victorian times.

DESCRIPTION AND HABITAT

Parsley is a biennial plant with dark green foliage. The curly varieties have deeply divided leaves, each division curling over giving the plant a crinkly, decorative appearance. There are fern leaf varieties which are also deeply cut and lacey, but not curling. Parsley is grown in the USA, Canada, England and many European countries. The plain leaved types are generally chosen for surviving the severest winters. Parsley is native to the Mediterranean region and may be found near cultivation as an 'escape' though it should not be confused with 'Fool's Parsley' (*Aethusa cynapium*) a highly poisonous wild plant.

CULTIVATION

Parsley is not difficult to grow once it is understood that the seeds are very slow to germinate. Soaking the seeds in lukewarm water before sowing may soften their hard outer coats and hasten germination. Parsley prefers the shade and moist soil, rich in humus. Heavy or difficult soil should be lightened with garden peat and watered well. Sow the seeds annually in spring and successively through the summer, keeping the seedlings well watered in dry spells. In areas with heavy soil it is advisable to sow seeds broadcast in John Innes Compost No. 2 or one of the modern soil-less composts. Water well after sowing and cover with a sheet of glass, and shade them. The glass is turned every day and the soil kept humid as necessary. The seedlings are pricked out, approximately thirty-five to a seed tray for later transplanting to their ultimate site before they become too leggy. Water again after transplanting. When fully grown, the flower stalks should be cut off to prevent the plant from flowering and going to seed. The foliage should be frequently harvested to encourage new growth. Curly parsley may have to be protected with cloches in very severe winters. The roots of Hamburg parsley are harvested during the plant's second year. The dwarf curly varieties are especially suitable for growing in pots indoors, or in window boxes.

FLAVOUR AND HOW TO STORE
Parsley has a tangy, sweet flavour. It also helps to bring out the flavour of other herbs and seasonings, particularly in soups and stews. The leaves have to be dried quickly in order to retain their natural colour and aroma, and domestic drying is best done in a cool oven with the door left ajar. Dried parsley flakes are now available in the shops. The roots of Hamburg parsley are not easily dried at home since they require a constant temperature of 170°F until they are dried through, but where available, pieces of dried root are useful for flavouring stews and casseroles.

USES
Parsley is included in most herb mixtures and bouquet garnis. It can be chopped and eaten raw in salads, added to stews, soups, casseroles and vegetable dishes and used as a garnish. Parsley sauce is a well known accompaniment to fish and can be made more piquant by the addition of lemon balm. Parsley leaves may be infused in water to make a tea which has a reputation as a carminative, an aid to digestion and also as a diuretic for the treatment of kidney and bladder complaints, arthritis and rheumatism. Externally, parsley water is reputed to help remove moles and freckles.

RECIPE SUGGESTION
To make Persillade sauce for cold lamb and butter beans: chop finely one hard-boiled egg and mix it with 3 tbs French dressing and 6 tbs fresh or dried parsley. Permeate for ½ hr before serving.

PEPPER
Botanical name: *Piper nigrum*
Family: Piperaceae

GENERAL
Pepper today is in such constant daily use as a condiment and seasoning it is hard to realise that

in Roman times it was a highly prized luxury. There are very few savoury dishes which do not include pepper in some form, and it is probably the most widely used spice of all. The pungent flavour of the pepper is due to the volatile oil and the aroma is due to the alkaloid known as piperine. These properties have medicinal value for they help in the digestion of rich meats and high protein foods by stimulating the digestive juices.

Coming originally from the Malabar coast of India, pepper was probably the earliest spice known to man. It was a very costly article of trade and became of such enormous value that from ancient times it was used in payment of levies and taxes instead of coins. Alaric, the king of the Visi-goths in 408 AD demanded 3,000 pounds of pepper as part of the ransom for the city of Rome. During the Middle Ages pepper was the most important commodity traded between India and Europe. The Venetian and Genoese merchants held the monopoly of that trade, and became exceedingly wealthy. In England the peppercorn rents were introduced— payment of rents being demanded in pounds weight of pepper—and were a great burden to many people.

As the demand for pepper increased the price soared and this encouraged the Portuguese explorer Vasco da Gama to search for the sea route to India and the Spice Islands around the Cape of Good Hope. The Portuguese then dominated the pepper trade until the eighteenth century when other countries found ways of sharing in the valuable trade. Wars were lost and won over the pepper trade and its history has been a turbulent one.

DESCRIPTION AND HABITAT
The black pepper plant is a vine, a perennial climbing shrub with smooth woody stems and leathery leaves. The flowers grow in long clusters and are followed by bright red berries or fruits. These berries are the black peppercorns; they are picked whilst still unripe, then dried until they become black and wrinkled. White peppercorns are ripe berries from the same plant which, after drying, are soaked and cleaned to remove the black outer skin and flesh. There are many different varieties of black and white pepper and these are named according to the district in which they are grown. In England a high quality white pepper is produced from good grade imported berries and is shipped all over the world. Pepper is nowadays extensively grown in the tropics and the main sources are India, the East Indies and south east Asia.

CULTIVATION
Pepper grows only in a rich soil in a moist tropical climate. Propagation is by cuttings taken from high up the vines, which can climb 20 ft (6½m) or more. The vines do not produce a worthwhile crop until about the seventh or eighth year, but they continue to bear for a good fifteen years. After harvesting, the berries are dried in the sun.

FLAVOUR AND HOW TO STORE
Black pepper has a very characteristic fragrant aroma with a hot, biting pungent flavour;

white pepper is milder and warmly aromatic. Both black and white pepper can be bought whole, coarsely or finely ground, and should be stored in the usual way in glass jars in a dry place.

USES

Pepper flavours nearly all dishes other than desserts and though it needs to be used sparingly, can make an enormous difference to the flavour of foods. It is an important seasoning in salt-free diets.

As a general rule white pepper is added to pale-coloured foods and sauces where specks of black pepper would spoil the appearance. Whole peppercorns are added to pickles, marinades and court-bouillon, to meats and fish. Ground pepper, both black and white, is used in all meat and vegetable cooking, in egg and cheese dishes; also with rice, in salad dressings and with spiced fruits and dates.

Medicinally pepper is a stimulant, helpful for indigestion and flatulence, and it relieves congestive colds and fevers.

RECIPE SUGGESTION

Mince finely 4 oz (120g) ham. In a pan mix together 2 oz (60g) cream cheese, 1 beaten egg and 4 tbs mashed potato. Stir in the ham and add ¼ tsp fresh ground black pepper, 1 tbs parsley and 1 tbs chives. Heat through, then place on rounds of toast and brown under grill.

PLANTAIN—Greater Plantain, Waybread
Botanical name: Plantago major
Family: Plantaginaceae

GENERAL

The plantain, known mostly as a troublesome lawn weed, is one of the commonest plants everywhere, with so much virtue that nature seems to have made it as a special gift. There are several species—P. lanceolate (ribwort plantain) known also as 'Soldier Herb' to children, P. coronopus and P. maritima, both found in Mediterranean countries and once used as a salad vegetable, as well as P. psyllium, the seeds of which are used in medicine. The seeds and leaves of the greater plantain can also be eaten and the whole herb contains a wealth of medicinal properties, among them potassium, lime and soda. Its action is cooling, alterative and diuretic. A Chinese herbal describes it as antirheumatic and tonic, good for wasting diseases and fertility, nourishing the liver, a help for difficult labour, diarrhoea and internal haemorrhage. The astringent quality of the leaves is used externally for all wounds and bleeding, insect bites and nettle stings.

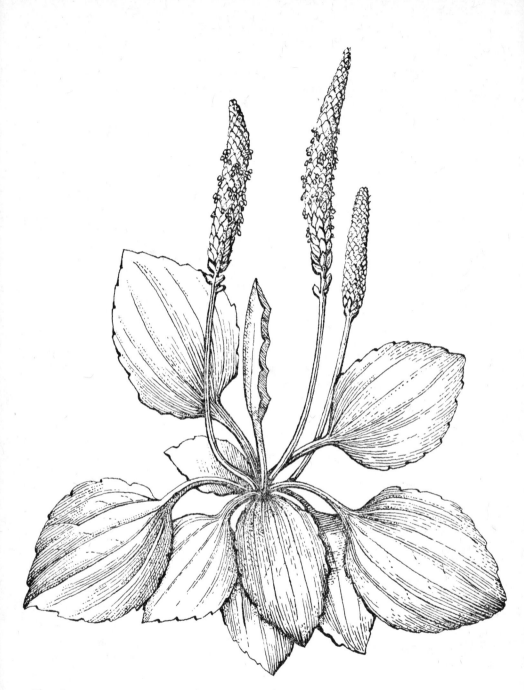

Plantain

Plantain has been known from ancient times in all parts of the world. Long ago in China it was once used as a potherb. Pliny and Dioscorides both mentioned it, giving it a long list of uses, and in England it was a medicinal herb. Shakespeare mentions it when Romeo says 'Your plantain leaf is excellent for broken skin'.

DESCRIPTION AND HABITAT
The greater plantain is a perennial plant, flowering in June and July. The deeply ribbed ovate leaves all grow from the base, and the straight flowering spike is dense with pinkish to purple flowers, four-parted with each cell containing four seeds. A native of Europe, it grows everywhere, especially on lawns.

CULTIVATION
It grows wild everywhere.

FLAVOUR AND HOW TO STORE
The plantain has no scent and the taste is rather astringent. The leaves can be dried and stored in glass screw-top jars.

USES
Fresh plantain leaves rubbed on the skin will give immediate relief to nettle stings and insect bites. Pulped leaves can be used externally to stop the irritation of haemorrhoids. An infusion of the leaves is a helpful diuretic if taken regularly. Psyllium seeds are used as a gentle laxative. They are soaked in water and swell to form a jelly-like substance which can either be swallowed with water or made up into a drink.

RECIPE SUGGESTIONS
To make an infusion, use 1 tsp of fresh chopped plantain leaves to 1 teacup of boiling water—allow to cool, strain and use, drinking 1 cupful a day.
For the psyllium seed drink, add 2 or 3 tsp of seeds to a tumblerful of hot water. Stir and take when mixture thickens. Orange or prune juice can be added to make it more palatable.

POPPY
Botanical name: *Papaver somniferum*
Family: Papaveraceae

GENERAL
The narcotic properties of the opium poppy have been known to many different civilisations.

Its Latin name 'somniferum' means 'sleep-bearing'. The drug opium is contained in the juice in the wall of the ripening poppy capsule up to twenty days after flowering. Amongst other active principles, this juice contains the important alkaloids morphine and codeine. The seeds however, contain no drug as the opium yielding power of the plant is lost before the seeds ripen.

The sedative properties of opium were used by the ancient Egyptians, and by the women of Crete, who worshipped a Poppy Goddess in 1400 BC. The poppy was also known to the ancient Greeks and Romans both as a medicinal and ornamental plant. Its powers were appreciated by the Arabians at the time of Mohammed (570–632 AD) and his missionaries were largely responsible for spreading its cultivation to Europe and the East. It was widely used in the treatment of cholera and dysentery and did not become an abused drug until the seventeenth century when the opium-smoking habit swept China. The use of poppy seeds as a spice spread to Europe during the Middle Ages.

DESCRIPTION AND HABITAT

The opium poppy is a stiff erect annual growing to quite a height. The flowers are white or lilac with a darker patch of colour at the base of each petal. The flowers are succeeded by the egg-shaped seed capsules containing countless tiny seeds of blue-grey colour. When ripe, the seed capsules are yellowish brown. Indigenous to the East Mediterranean region, Asia Minor and Central Asia, poppies are widely cultivated in temperate regions, including Europe, the USA and Britain and the best quality seeds for flavouring are considered to come from Holland. Opium poppies may occasionally be found wild on hillsides and waste land in some eastern counties of Britain.

CULTIVATION

Poppies flourish in fairly rich, moist soil with plenty of sunshine. Seeds sown in March should produce plants in flower in July and seeds ready for harvest in September. However, in Britain and the United States a permit from the authorities is required for growing opium poppies.

FLAVOUR AND HOW TO STORE

Poppy seeds have a pleasant nut-like flavour. They are generally available whole and may be stored in dry, airtight containers.

USES

Poppy seeds are frequently sprinkled on bread and rolls and included in recipes for cakes and pastries. Crushed poppy seeds are used in curry dishes to add flavour and thicken the gravy. Poppy seed butter adds extra flavour and aroma to noodles, rice, vegetables and fish. They are also crushed to provide an edible oil for flavouring purposes or as a substitute for olive oil. The seeds may be infused in water to be taken to relieve pain, soothe nerves. As a lotion, it may be applied to soothe skin and mouth irritations, ear or toothache.

RECIPE SUGGESTIONS
Try adding a tbs of poppy seeds to 8 oz (225g) of cooked noodles tossed in butter. Poppyseed butter: make with 1 tbs olive oil and 2 tbs butter to which is added 1 heaped tsp roasted poppy seeds, 2 tbs breadcrumbs, the juice of a lemon, and season it with salt and cayenne pepper.

PURSLANE

Botanical name: *Portulacca oleracea*—Common or Green Purslane
Portulacca sativa—Yellow Purslane
Family: Portulacaceae

GENERAL
Purslane is both a wild and cultivated plant containing valuable vitamins, minerals and essential trace elements. One of the few plants which are equally interesting in normal times as in emergencies when wild plants may come into their own as valuable food additions. It has been widely used since early times as a flavouring potherb and as a tisane. For generations it has been cultivated and eaten in India and in the Middle East.

DESCRIPTION AND HABITAT
Purslanes are half-hardy annuals of low spreading growth and the small ovate leaves are thick and fleshy. The flowers are yellow, growing on erect stems and bloom in July.
    Purslane can be found growing throughout the world in dry, sandy places. Cultivated purslane is a much taller plant. There are other varieties indigenous to North America and one variety with the name of the Italian botanist J. de Monti, but they have now spread to other regions in the world.

CULTIVATION
Purslane is propagated by seed, cuttings or division of roots and should be sown or planted out in the middle of April—successive sowings can be made at monthly intervals up to August. Purslane prefers light rich soil in a sunny well-drained position. The leaves are usually large enough for picking after six weeks. Young shoots can be gathered when about 2–3 in (5–7½cm).

FLAVOUR AND HOW TO STORE
Purslane has a sharp not unpleasant taste blending well with other herbs. Mostly used fresh, the leaves can also be dried and stored in the usual way for making tea.

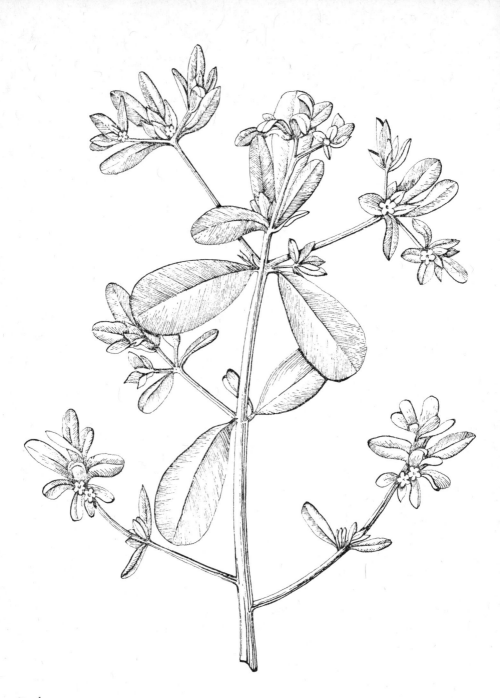

Purslane

USES
Young purslane leaves can be stripped from their stalks and added sparingly to green salads. The young shoots, tied in bundles of equal length can be cooked as a vegetable. Medicinally purslane tea is a tonic and helpful for blood disorders. Our recipe comes from a seventeenth-century book by one of the master cooks to Charles II.

RECIPE SUGGESTION
Summer salad: Mix together young chopped purslane leaves with twice the amount of lettuce leaves. Add chervil, borage flowers and marigold petals and serve with oil and lemon dressing.

QUASSIA—Bitter Ash
Botanical name: *Picraena excelsa*
Family: Simarubaceae

GENERAL
The bitter tasting wood chips from the quassia tree contain glucosides and essential oil. They are used medicinally, and for flavouring tonic wines, aperitives and in brewing beer. Cups made out of the wood can be obtained and water, left to stand in them, will soon take up the bitterness from the wood and provide a tonic to stimulate the flow of gastric juices in the stomach and sharpen the appetite. At one time brewers used the quassia chips as a substitute for hops.

DESCRIPTION AND HABITAT
The quassia tree grows very tall and has a thick trunk. It resembles the ash but the quassia has a grey, smooth bark and unequally pinnate leaves. The flowers are small and a pale yellowish-green. The tree is native to Central America and the West Indies.

FLAVOUR AND HOW TO STORE
Quassia chips have a very bitter taste and no smell. When added to water or alcohol they produce a yellow colour with an intense bitterness.

USES
Quassia is used in the manufacture of bitters. Medicinally its strong tonic qualities help the digestion and are especially useful in cases of dyspepsia.

RECIPE SUGGESTION
Quassia tea: Steep 1 oz (30g) quassia chips in 20 fl oz (575ml) cold water for 2 hr; strain and use.

Quassia

ROSE

Botanical names: *Rosa canina*—Wild Dog Rose
Rosa rubiginosa—Sweet Briar or Eglantine
Rosa rugosa—Shrub Rose
Family: Rosaceae

GENERAL

Roses, particularly the wild ones, produce the rusty-coloured, egg-shaped rose hips or 'false fruit' left after the bloom has died—'false fruit' because in fact the fruits are inside it, each one containing a seed. Rose hips of the *R. canina* variety are an important source of vitamin C, containing four times as much as blackcurrants and ten times the amount in oranges and lemons. Almost all varieties of rose produce valuable hips, but the most common is the wild dog rose. The more northerly the plant grows, the higher the content of vitamin C, and the hip of the Scottish dog rose contains four times as much as those grown in southern England. Rose hips also contain vitamins A, E, B and P.

For centuries European countries have used rose hips to make a purée, according to their own ancient traditions. It is evident that rose hips have been a part of British man's natural diet since as early as 2,000 BC—nearly a pint of rose hip and blackberry seeds were found in the skeleton of a Neolithic Essex woman. During Elizabethan times scented food was popular and rose hips and rose petals were used in great quantities in the kitchen, as well as for potpourris and scenting washing water. During World War II many countries made good use of their native sources of vitamin C in rose hips when supplies of foreign fruit were short. The British Ministry of Health distributed National Hip Syrup.

DESCRIPTION AND HABITAT

There are several varieties of wild dog rose not easy to distinguish. The tall deciduous bush has stems which bear hooked prickles. Fragrant pink or white flowers are borne in June and July, succeeded by the red hip, which is the swollen receptacle of the dead flower, containing the hairy fruits. Sweet briar rose is smaller; its sweet smelling leaves are usually hairy and sticky underneath. Roses are grown in all temperate climates. The wild dog rose is a common shrub in hedges, and sweet briar can be found on chalky limestone heaths in southerly regions.

CULTIVATION

The wild varieties are all easy to grow. The dog rose or shrub rose will form an impenetrable, decorative hedge. They are all fairly easy to obtain and should be planted one metre apart.

FLAVOUR AND HOW TO STORE

The characteristic hip flavour, sweet yet tangy, is a thirst-quenching favourite with children.

The vitamin C content is not harmed by short cooking, so they may either be made into purée or syrup and stored in jars, or dried.

For domestic purposes, the hips should be left on the bush until the first frost has touched them, and then picked when bright red and slightly soft to the touch. They should be carefully handled and quickly dealt with as loss of vitamin C starts with picking.

They should be cut in half lengthwise and speedily dried by hot air from an electric heater, care being taken that they do not lose their natural colour and burn brown. Store in a cool dry place after shaking them vigorously in a rough wire container to remove all the hairs. As vitamin C gradually decreases, no rose hip product should be stored for longer than a year.

USES
Rose hip syrup makes an excellent alternative to custard or chocolate sauce to pour over sweet dishes. The purée may be spread on bread like jam or added to cereals, especially Muesli. Rose hip wine may also be made. In preparing rose hips, only stainless steel, wooden and plastic implements should be used—the contact of other metals breaks down vitamin C. Rose hip syrup is a heart tonic and valuable in the treatment of dysentery and female disorders. Rose hips may be eaten raw (6 or 8 daily) or as a tea made from pips. This tea is mildly diuretic, a gentle tonic for kidneys and gall bladder.

RECIPE SUGGESTION
For Rose Hip Sauce: bring to boil 3 oz (90g) rose hip purée (bought or home made) 10 fl oz (275ml) water, clear apple juice or grape juice and 3 oz (90g) sugar. Add little lemon juice and 1 tsp each lemon balm and sweet cicely.

ROSE GERANIUM
Botanical name: *Pelargonium graveolens*
Family: Geraniaceae

GENERAL
The rose geranium, a scented flavouring herb, is probably the most popular of all the scented geraniums of which there may be over 200 aromatic varieties.

Rose geranium originated in South Africa and was introduced to Europe in 1690. The French perfumery industry first demanded its large scale cultivation for rose geranium oil in 1847.

DESCRIPTION AND HABITAT
A shrubby plant, rose geranium will grow to medium height. The soft, hairy leaves have

deeply cut edges and are divided into three main sections. The pink and lavender flowers bloom in loose umbels. All green parts of the plant are aromatic, but not the flowers. Rose geraniums grow in all warm climates and are grown chiefly in France, Spain, North Africa and Réunion Island.

CULTIVATION
Rose geraniums always require a warm sheltered position and will not survive frost. Plants should be taken indoors in winter and planted out again only when all danger of frost is past. Propagation is by cuttings taken in spring and started in pots indoors. These young plants should be gradually acclimatised by placing them out of doors on warm days only at first, and planting them into the permanent herb bed when strong and well established.

FLAVOUR AND HOW TO STORE
The leaves have the delicate taste and aroma of roses with a hint of spice. The leaves are generally used fresh. The larger the leaves, the more fragrant they will be. In drying, it is difficult to retain their natural colour, unless carefully and patiently done.

USES
Rose geranium leaves add a delicate sweet flavour to many summer fruit dishes. Jars of home-made jam are sealed with a large leaf, and one or two leaves placed in jars of apple or black-berry jelly before storing. For drinks they may be added to cool fruit drinks, crushed in warm water to make a tea or added to other herb brews, such as peppermint tea. They are also used in pot-pourris and for scenting water in finger bowls.

RECIPE SUGGESTION
Rose Geranium Apple Jelly is made by placing a small leaf at the bottom of each jar, then pouring on the hot juice and topping with another leaf before sealing.

ROSEMARY
Botanical name: *Rosmarinus officinalis*
Family: Labiatae

GENERAL
Rosemary is a lovely aromatic herb surrounded by tradition and legend, but with important culinary, medicinal and cosmetic properties. It was supposed only to grow in the garden of the righteous and because it was said to strengthen the memory, it has become the symbol of fidelity, friendship and remembrance.

Rosemary

It was first introduced to Britain by the Romans, and it is mentioned in an Anglo-Saxon herbal of the eleventh century as being recommended for use in clothes chests to keep the moths away. Knowledge of it was then lost and it was reintroduced to this country by Queen Phillipa of Hainault in the fourteenth century. In times gone by, this herb was valued for its pungent scent which was thought to possess elements to fight infection. It was carried at weddings, funerals and other church festivals and burnt instead of incense when this was scarce.

DESCRIPTION AND HABITAT
Rosemary is a fragrant shrub with pretty white or blue flowers and the plant has a strong distinctive, aromatic scent. It will grow to a good size and has leaves like coniferous needles. Its habitat is European; it grows all around the Mediterranean in the salt sea spray and the Latin name means 'dew of the sea'. It can be successfully cultivated in many countries.

CULTIVATION
Rosemary can be grown from seeds, but as this is a slow process it is preferable to start with the young plant. To propagate, take cuttings in August and transplant them, or divide up the roots of the plant. Rosemary likes a light, sandy soil in a sunny position. In the winter, young plants should be protected from frost. You can also pot these in the autumn and take them indoors.

FLAVOUR AND HOW TO STORE
The flavour of rosemary is fairly strong, with a pleasant, pungent taste. Dry and store in the usual way.

USES
In Italy rosemary is always added to lamb, fish and shellfish, veal and in chicken and rabbit dishes which are flavoured with wine and garlic. It is also recommended for use in fried potatoes, vegetable stock, risotto, raw and boiled vegetables. It can be used in sweet dishes as well as savoury, in biscuits, jellies, jams, fruit salads and cider and claret cups. It is a fairly strong flavouring and should be used with care.

Medicinally, rosemary has a reputation for strengthening the brain and the memory if applied to the outside of the head, and Greek students often wore garlands of it in their hair while taking examinations. This is because it has properties which expand the tissues to which it is applied, thereby increasing the blood supply to those tissues, which will have a stimulating effect. For the same reasons, added to wine or liqueur, or as an infusion, it is beneficial for the heart and circulation. As a rinse, it is said to stimulate the growth of hair, and is also a good tonic for skin conditions. In the USA it is cultivated for the essential oil it contains, which is used in perfumery.

RECIPE SUGGESTIONS

Rosemary biscuits: To a biscuit dough made of 4½ oz (120g) butter, 2 oz (60g) sugar and 6½ oz (180g) flour, add 2 tbs fresh or dried crushed rosemary when adding the flour. Cut into rounds and bake in hot oven for 10–12 min until golden and firm.

Baked rosemary potatoes are delicious—cut scrubbed potatoes lengthwise, dip cut surfaces on to rosemary leaves and salt, then place face down on oiled tin, brush with vegetable oil and bake in oven.

RUE—Herb of Grace
Botanical name: *Ruta graveolens*
Family: Rutaceae

GENERAL

Rue, a strong bitter aromatic herb, is used medicinally for its volatile oil. The ancient Greeks and Romans used it to season food and in medicine. The Romans brought it to Britain where it was used for relieving indigestion, easing eye strain and for many other complaints. Rue was one in the bunch of herbs carried by judges into court to guard them against infection from the prisoners, and Shakespeare called it the Herb of Grace.

DESCRIPTION AND HABITAT

Rue is an evergreen perennial shrub growing to medium height. It has a smooth branching stem and the leaves are bipinnate, the leaf segments small and blue-green containing small oil glands. The little yellow flowers grow in umbels and flower throughout the summer. The plant is native to southern Europe but can be successfully cultivated in many countries of different climates.

CULTIVATION

Rue will grow in the poorest of soils but needs a sunny position. It can be propagated by seed sown in spring, division of roots or from cuttings and layers. Allow sufficient space between these shrubby plants when putting into their permanent beds.

FLAVOUR AND HOW TO STORE

The rue plant has a strong aromatic scent and a pungent acrid taste. The herb is best used when fresh for it loses some of its active principle in the drying. It can be dried however, and should be stored in glass screw-top jars.

USES

Chopped leaves of rue can be added to salads as a strong seasoning. Medicinally it is a valuable

Rue

tonic and an aromatic stimulant when taken in small doses only. It relieves flatulence and is helpful for menstruation difficulties. The Chinese use it as an antidote for malarial poisoning.

RECIPE SUGGESTION
To make an infusion: use a teaspoonful of the chopped leaves to a teacup of boiling water; allow to become cold; strain and use. Not more than 1 teacupful should be taken during the day.

SAFFRON
Botanical name: *Crocus sativus*
Family: Iridaceae

GENERAL
The most expensive of the spices, true saffron is contained in the orange-red stigmas of the crocus flower. The stigmas are picked by hand and it requires 70,000 flowers to obtain one pound avoirdupois of saffron, so the cost of production is high.

In ancient times the spice was much more widely used for its medicinal properties, in food, in perfumes and as a dye. Greeks and Romans would strew saffron on the floors of public meeting places to scent the air and saffron tea was drunk to refresh the spirits.

Originally from Asia Minor, the saffron crocus has been widely cultivated in southern Europe since ancient times. By the sixteenth century it was popular in Britain and grown in quantity in Essex near Saffron Walden.

DESCRIPTION AND HABITAT
The saffron crocus, a perennial bulb, has pale lilac-coloured flowers and narrow deep-ribbed leaves. The stigmas, which are the saffron, are a bright orange-red and grow in three thread-like open-ended tubes from the style of the flowers.

Native to Asia Minor and the Mediterranean countries, saffron is now grown in many parts of the world and the finest saffron comes from south-eastern Spain.

CULTIVATION
The saffron corms grow best in a rich sandy but well-drained soil in a sheltered position. They are propagated by division of bulbs or by seed—but the seed takes three years before flowering. The corms are planted in August. Flowering takes place in autumn and as soon as the flowers open they should be harvested. The stigmas are picked out by hand and immediately dried either in the sun or on sieves over a low heat. When dried, the saffron is stored at once in airtight containers.

FLAVOUR AND HOW TO STORE

True saffron has a spicy, aromatic, pungent and slightly bitter taste with a penetrating characteristic scent. Very little is required to give colour and flavour to food. Saffron contains riboflavin and the pigment crocin which is very strong.

Saffron can be bought whole or as a powder. It should always be kept in airtight glass screw-top jars and away from the light to prevent bleaching.

USES

Saffron is mainly used today for flavouring and colouring foods. It is used a great deal in Spanish dishes, especially with rice and in the Provençal dish Bouillabaisse. It colours butter, cheeses and is used in confectionery.

Medicinally saffron is carminative and promotes perspiration when taken as an infusion.

RECIPE SUGGESTION

Saffron tea: Pour 20 fl oz (575ml) of boiling water over a pinch (4g) of saffron and leave to stand for 3 min. Drink a wineglassful whilst warm.

SAGE

Botanical name: *Salvia officinalis*
Family: Labiatae

GENERAL

Sage is a universal flavouring herb, yet it has been regarded as an all-round healing herb for many centuries, and there are now over 500 species of Salvia, the variety *officinalis* being the most important for culinary purposes. It is sometimes called 'true sage' or 'garden sage'. Red sage and narrow-leaved sage are among the best known of the other varieties. 'Salvia' is derived from the Latin *salvare* to save, an illusion to the powerful healing properties ascribed to it by the ancient civilisations.

The Romans called it 'herb sacra' and the Arabs had a proverb 'Why should a man die who grows sage in his garden?' The ancient Greeks and Romans used it as a remedy for snake bites, to enliven the brain and as a general tonic for the mind and body. In the Middle Ages sage was used as a remedy for constipation, cholera, colds, fevers, liver trouble and epilepsy. An old English couplet declares 'He that would live for aye, must eat sage in May' (the leaves are at their best in spring). Emperor Charlemagne promoted its cultivation, its use spread and it later became a great favourite of the Chinese. It was brewed as a beverage long before the tea we know today became popular. As its popularity in the kitchen increased, so its medicinal uses declined.

DESCRIPTION AND HABITAT
Sage is a hardy medium-sized perennial shrub and the entire plant is fragrant. It has greyish-green oblong leaves which are hairy with a 'pebblish' texture above. Pale blue or lilac flowers bloom in high summer, starting with the plant's second season. Red sage with its reddish stems, is less used for culinary purposes. Narrow-leaved sage has narrower, slightly wavy leaves. Sage is indigenous to northern Mediterranean regions but is grown in most temperate climates including Albania, Italy, USSR, Greece, USA, England and in the Dalmation region of Yugoslavia where it is an important peasant industry, reputedly producing the best sage. In Greek villages, sage tea is frequently served in cafés.

CULTIVATION
Although it will grow in most soils, sage does best in rich clay loam with good drainage in a sunny position. Propagation is by cuttings taken in April or May from well-established plants, and planted well-spaced, directly into their permanent positions. They should be harvested just before the flower spikes are produced. After about four years the plants tend to become woody and should be replaced with new plants. Sage is resistant to insects and bad weather, but in winter it should be mulched. A bushy growth will be encouraged if woody stems are cut back in early spring. Sage may be grown in a window box or indoor pot, and should be frequently cut to keep it bushy.

FLAVOUR AND HOW TO STORE
The flavour may be described as warm, pungent, slightly bitter with a hint of camphor. Careful drying is essential to preserve its natural grey-green colour and the oil content. Badly dried sage acquires a musty flavour. It takes longer to dry than other herbs, and will quickly discolour if you attempt to dry it too quickly over too high a heat. Dried sage leaves may be rubbed down or stored whole in the usual way.

USES
The combination of sage and onion for stuffing poultry is very well known. Sage is frequently used with rich and fatty dishes such as roast pork and eel, and is especially recommended with duck. Whole leaves may be put round joints or dried leaves sprinkled into casseroles or mixed with sausage meat. Chopped fresh leaves are also added to salads, kebabs, pickles and cheese. When the plants are in bloom they are much visited by bees and sage honey is in great demand for its excellent flavour. Sage tea is considered a tonic for the nerves and blood, and used as a lotion, is said to improve the condition of hair and skin. As a mouthwash, it helps to keep teeth white. Leaves among clothes discourage insects and rodents. Red sage tea is an old remedy for sore throats.

RECIPE SUGGESTION
Try Sage Fritters using fresh whole sage leaves. Dip in batter and fry till golden. Serve with a herb sauce or remoulade dressing or a home-made tomato sauce.

ST JOHN'S WORT
Botanical name: *Hypericum perforatum*
Family: Hypericaceae

GENERAL
St John's wort is most definitely a healing and not a culinary herb. Indeed, the reputation of its famous healing red oil has been known for many centuries. *Perforatum* in its Latin name refers to the tiny transparent dots in the leaves which are the oil producing glands. The herb's English name comes from its ancient association with St John the Baptist. There was an ancient tradition that to hang St John's wort in doors and windows would protect a home from damage or loss by keeping away evil spirits, and the herb was often used in magic charms. In the Middle Ages the healing red oil was widely employed by the Crusading armies to soothe and heal their wounds.

DESCRIPTION AND HABITAT
St John's wort is a wild medium-sized herbaceous perennial, common on grassland, woods, hedges and meadows, generally preferring some shade. It has pale green leaves dotted with oil glands and bright yellow flowers from July to September. St John's wort may be found in Britain, throughout Europe and Asia.

CULTIVATION
A widespread wild plant, St John's wort is not generally cultivated.

HOW TO STORE
The healing red oil may be stored in jars for up to two years.

USES
St John's wort's red oil has remarkable soothing and healing properties. Once used, you will never want to be without a bottle in the medicine chest. It can be rubbed on painful joints in cases of rheumatism, lumbago, gout, arthritis or strained muscles, bruises or tumours. It acts as a kind of embrocation, apparently directly intensifying the flow of blood to the injury wherever it is applied. It is especially effective when used as a compress on sprains and deep bruises, bringing quick relief. It may also be used to treat wounds, ulcers, inflammations and all kinds of skin rashes. Its nightly use on the hands prevents dark age spots and keeps the skin soft and in good condition. Internally the oil may be taken on a teaspoon of sugar cube for colic, worms, abdominal pains. Tea made from the leaves is a remedy for general nervousness and fainting fits, toothache, gastritis, insomnia, menstrual pains and for depression.

RECIPE SUGGESTION
To make the oil, the flowers and leaves should be placed in a large glass container. Cover

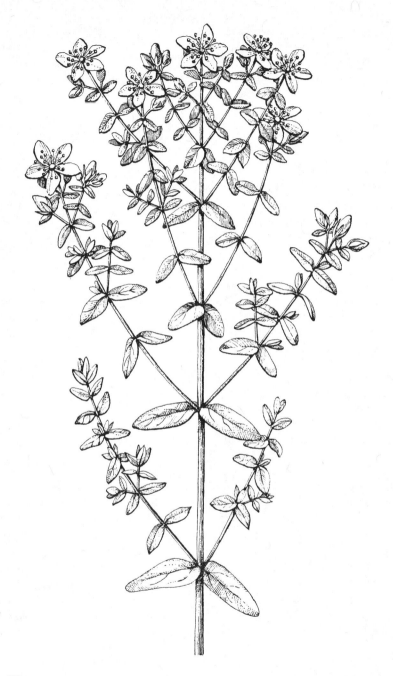

St John's Wort

them entirely with any cooking oil; cover with muslin and stand in the sun every day until the oil acquires a good red colour—but keep it in the dry overnight and protect from rain. Strain the oil through muslin into clean bottles and stopper. According to the amount of sunshine, it will take about 3-4 weeks to get the right colour.

SALAD BURNET

Botanical name: *Sanguisorba minor*
Family: Rosaceae

GENERAL

The delicate appearance of salad burnet, mainly a salad herb, belies its hardiness for it often remains with us all winter. It is a cousin of greater burnet (*S. officinalis*) and both herbs were used on the battlefields long ago to staunch bleeding wounds. Their Latin name, *Sanguisorba*, indicates this use. It was used also in cordials to promote perspiration and infused in wine or beer to help gout sufferers.

Salad burnet, originally from Mediterranean countries, naturalised in Asia and Europe and has been grown in Great Britain since the sixteenth century. Later it was cultivated in America, brought over by the Pilgrim Fathers.

DESCRIPTION AND HABITAT

Salad burnet's attractive appearance is due to its delicate lacy foliage. It is a small hardy perennial with reddish flowers which bloom from June to the end of August. Each flowerhead has female flowers at the top, bi-sexual in the middle and male at the bottom. They contain no nectar and are pollinated by the wind. Salad burnet grows wild by the roadsides and in meadows, especially on chalky soil.

CULTIVATION

Growing salad burnet needs no special requirements but it prefers chalky soil. The seed should be sown in April and covered lightly with soil. For a constant supply of fresh young leaves, keep cutting the plants back taking the first cutting when the flower shoots appear. Salad burnet is hardy and will even poke its head through a light fall of snow. It will self-sow if allowed to go to seed. Equally successfully it can be grown in a pot indoors.

FLAVOUR AND HOW TO STORE

The green leaves have a somewhat nutty flavour with a slight taste of cucumber. They may be dried and stored in the usual way.

USES
Salad burnet may be used generously in salads and is especially useful in winter when not many fresh green herbs are available. It is also used in soups and casseroles, vinegars, cream cheeses, for seasoning herb butters and as a garnish, and blends well with other herbs, especially rosemary and tarragon. The leaves are decorative and add a cool flavour to soft drinks and wine cups. Burnet tea is pleasant and mildly diuretic. Salad burnet improves the skin if added to a facial steam, and it is one in a mixture of herbs sprinkled over unfamiliar foods which might otherwise cause digestive upsets.

RECIPE SUGGESTIONS
Use salad burnet in combination with mint for a fish sauce. Melt 4 oz (120g) butter, add 2 tbs each chopped burnet and spearmint leaves and simmer for 10 min. Season with salt and pepper and pour over grilled sole or plaice.

For a cool, exciting whisky-based cocktail, bruise sprigs of burnet leaves in chilled glasses. Add another sprig to a combination of 1 tot whisky, $\frac{1}{2}$ tsp icing sugar and juice of $\frac{1}{2}$ a lemon per glass. Whirl in an electric blender with crushed ice and strain over more crushed ice in the glasses. Decorate with a further sprig of burnet and serve with straws.

SALSIFY—Vegetable Oyster
Botanical name: Tragopogon porrifolium
Family: Compositae

GENERAL
Salsify is included in the book for its outstanding value as a plant for survival. As a wild vegetable it was known for centuries and since 1300 AD has been described regularly in old herbals. Salsify is a valuable food plant, for not only can the roots be eaten, but the stems provide a natural sweetener. Its young flower stalks can be eaten raw or cooked like asparagus. Salsify is also a cultivated plant and the long, thin tapering roots are eaten as a delicacy in winter in the same way, and similar to, Scorzonera (Scorzonera hispanica) which is known as black salsify. Both are popular in America.

DESCRIPTION AND HABITAT
A tall erect plant, salsify is a hardy biennial with deeply veined leaves narrowing to a point. The flowers resemble those of the dandelion but are a purplish, pink colour. The long tapering roots are rather like parsnip though white and much thinner. It grows wild in the countries bordering the Mediterranean. Black salsify has long black roots and is indigenous to central and southern Europe.

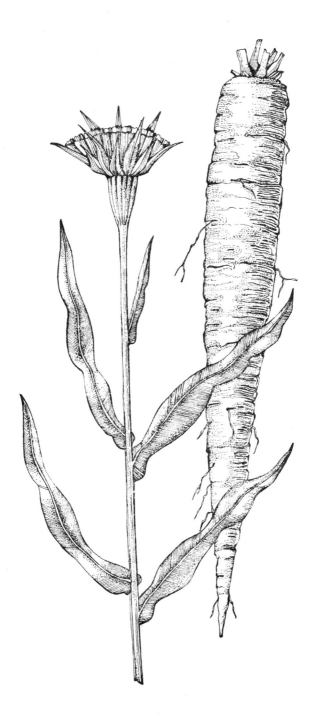

Salsify

CULTIVATION

Salsify is propagated by seed sown ½ in (1½cm) deep in drills 12 in (30cm) apart in rich soil at the beginning of April. They need a sunny open position. Seedlings should be thinned when 3 in (7½cm) high. To obtain the best roots the flower heads should be removed as soon as they appear. The roots are harvested in November, but some can be left in the ground to provide tender shoots in the spring.

FLAVOUR AND HOW TO STORE

The flavour of salsify is different from any other vegetable. It combines a slightly sour-sweetish taste with a mild, salty flavour similar to an oyster, hence the name vegetable oyster. On the Continent many people consider it a speciality like asparagus. After lifting, the leaves are twisted off and the roots stored in layers of sand in a dry shed away from danger of frost.

USES

As a vegetable the roots are first carefully scraped, tied in bundles and cooked for half an hour in boiling water containing salt, lemon juice and butter, and served with either a herb butter sauce, a béchamel sauce or with cream on toast. They can also be fried in butter after boiling and served with lemon, or the roots boiled, grated and formed into patties—the vegetable oyster. The young shoots can be cooked and eaten like asparagus. Black salsify roots should always be soaked well before using to remove the bitter taste.

RECIPE SUGGESTION

Cut boiled or steamed salsify into bite size pieces and mix with a good béchamel sauce to which meat balls can be added for a main dish. Heat well and serve with creamed or new potatoes. This is a traditional German dish.

SAMPHIRE

Botanical name: *Crithmum maritimum*—Rock Samphire, Sea Fennel
Family: Umbelliferae
Botanical name: *Salicornia herbacea*—Marsh Samphire, Glasswort
Family: Chenopodiaceae

GENERAL

Samphire is an aromatic succulent herb and an important plant for survival for it has both food and medicinal value and can be found in abundance on rocky shores throughout Europe. It is also a cultivated plant. It was once grown in English gardens for its leaves and used as a potherb, as a natural condiment, in salads or as a pickle. The seed pods were collected and made into a pickle. Samphire must not be confused with marsh samphire, a different family altogether found wild on saltmarshes. It is also a succulent food plant and eaten boiled as a vegetable or as a pickle. The name 'samphire' comes from the French 'Herbe Saint-Pierre'.

DESCRIPTION AND HABITAT
Samphire is a hardy perennial herb growing about a foot (30cm) high. The whole plant is thick and fleshy, the stem almost woody at the base. It is easy to recognise by its glabrous twice-ternate or segmented leaves and the umbels of tiny greenish-yellow flowers. Samphire grows in rock clefts close to the sea and extends from the Black Sea and the Caucasus along the Mediterranean and North Africa to England and Southern Ireland.

Marsh samphire is a small bright green erect annual without leaves. The fat stems are jointed with few branches and each of these ends in a spike. The flowers are green and tiny and form in the intervals between the branches and the stem. It grows on the salt marshes in all parts of the world.

CULTIVATION
A wild plant, samphire will also grow in a shady border in the garden especially if near the coast. It is propagated by seed sown thinly in sandy soil in March.

Marsh samphire is a wild plant only.

FLAVOUR AND HOW TO STORE
Samphire has a strong characteristic scent with a warm spicy taste. The leaves are full of aromatic juice. It cannot be stored dry. Marsh samphire said to be 'poor man's asparagus', because it is eaten in that way, has a mild salty flavour when cooked. It should be cooked when fresh, but if it is necessary to keep it overnight then it should be left dry and not placed in water or it will become slimy and inedible.

USES
The young shoots of samphire can be used fresh in salads or cooked as a vegetable and eaten with a butter sauce. The leaves and seed pods pickled in vinegar make a seasoning or accompaniment to cold meats.

Medicinally samphire is a diuretic herb and a helpful treatment for those suffering from overweight. An infusion made from 1 oz (30g) of the whole herb to 20 fl oz (575ml) boiling water is believed to be good for the kidneys. Marsh samphire is best cooked when fresh and eaten with melted butter. The tender young shoots can be added to a salad or the plant can be pickled in vinegar.

RECIPE SUGGESTION
Pick tender young shoots of samphire, wash well. Chop finely both leaves and stems and

sprinkle over a green salad. Or serve on their own with an oil and lemon dressing and a mixture of other green herbs.

THE SAVORIES

Botanical names: *Satureia hortensis*—Summer Savory
S. montana—Winter Savory
Family: Labiatae

GENERAL

Of the two varieties of savory, summer savory is the best for culinary use, and it is called 'the bean herb' on the Continent. The Romans used savory before the hot oriental spices were known and Virgil recommended that they be planted close to beehives. In Roman times a sauce was made with summer savory and vinegar which corresponds to our mint sauce of today. It was the Romans who brought the savories to Britain at the time of the Caesars and it became popular in Saxon cooking. Savory was a traditional flavouring for trout.

DESCRIPTION AND HABITAT

Summer savory is a tender, strongly aromatic plant. It is an annual which likes to grow in sunny places. The small, narrow leaves which grow sparsely along the stem, are dark green and a little thick. The white or lavender-coloured flowers are tiny and grow in fives in the axils of the leaves and bloom from July to September. It is a native plant of temperate and warm European districts.

Winter savory is a small hardy evergreen perennial, similar to summer savory with white or blue flowers and is a native of the mountains of southern Europe.

CULTIVATION

Summer savory is best grown from seeds sown in a sunny position. The young plants should be well spaced to allow them to become bushy. If sown in May or June the herb will be ready for use with all types of beans. The soil should be fairly rich but not containing fresh manure or compost. Winter savory which is propagated by divisions, cuttings or by seed sown under glass in April, prefers a light soil and makes a pleasant evergreen border.

FLAVOUR AND HOW TO STORE

Summer savory has a strong, piquant, slightly peppery taste. It can almost be described as spicy. For winter use the herb can be cut and dried in the airing cupboard. The best time to cut for drying is just before the plant begins to flower. If well dried at the right moment, summer savory will keep its flavour for a long time. Winter savory has a sharper taste and can be dried and stored like summer savory in the usual way.

Summer Savory

USES

In other languages, summer savory is known as the 'bean herb' because it is particularly recommended as an addition to all bean dishes, with broad, runner, French or haricot beans. It brings out the flavour of the beans without leaving any taste of its own. Both savories contain a strong volatile oil which aids digestion and are therefore recommended in dishes which are known to be difficult to digest, such as cucumber salad and pork. For bean dishes, use only summer savory, and now that frozen and tinned beans are available, it will bring back some of the natural flavour to these pre-prepared foods. Used alone or in combination with other herbs, it makes an excellent flavouring for poultry, meat, soups, eggs and salads. The savories' peppery flavour makes it a useful natural seasoning, and helpful in salt-free or salt-reduced diets. Crushed savory leaves can be applied to a bee sting to relieve pain and swelling.

RECIPE SUGGESTION

Summer savory is the main standby for all bean dishes however they are prepared. Blends nicely with other herbs in flavouring mixtures.
Horseradish sauce: Whip 8 fl oz (225ml) double cream until firm. Mix together 3 tbs grated horseradish, 2 tsp summer savory, 1 tbs wine vinegar, a good pinch of salt and a pinch of cayenne pepper. Fold mixture into cream and chill 10 min. Good with fish, roast beef and baked ham.

SEA HOLLY—Eryngo
Botanical name: *Eryngium maritimum*
Family: Umbelliferae

GENERAL

Eryngo root was a popular flavouring in Britain from Saxon times and was used medicinally and in the making of conserves and toffee. The edible roots are reputed to have nutritional value. Sea holly was a widely cultivated plant along the sea coasts.

DESCRIPTION AND HABITAT

Sea holly is a perennial growing to a medium height. The stem is solid and slightly ribbed. The leaves are irregularly lobed with sharp prickles on the ends and both leaves and stem are very pale grey green. The blue flowers grow in sessile heads in the whorls of the uppermost leaves, and flower in July and August. The long root is brown and coarsely fibrous. The plant grows wild in sandy soil along the sea coasts of Britain and other Atlantic shores, as well as in the Mediterranean.

CULTIVATION
Sea holly grows easily in the sandy soil of anyone living near the sea and is a worthwhile crop to grow. It is propagated by division of roots or by seed.

FLAVOUR AND HOW TO STORE
Eryngo root has a sweetish taste and the texture is mucilaginous. The plant is not scented. The roots are harvested either in the spring or after seeding in the autumn. They are washed and parboiled, then sliced and preserved by candying or by drying. The remainder of the plant can be dried and used as indoor winter decoration.

USES
The root can be used to flavour jams or jellies and toffees. When boiled or roasted, it is similar to chestnuts. The young shoots and leaves can be boiled and eaten like asparagus. Medicinally it is diuretic, expectorant and promotes perspiration; it is used in nervous diseases and for bladder complaints, especially where there is painful micturition. An ointment can be made by boiling the root in salted lard; this draws out the poisons from gatherings in the skin caused by splinters, thorns, bites or stings.

RECIPE SUGGESTION
Cough Syrup: Cover 9 oz (250g) eryngo root with 40 fl oz (1 litre) cold water. Bring slowly to boil and simmer gently until tender. Strain through a jelly cloth. To each 20 fl oz (575ml) extract add the juice of 1 lemon, the grated rind of half a lemon and 1 lb (450g) sugar. Boil hard for 10 min and test for jelling. Pot and cover. Use a teaspoonful at a time in a little hot water.

SESAME—Benne
Botanical name: *Sesamum indicum*
Family: Pedaliaceae

GENERAL
Sesame was one of the very early plants to be used by man both for the seed and for the oil contained in the seeds. The oil today is still the main source of fat used in cooking in the near and far East. In Europe it is used in the making of margarine and because it contains polyunsaturated fats is the best salad oil for use by those on a low cholesterol diet. Sesame also has a high protein content so is widely used by vegetarians and it is one of the staple foods in China and India.

Sesame originally came from the East Indies but records show it has been cultivated in parts of India as far back as 1600 BC. From there it was brought to Europe, grown in Egypt, and its value both medicinally and for cooking gradually spread throughout Europe. In Africa the seeds, called *benne*, were eaten as food as well as being used for oil and the seeds were taken by the slaves to America where it has been a cultivated food crop ever since.

DESCRIPTION AND HABITAT
Sesame is a tall erect annual. The ovate leaves grow alternately up the stem and are deeply veined. The flowers are white and shaped like a trumpet. The seed capsule is about 1 in (2½cm) long. When the seeds are ripe the capsule bursts open suddenly and scatters its seeds—perhaps the origin of the magic saying 'open sesame' in the tale of Ali Baba and the forty thieves. The tiny seeds are flat, shiny and egg-shaped and according to the variety, are either greyish-white, red, brown or black. To prevent loss of seed through the popping of the capsule, non-shattering varieties of sesame have been developed and the crop is harvested while the pods are still green. Native to Indonesia, India, China and tropical Africa, sesame is also cultivated in hot regions of North and South America.

CULTIVATION
Sesame grows best in sandy well-drained soil and a hot climate with moderate rainfall. It is propagated by seed sown in spring and it takes about four months for the seeds to ripen fully. Harvesting is begun when the seed capsules are well formed but still green. The crop is then cut, tied in bundles and threshed. After threshing the seeds are cleaned and dried and usually hulled to produce the familiar white seed.

FLAVOUR AND HOW TO STORE
Sesame has a pleasant nutty flavour which comes out more strongly when toasted or fried gently. The oil has a bland taste. Sesame seed can be bought whole or ground, which is known as sesame meal, and should be stored in a closed jar.

USES
An emulsion made from the ground sesame seed is called Tahini used a great deal in Greek and Lebanese foods as well as by the Arabs and Egyptians. Tahini is also used in making the Jewish Halva, a rich sweet confection usually eaten with coffee. On the Continent, sesame seed is sprinkled onto bread, rolls, biscuits and scones.

When toasted, sesame seed can be added to green, vegetable or potato salads; to cottage or cream cheese; as a garnish or instead of breadcrumbs on fish pies, chicken or meat fricasées and on cream coups. They can take the place of nuts in some recipes. Sesame oil can be used as a salad or cooking oil.

Medicinally sesame oil is mildly laxative. The fresh leaves of the sesame plant form a mucilage when steeped in water and in India this is drunk in cases of diarrhoea and for kidney and bladder disorders. It is also used for bathing the eyes and for skin complaints.

RECIPE SUGGESTION
Add 1 to 2 tbs sesame seeds to creamed spinach. Place in buttered dish and bake, covered, in a moderate oven for 20 min.

SILVERWEED—*Goose Grass, Wild Tansy*
Botanical name: *Potentilla anserina*
Family: Rosaceae

GENERAL
Silverweed is a common wild plant which, years ago, was used medicinally as an astringent and tonic. It has an edible root which was once used for making a red dye. Geese loved to eat it—hence the name goose grass.

Mentioned by Gerard in his *Herbal*, silverweed was thought to be good for the skin on the face, taking away freckles, spots and pimples. In the Middle Ages it was mostly eaten as a vegetable and the dried leaves used as medicinal remedies.

DESCRIPTION AND HABITAT
Silverweed is a small perennial with little yellow flowers which bloom all summer long. The leaves each consist of many deeply toothed leaflets which are covered with a shining silvery-white down. The plant grows by the roadside and on waste pastures where the ground is damp and low lying. It grows abundantly in Britain and throughout Europe, Asia and North America.

CULTIVATION
Grows wild abundantly.

FLAVOUR AND HOW TO STORE
Silverweed herb has no scent and the taste is sharply astringent. The root tastes like turnip when boiled or roasted. The herb can be dried and stored in glass screw-top jars.

USES
Silverweed root can be used as a famine food in place of root vegetables. Medicinally its effects are astringent and tonic. It can be used on the skin and as a mouthwash. Internally it can be taken for diarrhoea, fever and sciatica.

RECIPE SUGGESTION

Silverweed tea: Place a teaspoon of the dried herb in a teacup and pour over boiling water. Allow to become quite cold, strain and drink 1 or 2 cupfuls a day.

SOLIDAGO—Golden Rod
Botanical name: *Solidago virgaurea*
Family: Compositae

GENERAL

Solidago, or golden rod, has an old reputation as a wound herb. More recently, solidago tea has been considered useful in the treatment of kidney and bladder complaints. Another variety of solidago *S. canandensis* is often cultivated in gardens for its perennial beauty.

Its old name was 'Heathen Wound Herb' as the Saracens deplored going into battle without it. The American Indians had the same faith in it as a wound herb. During the Middle Ages it was spoken of as 'the gangrene herb'. It was imported into Britain from the Middle East and was very expensive until Tudor times when Gerard discovered it growing 'in Hamsted Wood ... near a village called Kentish Towne'.

DESCRIPTION AND HABITAT

Solidago is a tall hardy perennial with narrow pointed leaves. Flowers grow in spikes formed of tiny yellow daisy-like flowerets and bloom from July to October. The flowers are much visited by bees and other insects and are self pollinating. Solidago is found in dry woods, heaths and on hedgebanks and rocks throughout the British Isles, although rarely in the south-east.

CULTIVATION

Solidagos are easily cultivated. Propagate by division of the roots in autumn. The entire herb (except root) is harvested during the flowering period.

FLAVOUR AND HOW TO STORE

Tea made from solidago has a mild, pleasant taste. The leaves and flowers have to be carefully dried at a low temperature to ensure they retain their natural colours, and when dried can be rubbed into fairly coarse pieces and stored in dry, airtight containers.

USES

The crushed fresh herb, or the tea used as a lotion, has an anti-inflammatory effect on wounds, and staunches bleeding. If the tea is taken internally it is mildly diuretic and aids the functions of the kidneys and bladder, and is believed to help dispel gravel stones from these organs.

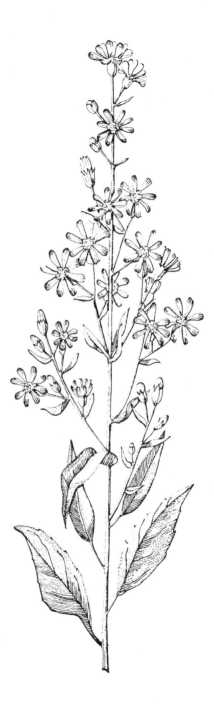

Solidago

RECIPE SUGGESTION

For gentle and effective treatment of inflammation of the bladder and kidneys, use 1 tsp of the cut-up herb with flowers per cup, boil for 1 min and steep for a further 10 min before straining. 2 to 3 cups of the tea daily are suggested.

SORREL

Botanical names: *Rumex scutatus*—French Sorrel
R. acetosa—Garden or Wild Sorrel
Family: Polygonaceae

GENERAL

Of the two varieties of sorrel mentioned, French sorrel is considered the finer and the one more often used as a culinary and medicinal herb. Both are members of the dock family and known for their high content of oxalic acid and vitamin C. Oxalic acid was formerly known as 'salts of sorrel' and used as a stain remover. The green parts of the plant are edible so long as they are tender and juicy, but while French sorrel is especially valuable as a source of spring greens and is less acid, the flavour of *Rumex acetosa* is not fully developed until the plant is in full season. French sorrel is used in the famous sorrel soup, a speciality of that country where sorrel has been used since the beginning of their recorded history. The Egyptians and Romans ate it to offset the richness in some of their food. The Greeks and Romans used the leaves for diuretic treatment, particularly to eliminate kidney stones. French sorrel is said to have been introduced to Britain in 1596.

DESCRIPTION AND HABITAT

Sorrel is a hardy perennial with arrow-shaped lobes at the base of the leaves. French sorrel grows to a medium height, the leaves are broad, shaped like a shield and the flowers grow in whorled spikes of reddish-green from May to July. Garden sorrel (*R. acetosa*) with its ridged reddish stalks and long slender leaves, is a common plant found in meadows, by streams and ditches in most countries with temperate climates.

CULTIVATION

Sorrel can be easily cultivated; propagation is by division of the roots in spring or autumn. The plants, well spaced, prefer light, rich soil in sun or shade with some shelter. The flowering plants should be cut back to prevent them going to seed and the old plants replaced with new ones after four years, when they become woody. Sorrel may be harvested 3-4 months after planting and cutting may continue during winter if the plants are placed under glass once frosts set in.

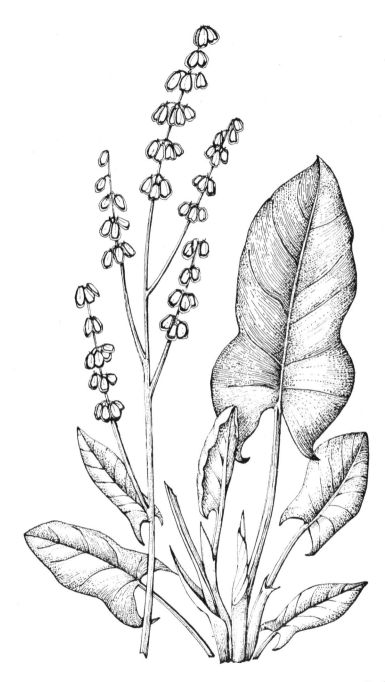

Garden Sorrel

FLAVOUR AND HOW TO STORE
Sorrel tastes bitter and a little sour, but is nevertheless a good condiment. The young spring leaves of French sorrel have a hint of lemon flavour. The leaves may be dried and stored in the same careful way as other herbs to preserve their natural colour and flavour.

USES
French sorrel may be used as a tangy seasoning in many dishes such as omelettes, vegetables and lamb and beef stews. It is particularly delicious in soups. The fresh, raw leaves are combined with other herbs in salads. The young spring leaves are cooked and served like spinach, but not in an iron pan or they may acquire a metallic taste. The crushed leaves and stems, or a strong decoction from them, are used to curdle milk and make junket. Sorrel tea is considered diuretic and useful in the treatment of kidney, liver and blood disorders and fevers. It is also used to treat mouth ulcers, boils, sores and other infested skin eruptions and festering wounds.

RECIPE SUGGESTION
French Sorrel Soup: Sauté 1 onion or ½ leek in a little butter or oil without browning. Add and sauté 2 tbs fresh or dried sorrel (re-constituted), 1 cup spinach and 1 large chopped lettuce. Add 4 quartered potatoes, 40 fl oz (1 litre) boiling stock or water and simmer for 45 min. Pass through coarse sieve, or mash. Return to pan and add 1 tbs chopped chervil (fresh or dried).

SOUTHERNWOOD— Old man, Lad's Love
Botanical name: *Artemisia abrotanum*
Family: Compositae

GENERAL
Southernwood, a relative of wormwood (*A. absinthium*), tarragon and mugwort, is both a flavouring and a healing herb, having stimulant, antiseptic and detergent properties. Its name is a shortened version of southern wormwood—the wormwood of northern climates being a harsher plant altogether. This attractive, familiar garden plant was grown in the 'physic' gardens from Elizabethan times when it was used as a remedy for women's ailments and for worms in children.

DESCRIPTION AND HABITAT
Southernwood is a perennial growing to a medium height, with a tough woody stem. The feathery grey-green leaves are slender and covered with short white downy hairs. Except in a good summer the plant rarely flowers in temperate climates, but when it does, the small yellow flowers appear in August. It is native to southern Europe and grows wild in Spain and Italy.

CULTIVATION

Southernwood prefers a sandy soil in a sunny position in the garden. Propagation is usually by cuttings about 10 in (25cm) long being taken in April. Half the leaves are stripped off from the bottom of the cutting and the stalk planted in light sandy soil. Rooting powder can be used to ensure success. The whole herb can be dried and it should be picked in early August.

FLAVOUR AND HOW TO STORE

The leaves of southernwood have a bitter lemony taste. The scent, again of lemon, is strongly aromatic and pleasant. The bitter taste comes from the essential oil which is contained in the leaves, known as absinthol, and it is this ingredient of the herb which repels moths and other insects. The leaves can be dried and stored in the usual way.

USES

The fresh young shoots of southernwood are used for flavouring cakes in Italy, and in France, where the herb is called 'garderobe', the dried leaves are used as a moth and insect repellant. Its medicinal value is however of greater importance, for southernwood is a tonic, astringent and a stimulant. As an infusion it has a special tonic action on the female reproductive organs and aids the menstrual flow. It is also useful in nervous diseases.

RECIPE SUGGESTION

Infusion of southernwood: to 2 tsp of the dried leaves add 20 fl oz (575ml) of boiling water. Allow to steep for 5 min. Strain and drink hot.

STAR-ANISE

Botanical name: *Illicium verum*
Family: Magnoliaceae

GENERAL

Star-anise differs in the botanical sense, from anise being an evergreen tree rather than an annual herb. Yet the fruits have the same composition, taste very much alike and can be used in the same way. It is the shape of the fruit which gives star-anise its name, being that of a perfect star. The fruit and seeds of this oriental tree are used in China today for seasoning their dishes and in medicines for various ailments. Star-anise, which originated in the East Indies and was brought to southern China, has a characteristic anise aroma. It contains an essential oil known as oil of anise, used in France, Germany and Italy to flavour liqueurs.

The Japanese star-anise (*I. religiosum*) is a smaller tree altogether and the fruit has poisonous properties. It can be easily distinguished from the true star-anise by its smell, resembling turpentine.

Star-anise

DESCRIPTION AND HABITAT
The star-anise tree is a small evergreen magnolia with a white bark similar to a birch, and a mass of little yellow flowers. The star-shaped fruits consist of eight brown individual fruits grouped round the short axil. Each fruit contains a shiny seed which is hard, wrinkled and light brown in colour. It is grown only in southern China where there are forests of star-anise trees.

CULTIVATION
The seeds are harvested after the sixth year and at fifteen years can be harvested three times in one year. The trees continue to bear fruit for many years.

FLAVOUR AND HOW TO STORE
The spicy sweet flavour of star-anise is stronger and more pungent than ordinary anise. For storing, the seeds should be kept in glass screw-top jars.

USES
Star-anise, being a spice, is an essential ingredient in many Chinese meat and poultry dishes, especially pork and duck recipes. They also mix the fruit with tea and coffee to improve the flavour, and the seeds are chewed for sweetening the breath. The oil too, is used to flavour drinks. In cooking, where a strong anise flavour is desired it can be used instead of anise. Medicinally it is a stimulant and a diuretic, helpful for flatulence and nausea. In China the seeds are recommended for constipation, lumbago, hernia and bladder troubles.

RECIPE SUGGESTION
Infusion of star-anise to ease a sore throat: add a cupful of boiling water to a teaspoon of star-anise. Cool and strain. Drink cold 1 or 2 cups a day.

STONECROP

Botanical names: *Sedum acre*—Wallpepper, Biting Stonecrop
Sedum roseum—Rose Root
Family: Crassulaceae

GENERAL
The stonecrops, of which there are more than 300 species, are of special interest nowadays. This wild plant, a succulent, found in all regions of the world, could provide valuable food and condiment in times of shortage, emergency or survival, particularly in arctic and desert regions where edible plants are scarce. The *sedum acre* is so-called because of its peppery taste

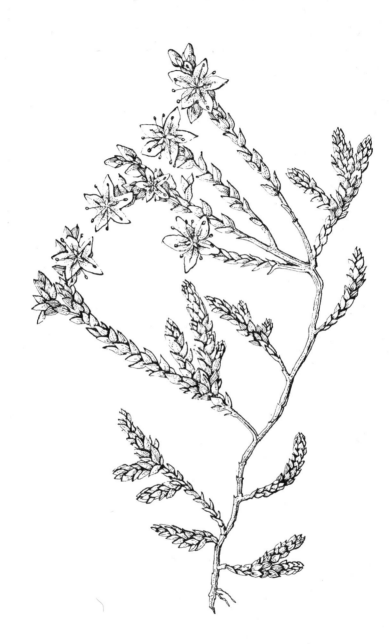

Stonecrop

and low-growing habit. The common stonecrop in former times was used medicinally as an emetic and in cases of scurvy. The crushed leaves can produce a sore, red skin, and if eaten to excess results in headaches, nausea and slight intoxication. Many varieties of sedum are edible, and the *sedum roseum*—rose root, is an alpine and arctic species used as a salad in Greenland.

DESCRIPTION AND HABITAT
Stonecrop is a perennial plant and, as its name suggests, grows largely on stones and rocks in dry, sandy, rocky places. It grows in all parts of the world even in the coldest or driest regions. The small thick egg-shaped leaves are succulent and crowded closely together. The plant lives on its own moisture, and even when picked and hung up, it continues to grow, sending out new shoots without any water. Stonecrop grows along the ground and the whole plant has a yellowish tinge. The tiny star-like yellow flowers grow on short erect stems and bloom in May and June. The stonecrops flourish throughout Europe and western Asia from the Mediterranean north to the Arctic regions.

CULTIVATION
A wild plant but easily transplanted and grown in the garden. There are many species of rockery and herbaceous plants and some make a good ground cover. Some nurseries stock, even today, ten to twenty different varieties.

FLAVOUR AND HOW TO STORE
Stonecrop has an acrid bitter taste when fresh. It is better to dry the leaves which then have a hot peppery flavour. The drying takes some time because of the amount of moisture in the leaves. They can be stored in the usual way.

USES
Stonecrop is a natural seasoning and the dried finely ground leaves can be used in place of pepper. The leaves of the yellow recurved stonecrop (*sedum reflexum*) and the white stonecrop (*sedum album*) can be used fresh in salads or cooked as a green vegetable. Orpine stonecrop (*sedum telephium*) adds flavour to soups and stews. Also having medicinal properties the orpine is an astringent and was believed to be good for intestinal troubles.

RECIPE SUGGESTION
In a survival situation the dried leaves can be ground to a fine powder between two stones and used sparingly as a seasoning with other wild foods.

SUNFLOWER
Botanical name: *Helianthus annuus*
Family: Compositae

GENERAL
The tall, handsome yellow sunflower is indigenous to North and Central America and was brought to Europe by the Spanish explorers. The sun-worshipping Aztecs of Peru were thought to have crowned their priestesses with sunflowers which were frequently represented in Aztec art, usually in pure gold. Today, sunflowers are common garden plants everywhere.

All parts of the plant can be used, and it is therefore a valuable crop as well as a decorative one. The seeds which are both edible and medicinal, provide a high quality oil, the first pressing being used for cooking, and subsequent pressings for making soaps, candles, in wool dressing and as poultry and cattle fodder. The stems, an excellent source of potash when burnt, provide a fibre used in textiles and paper-making as well as poultry litter. The flowers yield a yellow dye and the flower buds were once boiled and eaten like artichokes. The leaves too, have many uses for agriculture and in medicines.

DESCRIPTION AND HABITAT
An annual, the sunflower can grow to a great height, their stout stems holding them erect. Each stem bears one large yellow flower about 12 in (30cm) across. The leaves are large, heart-shaped and deeply veined, growing alternately up the stem. The seeds are yellowish-white, flat and broader in the middle than at the ends. There is a black variety which has a glossy surface and is thinner and longer. The sunflower is a cultivated plant throughout Britain, Europe and America, the largest crops being grown in Russia and other East European countries.

CULTIVATION
Sunflowers will grow well in any fertile soil and enhance every garden with their big decorative flowers. Propagation is by seed sown in April and planted out in June. The huge flowers bloom in July and August and later the seeds are ripe when the flowerheads droop down. The heads are then cut, left to dry, and when the seeds are fully dried they will fall out easily.

FLAVOUR AND HOW TO STORE
The sunflower seed has an oily taste which is pleasantly nutty; it has no smell at all. Dried sunflower seeds are easily obtained from Health Food Stores and they keep well stored in a dry cool place.

USES

Roasted sunflower kernels have a deliciously nutty flavour and these, when ground, can be blended with coffee. The oil extracted from the seeds makes a good nutritious salad or cooking oil. The oil also contains polyunsaturated fats, which is good for those on a low cholesterol diet. Medicinally, sunflower is diuretic and expectorant, successful in the treatment of coughs colds and bronchial complaints, and for these about 16 drops of the oil may be taken 2 or 3 times a day.

RECIPE SUGGESTION

Sauté 2 oz (60g) sunflower kernels in one tbs of oil until browned. Drain and roll in salt.

SWEET CICELY
Botanical name: *Myrrhis odorata*
Family: Umbelliferae

GENERAL

Sweet cicely is such an attractive plant, it should have a place in every herb bed; it is the first one to appear in the spring and the last to disappear in autumn. One of the 'sweetening herbs' sweet cicely is of enormous value to diabetics and those on slimming diets. It has been grown for many years in Europe, Asia Minor and Britain and used as culinary herb, all parts of the plant being eaten. In England in the sixteenth and seventeenth centuries the crushed seeds were used for polishing furniture for it produced a high gloss and agreeable scent.

DESCRIPTION AND HABITAT

Sweet cicely is a perennial, strong growing herb and will grow to a good height. It has a furrowed and hollow stem with large, light green, feathery leaves which turn almost purple in autumn. White flowers appear in clusters in May and June. It grows well in any British climate and can be seen growing wild in the north of England and in Scotland.

CULTIVATION

Sweet cicely can be grown fairly easily in any kind of soil from seeds sown in March or April, and freely re-seeds itself. Dig the ground over and clear it of weeds. Plant the seeds just under the surface, pressing them firmly in with the thumb and then level and smooth over the surface of the soil. Allow some space between for the development of the plants. Roots can be divided in the spring or autumn and transplanted to another position. Sweet cicely dies down in November and reappears in February, otherwise the leaves can be picked all the time. It is a plant which flowers profusely, but the flowerheads should be cut off as soon as they appear; otherwise there is little goodness left in the leaves and it will go to seed too quickly.

Sweet Cicely

FLAVOUR AND HOW TO STORE

Sweet cicely has a lovely sweet flavour and for diabetics and people who have to avoid sugar it is a natural substitute. The flavour is reminiscent of anise. There is little need for storing sweet cicely since it remains fresh in the garden for such a long time. For the two missing months, cut off the leaves in spring and dry them on a wooden frame with some nylon netting in the airing cupboard. Store in the usual way in airtight jars.

USES

Ancient herbalists have said that 'it is so harmless, you cannot use it amiss'. It helps with mild digestive troubles and coughs, but it is most valuable for its sweet flavour and can be used to take tartness away from any food, saving a fair amount of the sugar that you would expect to use in fruit pies and natural fruit juices. It is an important member of herb mixtures, eg bouquet garni. The leaves can be boiled in soups and stews, and also used fresh in salads. If added to cream, the cream will lose its fatty taste and become sweeter. The roots can be used, boiled and then eaten with oil and vinegar in a salad.

RECIPE SUGGESTION

Refreshing Fruit drink: Mix together the juice of 2 oranges, a grapefruit and half a lemon. Add 1 tsp finely chopped fresh sweet cicely. Stir well and chill in refrigerator for 15–20 min.

TANSY

Botanical name: *Tanacetum vulgare*
Family: Compositae

GENERAL

Tansy is a common wild plant, although many decorative garden varieties have been developed. Nowadays, tansy has hardly any culinary uses, but is known for its medicinal properties which are tonic and stimulant.

The ancient Greeks and Romans regarded tansy as a symbol of immortality and used it at burials. In Tudor England it was one of the 'strewing herbs'. It was said to be effective in keeping away flies, especially when mixed with elder leaves. At Easter, tansy cake and other foods were made as traditional fare after the Lenten fasts were over. Tansy frequently appeared in recipes of the sixteenth and seventeenth centuries.

DESCRIPTION AND HABITAT

Tansy is an attractive plant with outstandingly beautiful leaves, fern-like and delicate. A hardy perennial with an erect leafy stem and feathery leaves, the clusters of flat yellow flowers or 'buttons' appear from July to September. The herb has a unique pungent scent, a mixture of lemon and camphor. Tansy is widespread in Britain and Europe in hedgerows, waste places and by the wayside. It has also been naturalised in America.

CULTIVATION
Tansy will grow in almost any soil and is propagated by division of roots in spring or autumn.

FLAVOUR AND HOW TO STORE
The flavour of the tansy herb is hot and peppery, largely disliked. As a perennial, fresh green leaves are always available and there is generally no need to dry or store them.

USES
A tea brewed from the leaves and flowers is a general bitter tonic for failing appetite, nausea, menstrual troubles, jaundice, high blood pressure and heart weakness. However, it should not be taken regularly nor in large doses as some medical authorities consider it harmful. The tea may also be used as a lotion for toothache, eye and ear inflammations and swellings. Tansy leaves rubbed over meat where no refrigeration is available is said to keep away flies and to prevent decay. The flowers can be dried for winter decorations.

RECIPE SUGGESTION
For tansy tea: use 1 tsp of finely chopped leaves to every cup of water and take 1 tbs 3 times daily—or apply as a warm lotion on a cotton cloth.

TARRAGON
Botanical names: *Artemisia dracunculus*—French Tarragon
A. dracunculoides—Russian Tarragon
Family: Compositae

GENERAL
Tarragon is an important culinary herb and an essential ingredient in many famous French sauces such as béarnaise and hollandaise. It is said that tarragon came from Siberia, reaching Europe probably in the Middle Ages. French tarragon is known as 'true' tarragon and is preferable for culinary purposes. It is an interesting feature that although Russian tarragon never reaches the quality of the French, it is said to improve as the plant grows older, while French tarragon has to be divided up and replanted every three years to avoid deterioration.

An Arabian botanist and pharmacist Ibnal Bayter, living in Spain in the thirteenth century, mentioned tarragon by the name of *Tarkhun* meaning little dragon. The French called it

Tarragon

estragon—also meaning little dragon—and from this name the English word **tarragon** was derived; so called because it was thought to cure the bites and stings of venomous animals. Tarragon was introduced into Britain as a seasoning in about 1548 and was mentioned in Gerard's *Herbal*.

DESCRIPTION AND HABITAT

The Russian tarragon is tougher than the French variety, and grows to nearly 5 ft (1½m). French tarragon grows to 3 ft (1m), has darker, smooth shiny leaves and is altogether more fragrant. The flowers come in whitish woolly clusters in May and June but often do not open properly in colder climates. Both varieties are shrubby perennials, and the plants become larger and more profuse each year. The tarragons are native to Siberia and west and south Asia. French, or true tarragon, is widely grown in France where it is one of their favourite flavourings. It is also cultivated in southern England, Europe and temperate parts of the USA.

CULTIVATION

Some general nurseries stock Russian tarragon and do not distinguish between this and French tarragon, which can generally be obtained from herb nurseries. Propagation is by division of the underground runners, or the replanting of cuttings. It will grow in temperate climates, preferring warm, well-drained light soils in a sunny position. French tarragon needs a slightly richer soil than Russian and the addition of some organic fertiliser, and peat for heavy soils, may be desirable. As tarragon does not like having its feet in water, it is most important that the soil should be well drained. Plant the new tarragon plants when there is no danger of frost in April or September, about 18 in (45cm) apart. In very severe weather the ground around the roots should be protected with mulch. Do not over-manure as this causes succulent growth, weakening the plant and its roots which have to withstand frost in winter. French tarragon is inclined to deteriorate a little after some years and it is therefore advisable to divide and replant it from time to time. In good light soil tarragon can also be grown indoors, and should only require watering once or twice a week.

FLAVOUR AND HOW TO STORE

The flavour is sweet and slightly bitter at the same time, but with a definite hidden 'tang' which will become all too evident if it is used in too large quantities. French cooks only use French tarragon which has a delicate and aromatic flavour, slightly like anise. Russian tarragon is inferior and better avoided for flavouring as its taste is strong and bitter. When cutting for use in the kitchen or drying, never cut all the stems but leave a fair amount standing, perhaps a third, to facilitate further growth. Drying and storing can be done in the usual way and the dried tarragon stored in closed containers.

USES

The French like to combine tarragon with chervil in their cooking. It is the main flavouring in sauce béarnaise, and also in sauce tartare. Tarragon vinegar is made by saturating the fresh young shoots or the dried herb in wine vinegar, and is sprinkled over fresh salads and used in salad dressings. It also gives a special taste, similar to basil, to fresh tomatoes. Tarragon is much used in all herb mixtures such as fines herbes, in mayonnaise, preserves and pickles, in marinades for meat and in stuffings for meat and poultry. Asparagus and artichokes are delicious with tarragon butter, and it is recommended for use in a filling for avocado pear. In America, tarragon leaves are widely used with steak, chops and fish sauces. It goes particularly well with lobster and chicken—chickens are rarely roasted in France without tarragon. The Persians use Russian tarragon as an accompaniment with grilled meat.

RECIPE SUGGESTION
For Tarragon Dressing, delicious on tomato slices: beat together until light, 1 egg yolk, 1 tbs sugar and ½ tsp arrowroot. Add 2 tbs tarragon vinegar and ½ tsp fresh or dried tarragon. Stir over boiling water until thick. Cool, add 2 tbs double cream and stir again.

THYME

Botanical names: *Thymus vulgaris*—Garden Thyme
T. citriodorus—Lemon Thyme
T. serpyllum—Wild Thyme
Family: Labiatae

GENERAL
There are probably over 100 species of thyme all developed from wild thyme (*T. serphyllum*) the so-called 'mother of thyme'. They are grown as decorative, aromatic border plants, but for culinary purposes, garden thyme is the one most frequently used for its superior aroma and flavour. For culinary purposes the individual aroma of lemon thyme is often preferred for special dishes. The leaves contain volatile oil, thymol, which gives the herb a disinfectant quality and aids the digestion of fatty foods. In former times wild thyme was used for fragrant lawns. Golden thyme (*T. vulgaris aurea*) is another attractive, decorative variety.

It is said that the name thyme is connected with the Greek word *thymon* meaning fumigate as it was used for incense in temples. This herb has also been long associated with courage and Roman soldiers used to bathe in water infused with thyme to give them vigour. They introduced the herb to Europe and Britain where it quickly became popular. In the Middle Ages, ladies embroidered sprigs of thyme on to the tokens they presented to their knights-errant. In 1663 there was a recipe for making soup with thyme and beer to cure shyness! Its antiseptic qualities included it in the posies carried by judges and the nobility to protect them from the diseases and odours of the people.

Thyme

DESCRIPTION AND HABITAT
Garden thyme is a low, spreading perennial evergreen bush with woody, greyish roots. It has small leaves and pale mauve flowers throughout June, succeeded by numerous tiny seeds. The whole plant is fragrant, and bees are especially attracted to lemon thyme. Wild thyme and lemon thyme have broader leaves than garden thyme. Wild thyme is a native of the Mediterranean regions and Asia Minor and can be found growing over hillsides to quite a high altitude, even as far north as Iceland. In Britain it is found on dry heaths, usually on high ground. Garden thyme and other cultivated varieties are grown in temperate and sub-tropical climates.

CULTIVATION
Thymes are suitable for rock gardens since they prefer well-drained lime or chalky soil. Propagation is by division of established plants or sowing of seeds in spring. Cuttings should be planted out in April or May. Plants have to be replaced or divided up every three to four years as they become rather straggly and lose their aroma. It is generally recommended that cuttings be taken to increase lemon thyme plants. Winter protection for plants growing in cold areas is advisable. Thyme can be grown indoors and in window boxes. Frequent cutting will encourage bushy growth.

FLAVOUR AND HOW TO STORE
Thyme has a strong, slightly sharp flavour, and easily overpowers other more delicate flavours. Lemon thyme is less strong, with a lemony tang and is better in dishes for which garden thyme is too sharp. The plants should be harvested while in flower. In the first year only one cutting from the whole plant should be made, but two or more in subsequent years, the first in June and the second in August. The sprigs, with or without flowers, should be spread out to dry in the dark at a low temperature and when dry, they may be rubbed down and stored in dark, dry jars. Thyme dries and stores well, keeping most of its true flavour.

USES
Thyme is used to flavour a great variety of dishes; sausages, meat stews, stuffings and is especially excellent in dishes cooked slowly in wine. It is also used to flavour vegetables of all kinds, and makes a vast difference to plain creamed potatoes. It is an essential herb in bouquets garnis, and blends well with marjoram and rosemary. Lemon thyme adds a special tang to fresh fruit dishes. Thyme aids digestion of rich food and thyme tea sweetened with honey is an excellent soothing cough mixture. Lemon thyme is used in pot-pourris, perfumes and soap; also in mouthwashes and it is sometimes an ingredient in toothpaste or powder.

RECIPE SUGGESTION
A delicious liver dish is made by coating slices of liver (approx 1 lb, 450g) in seasoned flour

Lemon Thyme

mixed with 2 tsp thyme. When all pieces are sautéed in oil, add 5 fl oz (25ml) orange juice to the pan, cover and simmer for 3 to 5 min, then spoon over liver.

TURMERIC

Botanical name: *Curcuma longa*
Family: Zingiberaceae

GENERAL

Turmeric is a vivid yellow spice which, like ginger, comes from the underground rhizome of the plant but is sweeter and more fragrant than ginger. The roots yield an essential oil known as oil of curcuma, still used today in some perfumes. For many centuries turmeric has been used as a vegetable dye, as a food seasoning and in medicines and cosmetics. Today in Asian countries it is still used in the same ways.

The true origin of turmeric is in doubt as it grows nowhere in the wild state and has been a cultivated plant for more than two thousand years in Assyria, China and India. It is said that turmeric came into use in the west through the sun-worshippers of Persia. Their demand for the yellow saffron dye outgrew the supply and turmeric was used instead.

DESCRIPTION AND HABITAT

Turmeric is a sturdy perennial growing in the tropics. The large thin leaves grow from the base of the plant which has yellowish-white flowers. The underground rhizomes are short and thick, greyish outside and a brownish-yellow inside. The five known varieties differ slightly as to colour. Turmeric is today cultivated in south-east Asia, India, Jamaica, Haiti and Peru.

CULTIVATION

Like ginger, turmeric needs a tropical moist climate and a light, well-drained soil. Small pieces of rhizome are deeply planted and the crop is ready to harvest in about ten months. After the leaves have died down the rhizomes are dug up then cleaned and boiled, before being dried, to ensure equal colour throughout. After drying they are polished and either ground or left whole.

FLAVOUR AND HOW TO STORE

Turmeric has a delicate, aromatic, slightly peppery taste which is clean and refreshing, and the scent is fragrant. It should be stored in closed glass jars in the dark.

USES

Turmeric is an essential ingredient in curry powders, adding colour and flavour to them. It is also added to mustard powder, pickles and chutneys. Turmeric is used to give colour and flavour to devilled eggs, salad dressings and marinades, and it can be used as a substitute for saffron. It is widely used in colouring foods such as butter, cheese, margarine, fruit drinks and some liqueurs. When used for colouring, only a small amount is needed to give a brilliant yellow hue.

Medicinally turmeric is not now used in the West, but in India and other Asian countries it is taken boiled with milk and sugar for a cold and as a remedy for flatulence and liver complaints. In China it is used against haemorrhages. The wonderful yellow dye that turmeric yields is widely used in both India and China for colouring silks and cottons, and is mixed with alum to produce a fast colour.

RECIPE SUGGESTION

Marinade for Shrimps or Prawns: In a jug combine 5 fl oz (150ml) sunflower oil, 1 tbs red wine vinegar, 1 tsp turmeric, a pinch garlic powder and black pepper and 2 tsp chopped fresh mint. Pour this over 1 lb (450g) shrimps and leave for 2 or 3 hr. Sauté the shrimps in a little butter, remove and keep warm. Stir a little flour into the pan, mix well then gradually add the marinade stirring until it boils; simmer gently for 10 min, add the shrimps and heat through again; serve.

VALERIAN—All-Heal
Botanical name: *Valeriana officinalis*
Family: Valerianaceae

GENERAL

The root of valerian provides one of the best herbal sedatives and is an excellent tranquilliser. Its name is derived from the Latin verb *valere*, to be healthy, to fare well, and the old English name, All-heal is descriptive of its medicinal qualities. The roots have a peculiar smell, not pleasant to us, but it has a remarkable fascination for cats and other animals.

Although known by many different names throughout the course of history, valerian has been used as a medicinal herb for a very long time. It was recommended by Hippocrates in the fourth and fifth centuries BC and was included in Nordic and Anglo-Saxon herbal remedies of the eleventh century AD. During the sixteenth century valerian was greatly esteemed as a healing plant, it was grown in all monastery gardens and even used as a spice and in cosmetics,

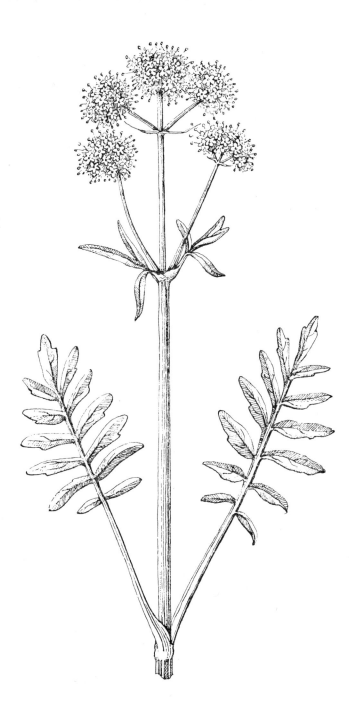

Valerian

though today its scent is not generally considered attractive. The first record of its being used in the treatment of epilepsy was in 1592. Traditionally valerian cultivation in England has been centred in Derbyshire.

DESCRIPTION AND HABITAT

Valerian is perennial, varying in height from medium to tall. It has bright green, much-divided leaves and the lowest have long stalks. Numerous small, pale pink flowers grow in clusters from June to August. The entire plant has a foetid odour, much accentuated when bruised. Valerian may be found growing wild throughout Britain, Europe and north Asia, generally in damp shady places, although it may be found in dry situations when a shorter variety with a stronger aroma and effect may result.

CULTIVATION

Many decorative varieties of valerian are cultivated, but only *V. officinalis* has the medicinal qualities. It is generally cultivated by division of roots; seeds may be sown but they are slow to germinate and have only a 50 per cent fertility rate. The plants will grow in any soil and should be well spaced. Many young plants will not produce flowers the first year and the roots should not be harvested until the autumn of their second year.

FLAVOUR AND HOW TO STORE

Valerian tea does not have a particularly pleasant taste, but it may be improved by sweetening with honey and one becomes quickly accustomed to it. The roots must be dried in the dark, the larger ones being first split into quarters and when thoroughly dry, the pieces should be stored in a cool place in airtight containers.

USES

Cold valerian tea is made from the roots and taken for the nerves, tense headaches, troubles typical at the change of life (menopause) and to induce sleep. It calms an upset digestive system and is especially effective in cases of sudden emotional distress or convulsions; it is sometimes helpful in treating epileptic fits. Valerian tea should be taken sparingly and made as suggested in our recipe, as taken too often or too strong will result in restlessness. Applied as a lotion, the tea will soothe sores, skin rashes, swollen joints and veins.

RECIPE SUGGESTION

Unlike other herbal infusions, valerian tea is more effective when taken cold about an hour before retiring. Soak a level teaspoon of the dried root in a cup of cold water. Cover and stand in a cool place for 12–24 hr, then strain.

VANILLA

Botanical name: *Vanilla planifolia*
Family: Orchidaceae

GENERAL

The vanilla pod is the fruit of the vanilla orchid vine and, with its delicate, spicy, aromatic flavour is a unique flavouring agent for sweet foods because there is nothing similar to it anywhere in the whole world. It is not a spice, having no essential oil. Its taste and aroma come from the vanillin crystals which form on the surface of the pod after fermentation.

During the last century the vanillin crystals were isolated from the pods and processing of the synthetic product was begun. This 'vanilla essence' was obtained by distilling oil of clove or by processing sucrose, waste paper pulp or coal tar. These are substitutes for vanilla but none has the delicate flavour of the true vanilla.

Cortez and his Spanish explorers first discovered vanilla in 1520 in Mexico where the Aztecs used it to flavour their chocolate drinks. The Spaniards began making vanilla-flavoured chocolate which immediately became popular and the use of vanilla for this and as a flavouring on its own spread throughout Europe. As the demand for vanilla increased, tropical countries elsewhere tried to produce it, but whilst the plants would grow, they produced no fruit. The reason for this, it was later discovered, was that the right pollinating insects were not found anywhere other than in Mexico. It was not until 1836 that a French botanist perfected the method of hand pollination of the flowers—still followed today. Then many plantations were started in Java, Brazil, the West Indies, the Seychelles and the Malagasy Republic, which today grows the bulk of the world's crop.

DESCRIPTION AND HABITAT

The vanilla vine is an exotic climbing orchid with pale yellow flowers and large fleshy oblong leaves. The slim stems climb and twine round trees or other supports. The green vanilla pod or bean grows to 10 in (25cm) long and contains a mass of tiny seeds. Native to Central America and Mexico, they are now grown in all tropical areas.

CULTIVATION

Vanilla will only grow in a hot moist tropical climate like other orchids. The vines, often grown on living supports planted the previous year, are grown from cuttings which root in ten to twelve weeks. They have to be pruned frequently to keep them low enough for the hand-pollinating. The first crop is harvested after three years, and the vines continue to fruit for a further nine. After picking, the pods go through the complicated process of fermentation, consisting of alternate sweating and drying. This takes anything up to five or six months, by which time the pods are soft and very dark brown.

FLAVOUR AND HOW TO STORE

The dried vanilla pod has a scent and flavour entirely its own, sweetly aromatic and delicate. True vanilla extract can be bought in bottles and the pods, bought whole, can be stored on their own or in a jar of sugar, permeating the sugar with its aroma. Pieces of the pod can be used several times if gently washed in warm water each time.

USES

Vanilla as a flavouring is very much part of the everyday cooking of sweet dishes, cakes and puddings. An essential ingredient in most of the sweet chocolate manufactured today, it is used also for ice-cream, soft drinks, tobacco, liqueurs and in perfumes. The Egyptians and the Turks use it in sorbets.

The medicinal value of vanilla has declined over the years but it was at one time considered to be a stimulant, an aid to digestion and to arouse the passions!

RECIPE SUGGESTION

Vanilla milk: Cut a short length from a vanilla pod and slit open. Pour over this a teacupful of boiling milk. Leave to stand for 5–10 min and strain. Sweeten with a little sugar if required, or use the milk to make hot chocolate drinks, rice or other puddings.

VERBASCUM—COMMON MULLEIN—
Aaron's Rod, Flannel Plant
Botanical name: *Verbascum thapsus*
Family: Scrophulariaceae

GENERAL

Verbascum, the common mullein, is a well known garden and wild plant which has bright yellow flowers. These are used either dried or fresh to make a tea with a particular reputation for easing chest complaints.

The plant's old country name, Aaron's rod, has Biblical connections, and it was also traditionally connected with fairies and the Devil. At one time, the strong stiff stalks were dipped in suet or pitch and used as funeral candles.

DESCRIPTION AND HABITAT

Verbascum is a tall beautiful biennial. The leaves grow in rosettes and are covered with white woolly hairs, earning the herb another name of flannel plant. Bright yellow flowers are nearly 1 in (2½cm) across and grow in dense spikes close to the stem of the plant, blooming from

June to August. Verbascum may be found wild in sunny dry situations throughout Britain Europe and Asia.

CULTIVATION
Verbascum requires little attention from the gardener, but grows best in well-drained chalky soil. In a sunny position sheltered from winds, the plants will grow tall and strong. The seedlings may be started in a frame or nursery bed and planted out into their permanent positions during August and September and will then produce flowers the following summer.

FLAVOUR AND HOW TO STORE
The flowers provide a pleasant tisane, but great care should be taken in gathering them, for if they are bruised their effectiveness will be lost. After picking, they should be either used fresh or dried immediately. When drying they should be neither heaped up nor pressed down, but laid out carefully in single layers and dried in the dark at a low temperature in order to retain their bright natural colour.

USES
The tea will remove clogged mucus from all tracts of the body and is therefore useful in treating and preventing bronchial troubles. The tea may also be used as a lotion and applied to inflamed eyes, wounds, skin rashes and burns. Verbascum root may be boiled in a little wine and taken as a cure for diarrhoea.

RECIPE SUGGESTION
Verbascum tea can bring quite dramatic relief in cases of persistent coughing. It can be taken over long periods and is made by infusing about 6 flowers, fresh or dried, in boiling water for 10 min.

VERBENA
Botanical names: *Verbena officinalis*—Vervain
Lippia citriodora—Lemon Verbena
Family: Verbenaceae

GENERAL
Some confusion exists between these two verbenas. Vervain is the only English native of the Verbenaceae which is a tropical plant family. Lemon verbena may also be grown in England and both are used to make health-giving herb teas. Lemon verbena tea is a popular drink in Spain and France.

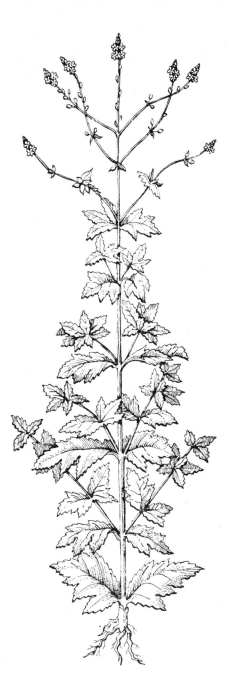

Verbena

Vervain's medicinal qualities were known to Hippocrates and it was held as sacred as mistletoe by the Druids. During times of the plague, vervain was one of the herbs recommended as protection. In fact, it was considered an all-round healing herb, though much of this reputation was attributable to superstition. It was even used in love potions. Lemon verbena was introduced to Britain from Chile in the eighteenth century.

DESCRIPTION AND HABITAT

Vervain is a hardy perennial plant of medium height, having stiff square stems. The small scentless lilac flowers grow on slender spikes from July to September. The leaves are greyish. Lemon verbena is a deciduous shrub with yellow-green leaves, shiny above and dull beneath, growing in threes. Pale lavender flowers grow in panicles. True to its name, lemon verbena has a lemon scent and flavour. Only vervain is found wild in England and Wales, common on waste lands, also in Europe and America.

CULTIVATION

Vervain is propagated by sowing seed in early spring, by cuttings or root division. It likes well-drained, rich soil. Lemon verbena can be grown in poor soil with the addition of some humus, but not manure. It is less hardy than vervain but can be grown successfully in mild climates if given a sheltered position. In winter the roots should be covered with wood-ash or leaf mould. Lemon verbena also makes a fragrant houseplant.

FLAVOUR AND HOW TO STORE

Vervain tea is slightly bitter but may be sweetened with honey. Lemon verbena is pleasantly tanged with lemon and makes a cooling and refreshing tisane. The side shoots of vervain should be harvested before the flowers are fully open in June, and carefully dried. All parts of lemon verbena may be harvested and dried in the usual way.

USES

Verbena or vervain tea is a sedative, digestive tonic, since it stimulates the production of bile. It will settle nerves, avert convulsions and soothe asthmatic coughs. As a lotion, it may be applied to inflamed eyes and sores in the mouth or throat. Lemon verbena leaves are refreshing in drinks, salads and may be used in sauce recipes which call for a lemon flavour. The tea, which is also considered sedative and soothing for bronchial and nasal congestion, may be drunk warm or cold, blended with ice and mint. Like lemon balm, the leaves may be used in summer fruit dishes and drinks. The scent of lemon verbena is also used in cosmetic and soap preparations.

RECIPE SUGGESTION

Both verbena teas are made by steeping a teaspoon of the fresh or dried herb per cup of boiling water for 3–5 min. Use lemon verbena leaves in the same way as suggested for rose geranium, putting them in the bottom of home-made ice cream or jellies.

VIOLET
Botanical name: *Viola odorata*
Family: Violaceae

GENERAL
The *viola odorata* or sweet violet is both a wild and cultivated plant with important healing properties. The leaves contain glucosides which are antiseptic, whilst the flowers, taken as a tea or syrup, are expectorant and make a good cough medicine.

Nowadays violet perfume is in many cosmetic products, and the crystallised flowers are a familiar sight on violet-flavoured sweets and chocolates.

Violet comes originally from Europe and since the days of Hippocrates has been in medicines, perfumes, love potions as well as in sweets. The Greeks chose violet as their flower of fertility and both Greeks and Romans drank quantities of violet wine, made violet conserves and cosmetics. It became so popular that it was cultivated on a large scale to supply the needs of all the Mediterranean countries. The ancient Britons are known to have used violet as a cosmetic, mixing the flowers with goats milk for a skin lotion.

In the Middle Ages violets were grown in the physic gardens, being used for insomnia, as a laxative and for many other ailments. Later violets were used in the still rooms of the large country houses as medicines, in cooking, for making into wine and filling sweet scented pillows.

DESCRIPTION AND HABITAT
The sweet violet has rough heartshaped leaves with a creeping rootstock and deep purple flowers. As a wild plant it is doubly prized for it flowers so early in spring and smells so sweet. A perennial, it grows in fields and on banks throughout Europe.

CULTIVATION
Violet is propagated by cuttings taken from the last season's runners. Plant in a half shady position in soil which has been dug over with compost, manure or leaf mould. The plants will need plenty of moisture until they have rooted. Leaves and flowers for drying should be gathered in the spring.

FLAVOUR AND HOW TO STORE
Violet has a sweet aromatic flavour and a highly fragrant scent. The leaves and flowers are stored in the usual way in closed glass jars away from the light.

Violet

USES

Candied violets are used as decoration for cakes and puddings and in ice-cream; the fresh flowers lend a delicate flavour to salads.

Medicinally violet tea and syrup, taken internally, are helpful for whooping cough in children, coughs and T.B. in adults. It has a soothing effect on the nerves and relieves head-aches and insomnia. Together with almond oil, the syrup is a mild laxative.

Externally a footbath, made from a decoction of the roots, and taken in conjunction with the tea, helps against sleeplessness. Violet infusion can be used as an eyebath and as a mouthwash. In folk medicine crushed fresh violet leaves make a compress for reducing swellings, for sore throats, gout and arthritis.

RECIPE SUGGESTION

To make a syrup: Put 3 oz (90g) of fresh violet flowers into a jug, pour on 5 fl oz (150ml) boiling water, cover and infuse for 24 hr. Strain, add 4½ oz (120g) sugar and heat to dissolve the sugar; bring to the boil and remove immediately; allow to cool.

WOODRUFF
Botanical name: *Asperula odorata*
Family: Rubiaceae

GENERAL

As its name suggests, woodruff is a herb found growing wild in the woods. In Germany it is called *Waldmeister*, the Master of the Wood and is used in a traditional punch known as the 'Mai Bowle'. It is an ancient herb, well known for its scent as well as its edible qualities and for centuries English folk used it as a 'strewing herb' for scattering among linen and clothes to keep away the moths and impart its refreshing scent.

DESCRIPTION AND HABITAT

It is a low carpeting perennial, with slightly shiny leaves which stand in whorls of six to eight on the stem. It has small white star-shaped flowers rising out of the dark green whorls of its leaves and this gives the plant its 'ruff' name. It flowers from April to June. Its scent resembles new-mown hay which comes from one of its constituents called cumarin, the content of which is highest in the spring, when the plant is in flower. This scent becomes stronger after cutting when the leaves are half dried and wilted. It prefers to grow in shady, woody places and will spread into any empty space it can find.

CULTIVATION

The seeds take a very long time to germinate so it is best to plant out young woodruff plants with good space between them in a shady place. Propagation can be done through the division of the roots of the older plants. Once established, woodruff will self-sow and spread to form a very attractive ground cover wherever grass does not encroach.

FLAVOUR AND HOW TO STORE

Woodruff has a distinctive scented flavour. Remove the leaves just as the herb comes into flower, or during flowering. Dry them at a low temperature so that they retain their green colour and do not become darker. Store the whole leaves loosely in airtight containers and as they should have retained their scent, they can be used throughout the year.

USES

For famous exhilarating Woodruff or May Cup, use the leaves dried, or after they have been picked some time and have wilted. A refreshing relaxing tisane can also be made from the dried leaves. In either of these forms woodruff has a wonderful effect of lifting the spirits and introducing a carefree atmosphere to any gathering. Its sweet scent is also valuable in pot-pourri and strewn in storage cupboards and amongst linen. Gerard said 'bunches hung up in the house in summer . . . make fresh the place to the delight and comfort of such as are there in'.

RECIPE SUGGESTION

Woodruff cup: Take a small handful of fresh woodruff and leave it to dry out in a heated airing cupboard for 3 hr. Cut off stems and put leaves into a large bowl. Pour over the juice of 1 lemon and ½ a bottle of light white wine so that the leaves are covered, and leave in a warm place for 3–4 hr. Add 4–6 tbs sugar according to taste, and 1½ bottles of the white wine. Chill in refrigerator. Just before serving, add 1 bottle sparkling white wine or champagne. For a stronger drink, add a measure of brandy when adding the sparkling wine. A lovely addition to the cup is strawberries, cut up and sprinkled with lemon juice and sugar, and floated on top.

WORMWOOD
Botanical name: *Artemisia absinthium*
Family: Compositae

GENERAL

Wormwood is a bitter aromatic herb of considerable medicinal value, for it contains a whole range of healing substances. The volatile oil is made up of various organic acids together with a bitter glucoside, absinthine.

Wormwood has a stimulating effect on the whole organism and improves the general health to a remarkable degree. It has been used for centuries for weak digestions and was an important vermifuge. In Britain during the Middle Ages bunches of wormwood were hung in rooms to prevent infection, rid the house of fleas and insects, and keep away evil spirits.

Wormwood

The bitter principle, absinthine, which the plant gives up when infused in water or alcohol, provided the basis for the French liqueur Absinthe. Nowadays wormwood flavours vermouth wines and tonic waters.

The wormwood mentioned in the Bible is a generic term given to a plant which has a strong aromatic smell and bitter taste. In the ancient Assyrian herbals wormwood is mentioned as being a useful expectorant; Hippocrates claimed it to be excellent for clearing the brain. Culpeper in the seventeenth century, recommended it to be taken with other herbs 'to keep a man's body in health'.

DESCRIPTION AND HABITAT
Wormwood is a bushy perennial with silvery-grey leaves and pale greenish-yellow flowers. Native to Britain and all Europe, wormwood now grows throughout the United States and Siberia.

CULTIVATION
Wormwood is an easy herb to grow and is propagated by seed, cuttings or root division. For best results, plant the divided roots in a shady position in spring, preferably in rather heavy clay soil. After flowering the plant should be cut back to encourage sturdier growth for next year.

FLAVOUR AND HOW TO STORE
Wormwood is an extremely bitter herb to taste and the odour is strongly aromatic and pungent. The flowering tops and leaves gathered from July to September, can be dried and stored in the usual way.

USES
Because of its bitter properties, wormwood is rarely used in the kitchen, but at one time it was used in brewing beer instead of hops. Wormwood flowers and leaves together make a tea which is diuretic and helpful against obesity, diabetes, fevers and for rheumatism; when infused in brandy it is a remedy for gout.

One of the most valuable medicinal herbs for stimulating the appetite and the digestion, wormwood is also a tonic remedy which activates secretions of the liver and gall bladder. It quickly removes flatulence and indigestion, whilst at the same time cleansing the intestines. It alleviates constipation, heartburn and other stomach troubles and decidedly improves the blood and circulation. Helpful to women, wormwood tea regularises menstruation.

Externally wormwood can be used as a fomentation for headaches, bruises and sprains.

RECIPE SUGGESTION
Wormwood Tea: 1 tsp of the herb per teacup of boiling water. Infuse for 3–5 min and sip 1–2 teacups a day slowly.

YARROW—Milfoil
Botanical name: *Achillea millefolium*
Family: Compositae

GENERAL

The high content of active, bitter substances and volatile oil to be found in the wild yarrow herb, make it an impressive all-round natural remedy without equal. It has the reputation as a general fortifier, helping to build up the body's natural resistance, and there is hardly an illness or symptom for which the different applications of yarrow are not beneficial. Traditionally, it was said that Achilles used it on the advice of the Centaur, and Chiron to staunch the bleeding wounds of his soldiers; hence its botanical name. It was also known as the 'military herb'. Its second name, milfoil, means a thousand leaves in reference to the feathery appearance of its foliage. Before hops came into use, ale was brewed with yarrow and it was thought that garlands of it would protect homes and churches from disease and evil spirits, due mainly to its reputation as an antiseptic all-healing plant.

DESCRIPTION AND HABITAT

Yarrow has a distinctive, spicy scent and bottle-green, feathery foliage. It is a perennial with creeping roots travelling underground and poking up fresh leafy branches. The ribbed stems of medium height bear white or pinkish flowers with strong aroma from June to October. Yarrow can be found almost anywhere as a garden weed or by roadsides and in meadows of Britain, Europe, Asia and America.

CULTIVATION

Yarrow will grow in any soil and one or two plants brought in from the wild and planted in the garden will help other plants to resist disease, since yarrow roots secrete beneficial substances into the soil. However, they must be watched and prevented from taking over too much ground. In a herb bed, yarrow will intensify aroma and flavour in its neighbouring culinary herbs.

FLAVOUR AND HOW TO STORE

Yarrow has a rather pleasant bitter taste. The leaves and flowers may be collected for use or drying during the flowering period.

USES

Yarrow stimulates the appetite, is antiflatulent and helps in treating intestinal troubles such as colitis, constipation and gastritis. It has diuretic qualities helpful to the functions of liver, gall bladder and kidneys. It is especially helpful to the circulation and heart function. It is also reputed to regulate the menstrual period and be good for all gynaecological complaints. It is

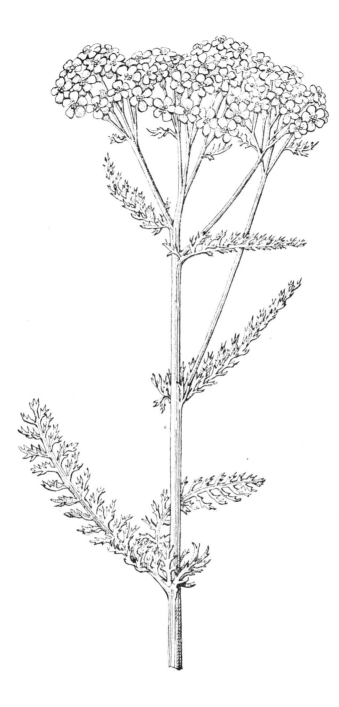

Yarrow

an ancient wound herb and will staunch bleeding in cuts and nosebleeds. It is also said to relieve gout and rheumatic pains. For all these purposes, yarrow tea can become a great help. It is particularly recommended as a cosmetic cleansing lotion for greasy skin. It can be taken internally, or the fresh herb chopped on to salads or eaten with bread and butter. The tea will induce perspiration and speed recovery from fevers and colds. Yarrow has been used as a safe substitute for quinine and chewing the leaves will relieve toothache. Fresh juice from the herb, rich in minerals and vitamins, has a blood improving quality of great importance in treating the first stages of diabetes. Yarrow in bath water has a general relaxing effect.

RECIPE SUGGESTION
Yarrow tea is made by pouring boiling water on a teaspoon of fresh or dried herb. This can be drunk or used for cosmetic purposes or as a bath addition.

PART THREE

CHARTS

HERB AND SPICE CULINARY CHART

There are many herbs and flavourings which belong to traditional dishes and bring out their flavour, such as dill with fish, basil with tomatoes and vanilla with chocolate. This chart gives information at a glance, and various ideas for different dishes. To make it easier to add the right amount of herbs or spice to a dish, the strength of each is marked M for mild or S for strong.

HERB OR SPICE		APPETISERS AND SALADS	EGGS AND CHEESE	SOUPS, SAUCES AND BEVERAGES
ALLSPICE	S	Grapefruit cocktail	Pickled eggs	Bouillons Soup stocks Spicy sauces Fruit punches
BASIL	S	Stuffed tomato Tomato salad French dressing Mayonnaise Green salad Tomato juice cocktail	Cheese soufflés Scrambled eggs	Tomato sauce, soup Bean soup Fish bouillon
BAY LEAVES	S	A pinch in salad dressing Rice salad	Macaroni cheese	Barbecue sauce In gravies and stocks Fish bouillon Meat soups
CHERVIL	M	Green, beetroot salads Salad dressing Crab cocktail	Omelettes Cottage cheese Savoury custard	Chervil, spring vegetable and sorrel soups Béarnaise sauce
CHIVES	M	In all salads and salad dressings Herb butter	Savoury pancakes Omelettes Devilled egg Cream cheese	A pinch in green soups Vichyssoise Tomato sauce White sauce
CINNAMON	S	Melon Grapefruit salad		Scotch broth Sweet sauces Coffee Mulled wines Chocolate drinks Milk
CLOVES	S	Beetroot salad	Stuffed eggs Cheese pancakes	Tomato sauce Mulled wines Potato, mulligatawny and tomato soups
DILL AND FENNEL	S	Cucumber salad Salad dressings Herb butters Stuffed eggs Fish pastes	Omelettes Sandwiches Savoury pancakes Stuffed eggs Dill seeds in cream cheese	Fish soups Cream sauces Bean soup Tomato soup Fennel in stock Fennel sauce

MEAT AND FISH	POULTRY AND GAME	VEGETABLES	PUDDINGS, PASTRIES CAKES AND PRESERVES
Stuffings for lamb, veal, pork Spiced meats Boiled, steamed fish	Poultry stuffings Jugged hare	Red cabbage Carrots Tomatoes	Fruit pies and puddings Fruit salads Pickles, mincemeat Chutneys Spiced cakes and biscuits Jams, jellies
Roast meat Beef pies and stews Stuffings for fish and meat	Venison stew Stuffings for poultry	Baked tomatoes A pinch to peas, potatoes and spinach	
Roast meat Pickled or smoked meats	In pan when roasting chicken or duck Stuffings	Add 1 leaf to water of potatoes, carrots, parsnips	In dill pickles
Garnish on steaks Veal casserole	Stuffings for poultry	Spinach, cabbage, carrots, potatoes	Herb jelly
Fish pie Shell fish Meat rissoles		New potatoes Garnish on vegetables Potato cakes	
Ham Meat chops		Haricot beans Pumpkin	Ice cream, stewed apples, pears, peaches, apricots Junkets, fruit pies Cakes, buns, biscuits Jams, jellies, chutney Rice pudding
Smoked meats Baked ham Marinades for beef	In marinades for venison	Beetroot Spinach Mushrooms	Fruit pies, rice puddings Cakes, buns, junkets Sweet pickles
Fennel with mackerel, eels, salmon Fish soufflés	Dill on poultry when roasting	Beans, cabbage, peas Fennel seeds with lentils, sauerkraut	Cucumber pickles

HERB OR SPICE		APPETISERS AND SALADS	EGGS AND CHEESE	SOUPS, SAUCES AND BEVERAGES
GARLIC	S	Salad dressings Garlic butter Rubbed round salad bowl	Curried eggs	Fish soups Meat sauces Vegetable soups Lentil soup
JUNIPER	S			Meat soups Spiced sauces Spiced vinegars Marinades Herb teas
LEMON BALM	M	Green salads Tomato, cucumber salad Tomato juice Seafood cocktails	Sweet omelettes Pancakes	Asparagus soup Cream sauces Herb tea Fruit cup, wine cups Lemonade
LOVAGE	S	Green salads Mayonnaise	Omelettes	Fish sauces Gravies Lovage soup Vegetable soups, stocks, broths Herb tea
MARJORAM	S	Stuffed mushrooms Green salads	Scrambled eggs Omelettes Soufflés	Onion soup Fish soups Meat sauces Lentil, split pea and butter bean soups
MINT	S	Green salads Celery salad Salad dressings Potato salad	Cream and cottage cheese Sweet pancakes	Mint Sauce Pea soup Wine punch, fruit cups Iced fruit drinks Herb tea Chocolate drinks
NUTMEG	S	Rice salad	Cheese fondue Sprinkle on to scrambled eggs	Meat soups Split pea soup Mushroom sauce Chocolate and milk drinks Mulled wine Eggnogs
PAPRIKA	M	Rice Celery salad Smoked salmon Vegetable salad	Cream cheese Welsh rarebit Scrambled eggs	Cream soups Chicken, meat, fish and vegetable soups

MEAT AND FISH	POULTRY AND GAME	VEGETABLES	PUDDINGS, PASTRIES CAKES AND PRESERVES
Kidneys, liver, pork Meat balls Lamb Curried shrimps Scallops	Curried chicken	Butter bean casserole Cabbage Spinach Kohlrabi Beans	Dill pickles
Braised meats, stews Pickled meats	Duck, goose Roasted wild duck, pheasant Marinade for venison Pickled game	Sauerkraut	Purée conserve Jam
Roast lamb Baked or boiled fish Meat stews	Chicken Stuffings for poultry and game	Mushrooms	Fruit salad Lemon jelly Baked custard Ice cream

Meat casseroles
Minced ham
	Roast chicken or
	  game
		Mix with all green
		  vegetables
			Lovage savoury
			  biscuits

Sausages, liver, lamb,
  beef, veal
Sweetbreads
Meat stews
Stuffings for veal, crab,
  baked fish
Smoked fish
	Chicken salad
	Rub over chicken,
	  duck, goose
	  before roasting
	Stuffings
	Venison, hare, rabbit
		Carrots
		Marrow
		Spinach
		Potatoes
			Milk puddings

Lamb Veal Baked, grilled fish Marinades for meat	Chicken	Peas Carrots New potatoes Green beans Spinach	Bananas Fruit salad Stewed fruit Ice cream sorbets, jellies Apply jelly Mint syrup

Fish mousse
Beef patties
Beef casserole
Meat balls
	Poultry stuffings	Sprinkle on to potatoes,
		  creamed spinach,
		  cauliflower, carrots
			Baked custard
			Spiced breads, cakes
			Fruit pies, rice
			Stewed fruits
			Chocolate and bread
			  puddings
			Fruit salads
			Chutneys

Pork spareribs
Beef, lamb, veal
Seasoning on baked or
  boiled fish
	Roast turkey, chicken,
	  duck, venison
		Garnish on potatoes,
		  cabbage, cauliflower,
		  turnips, swedes	

HERB OR SPICE		APPETISERS AND SALADS	EGGS AND CHEESE	SOUPS, SAUCES AND BEVERAGES
PARSLEY	M	Green salads Parsley butter Garnish on all salads Meat pâté	Cream and cottage cheese Omelettes Scrambled eggs	Fish bouillon Tartar sauce Garnish on all soups In sauces Herb tea
ROSEMARY	S	Vegetable cocktails	Omlettes Scrambled eggs Cheddar cheese savouries Cream cheese Pancakes	Pea soup Spinach soup Chicken cream soup Marinades Fruit cups, wine cups Herb tea
SAGE	S	Herb butter	Cheddar cheese Sage fritters	Fish bouillon Fish soups Marinades Meat sauces Herb tea
SUMMER SAVORY	S	Green salad Tomato salad Bean salad Herb butter	Omelettes Scrambled eggs Savoury pancakes	Bean soups Pea soup Consommé Horseradish sauce Fish sauces
TARRAGON	S	Mayonnaise Tomato and vegetable juices Seafood cocktails Herb butter Green salads Salad dressings Asparagus Tomato salad	Omelettes Scrambled egg Cheese soufflés	Chicken, mushroom and tomato soups Consommé Béarnaise sauce Tartar and hollandaise sauces Marinades Tarragon vinegar
THYMES GARDEN AND LEMON	S	Seafood cocktails Tomato juice Herb butter Beetroot salad A pinch in green salads	Cream cheese Pancakes	Tomato sauce Vegetable soups Minestrone

MEAT AND FISH	POULTRY AND GAME	VEGETABLES	PUDDINGS, PASTRIES CAKES AND PRESERVES
All meats, casseroles All fish, shellfish	All poultry	Fried parsley All vegetables	Savoury biscuits
Lamb, beef, pork and veal Halibut, eel	Chicken, duck, pheasant, venison, rabbit	Cauliflower, spinach, peas, potatoes, mushrooms	Fruit salads Rosemary biscuits Crab apple jelly Apple pie
Pork, beef, lamb, mutton Meat puddings and stews Baked or boiled fish Stuffings	Stuffings for chicken, goose, turkey Roast venison, rabbit	Tomatoes, butter beans, onions, peas, aubergines	Sage jelly
Meat pies Smoked meats Garnish on baked fish	Stuffings for chicken, duck, turkey Venison stew	All types of beans Dried peas Cabbage Sauerkraut	Pickled cucumbers
Garnish on steak Meat casseroles Baked and boiled fish Shellfish	Chicken salad Roast chicken, duck, hare, rabbit	Carrots	
Lamb, beef, pork Casseroles Baked and boiled fish Lemon thyme butter on lobster	Chicken, turkey pies and stuffings Venison and rabbit casseroles	Beans, beetroot, potatoes, mushrooms	Herb breads Cheese biscuits Lemon thyme in custards Fruit salads Apple puddings

CHART FOR HOME-MADE MIXTURES

MIXTURE	HORS D'OEUVRES AND SALADS	EGGS AND CHEESE	SOUPS, SAUCES AND BEVERAGES
Soups and Stews 1 tsp Parsley 1 „ Onion green ½ „ Bay leaves ½ „ Thyme	Stuffed tomatoes Sardines	Curried eggs Bacon pancakes Milk cheeses	Clear soups, broths Sprinkle over mixed vegetables and cream soups

Fish
1 tsp Parsley
1 „ Chives
1 „ Dill
	Kipper pâté
	Sprinkle over fish
	   and shellfish hors
	   d'oeuvres
	With sardines, tuna
	   salad
	Herb butter for fish dishes
		Fish and shellfish
		   soufflés
		Smoked salmon flan
		Fish mousses
		Kedgeree
			Fish soups and chowders,
			   sauces to go with fish
			Court bouillon

Poultry and Game
1 tsp Parsley
1 „ Onion green
½ „ Celery leaves
½ „ Tarragon
6 Juniper berries
	Chicken liver pâté
	Terrine of game
		Chicken, omelettes
		Soufflés
			Chicken broths, soups; add
			   to white sauce for serving
			   with boiled chicken

Meat
1 tsp Parsley
1 „ Onion green
½ „ Celery leaves
½ „ Marjoram
½ „ Thyme
	Meat pâtés
	Sausage rolls
	Liver paste
		Savoury pancakes
		Ham omelettes
		Cheese pie
		Herb cheese
			Add to gravies, brown sauces
			   meat broths, oxtail and
			   kidney soups

Salad
1 tsp Borage
1 „ Chives
1 „ Dill
1 „ Mint
	Green herb mayonnaise
	Sprinkle over salads
	French dressing,
	   vinaigrette
	Vegetable juices
		Stuffed eggs
		Cream cheese
			Cold cucumber or avocado
			   soups
			Mayonnaise, sauces
			Green sauce
			Herb vinegar

Sweet Herb
1 tsp Sweet Cicely
1 „ Lemon Balm
½ „ Lemon Thyme
½ „ Angelica stem
   (optional)
	In sweet dressings for
	   fresh fruit salads
	Herb butter
	Yogurt and pineapple
	   salad
		In pancakes, fritters,
		   sweet omelettes
		Cheesecake
			In fruit cups, chilled wine
			   drinks

A mixture of herbs give a pleasant overall flavour to the dish and can be added more generously than single herbs with their specific flavours. Mixtures may be prepared in advance and stored in the usual way, when they are ready for use at any time. With a little experience you will soon judge how much to add to the different dishes.

MEAT AND FISH	POULTRY AND GAME	VEGETABLES	PUDDINGS, PASTRIES, CAKES AND PRESERVES
Meat and fish casseroles, mutton hot pot Braised ham	Chicken and game casseroles	Vegetable casseroles Dumplings Savoury rice	Savoury bread
Hot buttered crab, with baked and boiled fish and shellfish Fish casseroles, on grilled fish In stuffings for fish, eg plaice In fish cakes, fish stews		Finocchio fennel Baked cucumber	Savoury pastry for fish fillings Pickles
	Coq-au-vin, chicken pies, chicken casseroles Rub over chicken before roasting Stuffings for all game Jugged hare, rabbit dishes	Red cabbage Haricot beans	
Meat casseroles Rub into joints before roasting On steaks, in marinades Stuffing for beef olives Beef pies, meat balls Meat curries	Roast venison	Stuffed green peppers, aubergine and marrow Baked beans	Savoury flan
Cold meat and fish Meat brawn Cold salmon and shellfish dishes	Chicken or turkey salad	Sprinkle over beetroot, celery, beans and courgettes when serving cold	Cucumber chutney
Lamb cutlets Ham roll	Minced chicken or turkey fricassée	Baked onions White cabbage	In fruit puddings, stewed fruits such as rhubarb, plums, gooseberries In custards, baked and boiled In jellies and jams Rice puddings

MIXTURE	HORS D'OEUVRES AND SALADS	EGGS AND CHEESE	SOUPS, SAUCES AND BEVERAGES
Sweet Spice 2 tsp Cardamom 2 ,, Cinnamon 2 ,, Cloves	Spiced vinegar for beetroots Melon salad Grapefruit	Sweet soufflés, pancakes and fritters	In sweet and sour sauces In mulled wines Iced coffee, fruit cups Spiced vinegars
Omelette 2 tsp Parsley 1 ,, Chives 2 ,, Dill 1 ,, Celery leaves 1 ,, Tarragon	Rice salad Stuffed egg salads Eggs in aspic Herb butter Salad dressing Potato salad	Herb cheese, omelettes, scrambled eggs, cheese soufflés With cream cheese dishes Savoury pancakes	Herb soup Fish sauces and soups
Barbecue 1 tsp Parsley 1 ,, Onion green or Chives ½ ,, Mint ½ ,, Tarragon ½ ,, Thyme	Barbecue butter Salad dressings Rice salads	Sprinkle lightly on scrambled eggs Welsh rarebit Pizzas Bacon and egg flan	Add to oil and tomato purée for barbecue sauce
Herb Bouquet 1 tsp Parsley 1 ,, Onion green or Chives ½ ,, Marjoram ½ ,, Celery leaves ½ ,, Tarragon ½ ,, Thyme	Salad dressings, beetroot, hors d'oeuvres In pâtés Tossed green salads Tomato juice cocktails	Scrambled eggs and soufflés, savoury custard With cream, cottage and home-made cheeses	Soups, brown sauces and meat gravies Espagnole and other tomato sauces Vegetable soups Marinades
Bouquet Garni (Fines herbes) 1 tsp Parsley 1 ,, Chives or Onion green ½ ,, Celery leaves ½ ,, Thyme	As garnish on hors d'oeuvres In salad dressings Red cabbage salad Herb butter	Omelette fines herbes Sparingly in other egg and cheese dishes	Béchamel sauce, gravies and to flavour meat and vegetable soups lightly Marinades
Curry ½ tsp Mustard ½ ,, Ginger 1 ,, Coriander ½ ,, Fenugreek 1 ,, Cumin 1½,, Turmeric ⅛ ,, Chili powder	Seafood cocktail Salad dressings Dips	Devilled eggs Curried eggs With cream, cottage, home-made cheeses	Mulligatawny soup Spiced cream sauces Herb curry soup

MEAT AND FISH	POULTRY AND GAME	VEGETABLES	PUDDINGS, PASTRIES, CAKES AND PRESERVES

Baked gammon
Pork chops
Potted ham
Add to pan when
  boiling mutton
	Chicken pie	Stuffed cabbage	In plum puddings, Christmas
			  baking, spiced cakes and
			  breads
			To flavour custards and
			  blancmanges
			Sprinkle over fruit pies
			Spices fruit and preserves

Meat rissoles
Fish soufflés
Shellfish dishes
	Chicken or turkey
	  salad
		Sprinkle over new
		  potatoes, mushrooms
		Vegetable casseroles
		Baked tomatoes
			Egg sandwiches
			Savoury turnovers

Add to oil for brushing
  steaks and chops before
  cooking
Sprinkle over broiled fish
  and mixed grills
Barbecued spareribs or
  pork
	Barbecued chicken
	  and stuffings
		Sprinkle over braised
		  celery and carrots
		  after cooking
			Cheese straws
			Savoury biscuits

In meat stews and on
  roasts
Boiled beef and ham
Meat galantines
	Rub inside chicken,
	  duck and goose
	  before roasting
	Use in turkey stuffing
	In rabbit, hare and
	  venison stews and
	  roasts, game casseroles
		Add to water when
		  cooking carrots,
		  spinach, cabbage,
		  beans, onions
			Herb scones, bread, cheese
			  biscuits
			Chutneys

When boiling meat or
  fish
	In stuffings and for
	  rubbing over chicken,
	  duck and goose before
	  roasting
	Chicken casseroles
	Rabbit, game of all kinds
		Add to boiling
		  vegetables and
		  remove before
		  serving
			Herb bread
			Herb biscuits

Beef, pork, lamb, veal Steamed fish Shellfish	Chicken, duck Devilled turkey	Stuffed green peppers Beans Lentils	Savoury cheese biscuits Savoury muffins, pastry

CHART FOR HERB TEAS

Herb teas, also called tisanes, are widely used on the Continent. German students love rosehip tea mixed with hibiscus which is sold in small, ready-mixed packets—as are most other herb teas. Many medicinal tisanes have become widespread today to relieve minor ailments. For instance, valerian tea for insomnia, verbascum for all bronchial troubles, lemon balm (melissa) tea as a general sedative and peppermint for digestion. These tisanes which are non-toxic and safe, should be taken regularly over a period of time. They are simple to make, in most cases just boiling water poured over the dried or fresh herb, and in principle the teacup should always be covered while steeping to keep in the flavour and heat. Where a measurement is given in teaspoons, it is meant for the dried herb. If fresh herbs are to be used, five to eight leaves according to their sizes, is a rough guide.

HERB	PARTS USED	DIRECTIONS	HOW TO TAKE	APPLICATIONS AND EFFECTS
BORAGE	Leaves	1 oz (30g) to 20 fl oz (575ml) boiling water; cover; infuse 5 min. Strain	Hot or cold—a wineglassful 3 times a day	Catarrhs Stimulant, diuretic, exhilarating
CHAMOMILE	Flowers	1 tsp per cup boiling water; cover; infuse 3–5 min. Strain immediately	Hot, a cupful after meals As a gargle and mouthwash	Sore throat, mouth infections Digestive, soothing
COLTSFOOT	Leaves	Boil 1 oz (30g) in 40 fl oz (1 litre) water uncovered until 20 fl oz (575ml) is left. Strain	Hot, a teacupful at a time	Catarrhs, colds Expectorant Source of vitamin C
COMFREY	Leaves Roots (dried and pounded or chopped)	1 oz (30g) to 20 fl oz (575ml) boiling water; cover; infuse 5–10 min; strain 1 tsp per cup of boiling water; cover, steep ½ hr Strain	Hot, a wineglassful at a time	Chest complaints, catarrhs, internal disorders, soothing, digestive
COWSLIP	Flowers	3 tsp per cup boiling water; cover; steep 3 min. Strain	Hot	Cramp, vertigo, restlessness Sedative
DANDELION	Leaves	1 tsp per cup boiling water; cover; steep 5–10 min. Strain	Hot	Gall bladder, liver, rheumatism Digestive, diuretic, tonic
	Dried roots	Same as above, steep ½ hr Strain	Cold, 1 or 2 cupfuls a day	

HERB	PARTS USED	DIRECTIONS	HOW TO MAKE	APPLICATIONS AND EFFECTS
ELDER	Flowers	Half fill a jug, pushing down flowers. Fill with boiling water; steep 10 min. Strain	Hot, at bedtime	Asthma, chills, colds, fevers Induces sleep, promotes perspiration
HORSETAIL (Equisetum)	Leaves	1 tsp per cup; soak 2 hr. Boil in this water 10–15 min. Strain	Hot or cold	Stomach troubles Kidney, liver Antiseptic, diuretic
HYSSOP	Tops and leaves	1 tsp per cup boiling water; steep 10 min. Strain	Hot or cold	Asthma, catarrhs, coughs Expectorant
JUNIPER	Berries	12–18 crushed berries per cup boiling water; steep 10 min. Strain	Hot	Chest complaints, intestinal troubles, kidneys, nerves, diabetes Antiseptic, stimulant, diuretic Builds up resistance (Over-use can cause irritation and inflammation of kidneys)
LADY'S MANTLE	Leaves	1 tsp per cup boiling water; cover; steep 5–10 min. Strain	Hot	Female disorders Helpful during pregnancy
LIME	Flowers	1 tsp per cup boiling water; cover; steep 5–10 min. Strain	Hot after meals or at bedtime	Chills, colds, digestive Expectorant, refreshing, soothing
MELILOT	Whole herb	1 tsp per cup boiling water; cover; steep 5–10 min. Strain	Hot	Flatulence Purifies bloodstream
MELISSA (Lemon Balm)	Leaves	1 tsp per cup boiling water; cover; steep 5–10 min. Strain	Hot, refreshing when cold	Relaxing, refreshing, soothing
MARSH MALLOW	Roots Leaves	3 tsp chopped root per cup cold water; cover; steep 8 hr. Strain. Heat to lukewarm 1 tsp per cup, otherwise as above	Lukewarm	Asthma, bronchitis, coughs Diarrhoea, dysentery, urinary complaints Soothing, demulcent
PARSLEY	Leaves	1 tsp per cup boiling water; cover; steep 5–10 min. Strain	Hot	Haemorrhoids, rheumatism Tonic, diuretic
PEPPERMINT	Leaves	1 tsp per cup boiling water; cover; steep 5–10 min. Strain	Hot, refreshing if iced	Diarrhoea, flatulence Headaches, heartburn, nausea, sickness Digestive

HERB	PARTS USED	DIRECTIONS	HOW TO TAKE	APPLICATIONS AND EFFECTS
ROSE HIP	Dried fruit and seeds	Separate seeds from fruits. Soak 2 level tbs in water 12 hr covered. Bring 40 fl oz (1 litre) water to boil, add hips, simmer 20 min. Strain	Hot	Gall bladder, kidneys Source of vitamin C Diuretic
VALERIAN	Roots (Dried and chopped)	Soak 1 tsp in cup of cold water, covered for 24 hr. Strain	Cold	Insomnia Relaxing, sedative
VERBASCUM	Flowers (Dried or fresh)	5-7 whole flowers per cup boiling water; cover; steep until tea is yellow (5-10 min). Strain	Hot, 2-3 cups per day	Bronchitis, colds, coughs

CHART FOR COSMETIC USE

Nowadays herbal cosmetics are becoming popular and it is quite easy to make your own at home. In the following chart quantities are given for the fresh herb. When these are not available use the dried herb and half the quantity. No special equipment is needed but avoid aluminium pans, and keep all equipment used scrupulously clean. Herbs are used in face packs, compresses and facial steams; in eye compresses, in hair rinses, nail baths and as bath additions. They can also be incorporated in cold creams, cleansing milks and hand lotions.

Face packs are usually made by adding a strong infusion of a herb—or crushed leaves of the herb itself, made into a mash—to fermented dairy produce such as yoghourt, buttermilk, curd or a powder like Fullers Earth and oatmeal, so that it forms a thick paste. The face and neck are thoroughly cleansed, the paste, which is cold, is spread over the skin and left for 10-15 min. Afterwards it is washed off with warm water and the face splashed with cold water.

Compresses, made of a strong infusion of herb into which is dipped cotton wool pads or pieces of lint, do more than just open and close the pores of the skin. They provide a tonic and an astringent and are very refreshing. For normal skins warm and cold compresses can be used alternately, leaving the cold one on for only a third of the time of the warm compress. For those with a dry skin lightly smooth on Johnson's baby oil before applying the compress. For dilated facial veins a warm compress only of Coltsfoot infusion is helpful.

A facial steam is perhaps the best of all beauty treatments and is one of the easiest to administer —but it is not for those with a very dry skin. Dried herbs are needed and can either be in a mixture or a specific herb for a special purpose, such as elderflowers for cleansing and softening. On normal and greasy skins the facial steam can be used once a week.

To make: Place about 2 handfuls of as many as possible of the following herbs in a bowl— sage, peppermint, chamomile flowers, lime flowers, elderflowers, lavender flowers, marigold petals, nettle, cornflowers, nasturtium flowers, salad burnet—onto these pour 40 fl oz (1 litre) boiling water. Cover hair and cleanse the face and neck. Hold head over the bowl and cover entirely with a bath towel for about 10 min. Wipe face and neck with a cold wet flannel and rest for a few minutes whilst the face cools down.

For eye compresses an infusion of the herb is always used. The following herbs are suitable either alone or in a mixture—eyebright, fennel, chamomile flowers, elderflowers and verbena. Onto 1 heaped tsp pour 5 fl oz (150ml) boiling water and allow to infuse for 10 min. Cut pieces of lint and place in warm infusion; squeeze lightly and cover closed lids. Leave for 5-10 min, then splash eyes with cold water.

A hair rinse of herbs stimulates the tissue and glands of the scalp, promoting healthy growth. The following herbs can be used—sage, fennel, chamomile, rosemary, yarrow, nettle, lime flowers—the greater part of the mixture being lime flowers, fennel and chamomile. To make: Onto 2 heaped tbs of herbs pour 40 fl oz (1 litre) boiling water. Leave until the right temperature for rinsing. Wash and rinse the hair in the usual way, finally pour over the strained rinse.

For splitting and brittle nails the following suggestion, applied twice a week for a few weeks will help. Have two small bowls ready, fill one with warm oil and the other with a strong infusion of horsetail. Thoroughly cleanse the hands, then immerse nails first in the oil then in the horsetail for a minute or two in each. Keep dipping the hands into alternate bowls for about 10 min altogether, ending with the horsetail. Dry hands on a soft cloth.

The addition of bath salts, oils and perfumes to the bath water is frequently practised today for softening the water and perfuming the body. When strong infusions of herbs are added instead, the bath can have a soothing effect on the nerves, be refreshing, tonic or astringent, and be helpful for those with skin troubles. Again herb infusions can be used singly or as a mixture, the following herbs being suitable—sage, fennel, peppermint, rosemary, yarrow, lovage, chamomile, horsetail and wild herbs such as nettle, dandelion, daisy and cowslip. How to make: Onto 13 oz (275g) pour 30 fl oz (825ml) boiling water, allow to infuse for 10 min—strain and add to bath.

Finally, it is best always to use the fresh herbs unless dried ones are specifically mentioned and green-dried herbs are available.

The following Chart gives more ideas and applications.

COSMETIC CHART

HERB	USED FOR	PARTS USED	DIRECTIONS	HOW TO USE
CHAMOMILE	Acne Hair rinse for fair hair Skin cleanser Tired eyes	Flowers	*Infusion:* Onto 3 tsp fresh flowers pour 5 fl oz (150ml) boiling water. Steep 3–5 min Strain	*Compress:* Dip lint pads in warm infusion. Leave on skin 8–10 min. Follow with cold water compress *Rinse:* Use lukewarm for final rinse after washing hair *Eyebath:* Use lukewarm
COLTSFOOT	Dilated veins Acne Puffy eyes	Leaves Flowers	*Infusion of leaves:* Onto 3 tsp chopped fresh leaves pour 5 fl oz (150ml) boiling water. Cover, leave to stand in warm place 10 min. Strain *Infusion of flowers:* As above *Poultice:* Crush or mince fresh leaves. Place between two layers of muslin on plate. Warm by standing plate on pan of boiling water for 10 min	*Compress:* Dip lint pads in infusion. Lay on affected skin until cold, twice a day *Eyebath:* Use lukewarm *Poultice:* Hot once a day for 15 min or until cold

HERBS	USED FOR	PARTS USED	DIRECTIONS	HOW TO USE
COWSLIP	Wrinkles Sunburn Spots	Flowers	*Infusion:* Onto 3 tsp dry cowslip flowers pour 5 fl oz (150ml) boiling water; cover. Leave to stand 3–4 min. Strain	*Compress:* Dip lint paids in cold infusion. Lay on sunburn until burning sensation is eased
DANDELION	Skin eruptions on face Bath addition	Leaves	*Infusion:* Onto 3 tsp chopped fresh leaves pour 5 fl oz (150ml) boiling water; cover, simmer for 5 min	*Compress:* Place hot infusion on face, when cold renew *Bath:* Add 10 fl oz (275ml) double strength infusion to bath water
ELDER	Bath addition Sunburn Wrinkles Freckles Skin tonic	Flowers	*Infusion:* Fill a jug with crushed flowers, cover with boiling water; cover. When cold, strain *Face pack:* Mix washed flowers or strong infusion with yoghourt; allow to permeate 15 min	*Compress:* Dip pieces of lint in warm infusion. Place on skin for 20 min *Face pack:* Put cold pack mixture onto muslin. Lay on face for 15 min *Bath:* Add 10 fl oz (275ml) double strength infusion to bath water
FENNEL	Tired eyes Slimming Wrinkles Skin tonic	Leaves	*Infusion:* Onto 3 tsp fresh leaves pour 5 fl oz (150ml) boiling water; cover, leave to stand 10 min. Strain *Face pack:* Mix strong infusion with equal quantities of yoghourt and clay powder	*Compress:* Dip pieces of lint in warm infusion. Leave on skin until cold *Face pack:* Clean the face, spread on pack; leave 15 min. Rinse off with lukewarm water and finish with cold water *Eyebath:* Use warm or cold infusion
HORSETAIL	Skin tonic	Whole herb	*Infusion:* Soak 3 tsp fresh herb in 5 fl oz (150ml) water for 2 hr. Boil in this water for 10 min; cover; allow to stand for 15 min. Strain	*Lotion:* Dip cotton wool pads in infusion and smooth over face before applying make-up or last thing at night
LADY'S MANTLE	Large pores Acne Freckles	Leaves	*Infusion:* Onto 3 tsp chopped fresh leaves pour 5 fl oz (150ml) boiling water; cover, leave to stand 5–10 min. Strain *Fresh juice:* Crush large handful of leaves until juice runs, or use juice extractor or electric blender Store in refrigerator	*Compress:* Dip pieces of lint in cold infusion and leave on skin for 10–15 min *Lotion:* Dip cottonwool pads in fresh juice, dab onto freckles night and morning

HERB	USED FOR	PARTS USED	DIRECTIONS	HOW TO USE
LAVENDER	Skin tonic Bath addition	Flowers	*Infusion:* Onto 4 tsp fresh lavender flowers pour 10 fl oz (275ml) boiling water. Cover; when cold, strain and bottle *Oil:* Cover 1 oz (30g) crushed flowers with almond oil. Leave for 2 weeks, stir once a day. Simmer gently until flowers are crisp, then strain and bottle	*Compress:* Pat cottonwool pads soaked in infusion onto skin once a day *Bath:* Add 10 fl oz (275ml) double strength infusion to bath water Add few drops oil to bath water
LIME (Linden)	Wrinkles Freckles	Dried flowers	*Infusion:* Infuse small handful of flowers in 5 fl oz (150ml) boiling water for 3–5 min. Strain	*Compress:* Dip pieces of lint in infusion, lay on face for 10–15 min or Dip cottonwool pads in infusion and pat gently onto face
MARIGOLD	Nourishing skin Large pores Pimples Chapped hands and face	Flowers	*Infusion:* Onto 1 oz (30g) petals pour 20 fl oz (575ml) boiling water; infuse 10 min covered. Strain *Ointment:* Melt 4 oz (120g) vaseline in pan, add 2 oz (60g) petals; cover; simmer gently for 30 min. Strain into pots. Use cold *Oil:* Soak 1 oz (30g) petals in 10 fl oz (275ml) almond oil	*Compress:* Dip pieces of lint in cold infusion and lay on face. Leave 10–15 min *Ointment:* Smooth gently onto skin each night *Oil:* Smooth onto hands
NETTLE	Hair tonic Skin tonic	Leaves	*Infusion:* Onto large handful of fresh leaves pour 10 fl oz (275ml) boiling water. Infuse 10–15 min. Strain *Pack:* Crush fresh leaves and sprouting tops; cover with water and simmer covered for 10 min	*Hair lotion:* Rub infusion into scalp 3 or 4 times a week *Face pack:* Spread warm pack mixture on muslin and place on face, protecting eyes. Leave 15–20 min. Wash skin with warm water, to which lemon juice is added
ROSEMARY	Hair tonic Bath addition	Leaves	*Infusion:* Onto 3 tsp fresh leaves pour 5 fl oz (150ml) boiling water. Steep 15–20 min	*Hair lotion:* Rub infusion into scalp 4 or 5 times a week *Bath:* Make up 10 fl oz (275ml) double strength infusion and add to bath water
SAGE	Large pores Hair tonic Whitening the teeth	Leaves	*Infusion:* Onto 3 tsp fresh bruised leaves pour 5 fl oz (150ml) boiling water. Infuse 10–15 min. Strain	*Compress:* Dip pieces of lint in cold infusion, leave on face for 10 min *Hair lotion:* Rub infusion into scalp 4 or 5 times a week *Teeth:* Rub teeth with fresh leaves

HERB	USED FOR	PARTS USED	DIRECTIONS	HOW TO USE
SALAD BURNET	Refining skin	Leaves	*Infusion:* Onto 3 tsp fresh leaves pour 5 fl oz (150ml) boiling water. Infuse 10–15 min. Strain	*Compress:* Dip pieces of lint in cold infusion. Leave on face 15 min
SOUTHERN-WOOD	Hair tonic Bath addition	Leaves	*Infusion:* Onto 3 tsp fresh leaves pour 5 fl oz (150ml) boiling water. Infuse 5–10 min. Strain	*Hair lotion:* Massage infusion into hair with fingertips 3 or 4 times a week *Bath:* Add 10 fl oz (275ml) double strength infusion to bath water
THYME	Bath addition Skin tonic	Leaves	*Infusion:* Onto 3 tsp fresh leaves pour 5 fl oz (150ml) boiling water. Infuse 10–15 min. Strain *Face pack:* To 5 fl oz (150ml) yoghourt add 1 tsp fresh leaves. Allow to stand ½hr. Use	*Bath:* Add 10 fl oz (275ml) infusion to bath water *Face pack:* Cover face with pack. Leave 10–15 min. Wash off with warm water
VERBENA	Puffy eyelids	Leaves	*Infusion:* Onto 3 tsp fresh leaves pour 5 fl oz (150ml) boiling water. Infuse 10–15 min. Strain	*Compress:* Dip cottonwool pads in warm infusion. Place on closed eyes for 15–20 min
VIOLET	Bath addition Cleansing and clearing skin	Leaves Flowers	*Infusion of leaves:* Onto a handful of fresh leaves pour 10 fl oz (275ml) boiling water. Infuse for 10–15 min. Strain *Lotion:* To 20 fl oz (575ml) milk add a handful of flowers; warm to blood heat, cool, then strain and use	*Bath:* Add 10 fl oz (275ml) infusion to bath water *Lotion:* Dip cottonwool pads in lotion and smooth over skin. Leave to dry
YARROW	Cleansing lotion for greasy skin Hair lotion against baldness Hair tonic Bath addition Chapped hands	Flowers Leaves	*Inufsion:* Onto a handful of fresh leaves and flowers pour 10 fl oz (275ml) boiling water. Infuse for 10–15 min. Strain *Face pack:* Crush fresh sprouts and buds, cover with water and simmer covered for 10 min	*Hair lotion:* Rub infusion into scalp 4 or 5 times a week *Bath:* Add 10 fl oz (275ml) double strength infusion to bath water *Face pack:* Spread pack mixture onto pieces of muslin and place on face. Leave for 15–20 min *Lotion:* Soak hands in infusion for 10 min. Pat dry

PART FOUR

APPENDICES

GLOSSARY

ACID	A sour substance.
ALBUMEN	Egg white. A dilute solution of protein in water.
ALEXIPHARMIC	Able to counteract poison.
ALKALOID	An organic constituent of plants containing nitrogen which has a biological action.
ALTERATIVE	Type of treatment, or substance, which gradually restores healthy functions of organs.
ANNUAL	A plant which lasts only one year or season.
ANODYNE	Soothing, painkilling.
ANTHER	The part of the stamen which produces pollen in flowers.
ANTIDOTE	A remedy that counteracts a poison.
ANTISCORBUTIC	Preventing scurvy, a disease caused by lack of vitamin C in the diet.
ANTISEPTIC	A substance that destroys bacteria or inhibits their growth.
ANTISPASMODIC	Prevents or counteracts spasms.
APERIENT	Produces a natural movement of the bowels.
AROMATIC	Having a fragrant, pleasant scent.
ASTRINGENT	Contracts and increases the firmness of skin, mucous membrane or organic tissue.
ATROPINE	Drug obtained from the deadly nightshade plant.
AXIL	Angle formed by leaf or bract with stem or branch.
BIENNIAL	A plant which lasts two years, flowering and fruiting only in the second year.
BITTER PRINCIPLE	Contained in bitter tasting herbs which stimulate the appetite, eg cetarin, lupulin, phulin, tannin, etc.
BRACT	Any type of leaf under a flower.
BULB	The underground stem of a plant, more or less globular, usually consisting of overlapping fleshy scales.
CALYX	The outer row of floral leaves enclosing the rest of the flower.
CAPSULE	A dry fruit which opens when ripe.
CARDIAC	Pertaining to the heart. A property of a plant having an effect on the heart.
CARMINATIVE	Relieves flatulence and eases griping pains.
CATALYST	A substance that accelerates a chemical change without itself undergoing any change.
CONCOTION	Mixture of different ingredients.
CONDIMENT	A seasoning which gives flavour to food.
CORDIAL	A fortifying drink which revives and comforts the heart, and stimulates the circulation.
CORM	An enlarged, round underground stem.
COROLLA	A collective name for the petals of a flower.
CORYMB	A flat-topped collection of flowers.
CRENATE	Leaves having scalloped edges.
CRYPTOGAM	The vegetable group of plants which have no stamens or pistils and therefore no flowers, eg ferns, fungi, mosses, lichen and algae.
CYME	Inflorescence where central flower, or branch of the whole, opens first.
DECIDUOUS	Shedding of leaves, petals etc at a certain period of growth.
DECOCTION	An extract of a substance obtained by boiling.
DEMULCENT	A preparation which soothes and protects the alimentary canal.

DEODORANT	Substance which reduces or removes smells.
DIAPHORETIC	A medicinal herb which promotes perspiration.
DISTILLATION	An extraction of the pure essence of a substance by a process of evaporation and condensation.
DIURETIC	A medicine that increases the output of urine.
EMETIC	A medicine that causes vomiting.
EMOLLIENT	A substance having a softening and soothing effect.
ENZYMES	Chemical substances present in living cells which produce changes whilst they themselves remain unchanged.
ESSENTIAL OIL	A volatile oil of complex composition contained in many plants giving them their characteristic scent, aroma and taste.
EXPECTORANT	A remedy that promotes the removal of secretions from the bronchial tubes.
FEBRIFUGE	A remedy for reducing fever.
FERMENTATION	A chemical change brought about by a process of effervescence and heat which alters the properties of two substances when mixed, eg the action of yeast on dough or sugary liquids.
FLATULENCE	The condition of accumulated gases in the stomach and alimentary canal.
FOMENTATION	Application of warm or medicated lotions.
FUNGUS	A mushroom, toadstool or one of the allied plants, including the various forms of mould. In botany, a cryptogamous plant, characterised by the absence of chlorophyll, and deriving its sustenance from dead or living organic matter.
GLUCOSIDE OR GLYCOSIDE	Compound of glucose and various substances in plants, eg acid, mustard oil, aromatic compounds.
HABITAT	A locality or region where a plant grows naturally.
INDIGENOUS	Native to soil or region. Produced naturally in a given place.
INFLORESCENCE	The mode in which flowers are arranged in relation to the axis of the plant.
INFUSION	A dilute liquid extract resulting from the steeping of a substance in water.
INORGANIC	Inanimate matter. Not having an organised physical structure.
INULIN	A white starchy substance found in Elecampane plants and other Compositae roots.
IRRITANT	Causing excitement of a bodily organ not amounting to inflammation.
LICHEN	Small cryptogamic plants, growing over rocks, trees and soil, consisting of algae in partnership with fungi which take their food from soil, air and inorganic mineral substances. Some are parasitic, feeding on their host, eg mistletoe.
LINIMENT	A kind of thin ointment or embrocation.
MOLLIFYING	Having a soothing effect.
MUCILAGE	Sticky, gelatinous substance found in certain plants.
MULCH	Horticultural term for protective covering of wet straw, leaves, peat etc spread round plant roots to keep in soil moisture.
NARCOTIC	Having the effect of producing sleep or stupor.
NERVINE	Relieves pain and nervous irritation; restores nerves to natural state.
NUTRITIOUS, NUTRITIVE	Nourishing.
OEDEMA	Swelling of tissue by increase of fluid content.
OFFICINAL PLANT	One used in medicine adopted officially by the Pharmacopoeia.
OINTMENT	A medicinal or cosmetic preparation applied to the skin.
ORGANIC	Having organs, or an organised physical structure. Applied to compound substances which are natural constituents of organised bodies, ie animals, or plants, all constituents being derived from hydrocarbons (compounds of hydrogen and carbon).
OVATE	Egg-shaped.

PERENNIAL	A plant lasting more than two years.
PETAL	A leaf of the corolla of a flower.
PINNATIFID	A leaf divided half-way to the midrib, like a feather.
PLASTER	Adhesive bandage. An external, local medicament of an adhesive nature, spread on muslin and applied to the skin.
POD	A long seed vessel usually applied to leguminous plants such as peas and beans.
POLLEN	The fertilising powder formed in the anthers of flowers.
POMANDER	A ball of fragrant or aromatic substances formerly worn as protection against infection.
POTHERB	A flavouring herb or vegetable grown for boiling in the pot as a natural seasoning.
POULTICE	A warm, soft moist substance usually prepared with boiling water, spread on a cloth and applied to an inflamed part of the body to draw pus or act as a counter irritant.
PROPHYLACTIC	Preventative remedy.
RACEME	Flowers with stalks of equal length growing from a central stem.
RHIZOME	A thickened underground stem of a plant.
SACHET	A small bag or wallet often used to contain perfumed powder or dried herbs.
SEDATIVE	A medicine which calms nervous excitement.
SEPAL	A botanical term for the leaves of the calyx.
SERRATE	Shape of leaves with notched or saw-like edges.
SIMPLE	A medicine derived only from one plant.
STAMEN	The male organ of a flower.
STELLATE	Star-like flower.
STIGMA	Botanically, that part of the pistil in a flowering plant which receives the pollen.
STIMULANT	A drug or other agent which temporarily increases the activity of an organ or some vital process of the body.
SYNTHESIS	The putting together of parts or elements to make up a whole, or a compound. Especially applied to artificial production (synthetics) of organic compounds formerly obtained by extraction from natural products.
THERAPEUTIC	Healing, curative treatment.
TINCTURE	A solution, usually in alcohol, of a medicinal substance.
TISANE	A tea prepared from any part of a herb or spice.
TONIC	An invigorating medicine, one which tones up the system.
TOXIC	Of a poisonous nature.
UMBEL	Flattened flower-head whose stalks radiate from one point.
VALVE	Anatomically, a membranous fold in an organ or passage of the body, eg heart and veins, which automatically closes to prevent flow-back of blood or fluid.
VALVULAR	Having the form or function of a valve, eg the heart valve.
VERMIFUGE	Substance that expels worms from the body.
VOLATILE	Evaporates or dissolves at ordinary temperatures. Easily changeable.
VOLATILE OIL	Essence obtained from plants by distillation. See ESSENTIAL OIL.
VULNERARY	A plant, ointment or drug for healing wounds.

BIBLIOGRAPHY

ARY, S. and GREGORY, M. *The Oxford Book of Wild Flowers.* OUP, 1970.

AUSTIN, THOMAS (ed). *Two Fifteenth Century Cook Books.* Early English Text Society, 1888.

BELL, J. W. *Nature's Remedies.* Pitman.

BENTHACH, H. G. *Anis bis Zim.* Usego Co Publications.

BENTHAM and HOOKER. *The Handbook of British Flora.* L. Reeve & Co, 1945.

BIRCHER-BENNER, CLAIRE LOEWENFELD (ed). *Eating your Way to Health.* Faber & Faber, 1961.

BRECHT, E. A. *Die Magische Droge.* Brecht-Karlsruhe, 1954.

BROWN, PROF O. PHELPS. *The Complete Herbalist.* Frederick W. Hale, 1907.

BUTLER and BROWN. *Illustrated Flora of the United States & Canada.*

CLARKSON, ROSETTA. *Herbs: Their Culture and Uses.* Macmillan, 1961.

FERNIE, W. T., MD. *Herbal Simples.* John Wright & Son Ltd, Bristol, 1914.

FLOWER and ROSENBAUM. *Apicius—The Roman Cookery Book.* Harra, 1958.

FLUCK, DR HANS. *Unsere Heilpflanzen.* Ott-Verlag, Thun, 1941.

GERHARD, H. *Moderne Kräuterkunde.* Deutscher Reform-Verlag, 1961.

GOSSNER, S. *Küchengewürze.* J. F. Schreiber.

GRIEVE, M. *A Modern Herbal, Vols I & II.* Jonathan Cape, 1931.

GRIGSON, GEOFFREY. *The Englishman's Flora.* Phoenix House, 1958.

HARRISON, R. H. *Healing Herbs of the Bible.* E. J. Brill, Leiden, Netherlands, 1966.

HATFIELD, AUDREY WYNNE. *Pleasures of Herbs.* Museum Press Ltd, 1964.

———. *How to Enjoy Your Weeds.* Muller, 1969.

HAYES, ELIZABETH. *Herbs, Flavours and Spices.* Faber & Faber, 1961.

HENSLOW, PROF. G. *The Uses of British Plants.* Lovell Reeve & Co Ltd, 1905.

HEMPHILL, ROSEMARY. *Fragrance and Flavour.* Darton Longman & Todd, 1963.

HILL, SIR JOHN, MD. *The Family Herbal.* C. Brightly & T. Kinnersley.

HOOKER, ALAN. *New Cookery.* 101 Productions, San Francisco, 1971.

HOGNER DOROTHY CHILDS. *Herbs from the Garden to the Table.* OUP (New York), 1953.

HOOPER, M. M. M., FRHS. *Wild Plants to the Rescue—For Food and Medicine.*

HUTCHINSON, JOHN. *Common Wild Flowers.* 1945. *More Common Wild Flowers.* Pelican, 1948.

JOHNS, REV C. A. *Flowers of the Fields.* Routledge & Kegan Paul Ltd, London, 1949.

KEBLE, MARTIN W. *The Concise British Flora in Colour.* Michael Joseph, 1965.

LEVY, J. B. *Herbal Handbook for Everyone.* Faber & Faber, 1966.

LEYEL, C. F. *Herbal Delights.* Faber & Faber, 1937.

LOEWENFELD, CLAIRE. *Britain's Wild Larder—Fungi.* Faber & Faber, 1956.

———. *Britain's Wild Larder—Nuts.* Faber & Faber, 1957.

———. *Edible Plants—Manual of Survival.* Marshall Cavendish Ltd, 1970.

———. *Herb Gardening.* Faber & Faber, 1964.

LOEWENFELD, CLAIRE and BACK, PHILIPPA. *Herbs for Health and Cookery.* Pan Books, 1965.

MABEY, RICHARD. *Food for Free.* Collins, 1972.

MACALISTER, CHARLES J., MD. FRCP. *Comfrey: An Ancient Medicinal Remedy.* (A detailed research in the chemical substance of allantoin in comfrey.) Henry Doubleday Research Association, 1936.

MCCLINTOCK, DAVID and FITTER, R. S. R. *Pocket Guide to Wild Flowers.* Collins, 1956.

MASSEE, GEORGE. *British Fungi and Lichens.* G. Routledge & Sons Ltd.

MEDSGER, OLIVER PERRY. *Edible Wild Plants.* Macmillan, USA, 1939.

MESSEGUE, MAURICE. *Of Men and Plants*. Weidenfeld & Nicolson, 1972.

MEYER, JOSEPH E. *The Herbalist*. 1960 edition.

MILORADOVICH, MILO. *The Art of Cooking with Herbs and Spices*. Doubleday & Co Ltd, New York, 1950.

MIN OF AG FISHERIES and FOOD CIRCULAR. *Culinary and Medicinal Herbs*. 1951.

——. *Culinary and Medicinal Herbs*. 1960.

MIN OF FOOD and AG (GERMANY). *Küchenkräuter und Gewürze*. 1967.

NIEBUHR, ALTA DODDS. *Herbs of Greece*, sponsored by The New England Unit of the Herb Society of America, 1970.

OSTMANN, K. *Die Gewürze und das richtige Würzen*. Karl Ostmann, Bielefeld.

RANSON, FLORENCE. *British Herbs*. Penguin Books, 1949.

ROSENGARTEN, F. *The Book of Spices*. Livingston Pub. Co, 1969.

ROYAL HORTICULTURAL SOCIETY DICTIONARY OF GARDENING. OUP, 1951.

SCHUPHAN, PROF WERNER. (Chief Director of the Federal Research Institute of Plant Products, West Germany) *Nutritional values in Crops and Plants*. Faber & Faber, 1965.

SMITH, DR F. PORTER. *Chinese Materia Medica*. Ku T'ing Book House, Taiwan, 1969.

STOBART, T. *Herbs, Spices and Flavourings*. David & Charles, 1970.

STURTEVANT, ed by U. P. HEDRICK. *Edible Plants of the World*. Dover Publications Inc, 1972.

USHER, GEORGE. *A Dictionary of Botany*.

WARD, HAROLD. *Herbal Manual*. C. W. Daniel & Co Ltd.

WASESCHA, C. *Richtig Würzen!* 1951.

WILKINSON, W. R. and CO LTD. *The Story of Liquorice*.

WILLFORT, R. *Gesundheit durch Heilkräuter*. Rudolf Trauner, Linz, 2nd ed 1961.

WREN, R. C. *Potters New Cyclopaedia of Botanical Drugs and Preparations*. Health Science Press, 1956.

INDEX

Page numbers in bold indicate the main section on each individual herb